Edge Hill Learning Services

Renew Online: http://library.edgehill.ac.uk

24/7 telephone renewals: 01695 58 4333

Help line: 01695 58 4286

Edge Hill University
LEARNING SERVICES

449089

Law in Context

Below is a listing of the more recent publications in the Law in Context Series

Editors: William Twining (University College, London) and Christopher McCrudden (Lincoln College, Oxford)

Ashworth: *Sentencing and Criminal Justice*
Bell: *French Legal Cultures*
Bercusson: *European Labour Law*
Birkinshaw: *Freedom of Information: The Law, the Practice and the Ideal*
Cane: *Atiyah's Accidents Compensation and the Law*
Collins: *The Law of Contract*
Elworthy and Holder: *Environmental Protection: Text and Materials*
Fortin: *Children's Rights and the Developing Law*
Harlow and Rawlings: *Law and Administration: Text and Materials*
Harris: *An Introduction to Law*
Harris, Campbell & Halson: *Remedies in Contract and Tort*
Harvey: *Seeking Asylum in the UK: Problems and Prospects*
Lacey and Wells: *Reconstructing Criminal Law*
Moffat: *Trusts Law – Text and Materials*
Norrie: *Crime, Reason and History*
O'Dair: *Legal Ethics – Text and Materials*
Oliver and Drewry: *The Law and Parliament*
Oliver: *Common Values and the Public-Private Divide*
Palmer and Roberts: *Dispute Processes: ADR and the Primary Forms of Decision Making*
Reed: *Internet Law – Text and Materials*
Scott and Black: *Cranston's Consumers and the Law*
Turpin: *British Government and the Constitution: Text, Cases and Materials*
Twining and Miers: *How to Do Things with Rules*
Twining: *Globalisation and Legal Theory*
Ward: *Shakespeare and the Legal Imagination*
Zander: *Cases and Materials on the English Legal System*
Zander: *The Law Making Process*

Reconstructing Mental Health Law and Policy

Dr Nicola Glover-Thomas
Lecturer in Law, University of Liverpool

Butterworths
LexisNexis™

Members of the LexisNexis Group worldwide	
United Kingdom	LexisNexis Butterworths Tolley, a Division of Reed Elsevier (UK) Ltd, Halsbury House, 35 Chancery Lane, LONDON, WC2A 1EL, and 4 Hill Street, EDINBURGH EH2 3JZ
Argentina	LexisNexis Argentina, BUENOS AIRES
Australia	LexisNexis Butterworths, CHATSWOOD, New South Wales
Austria	LexisNexis Verlag ARD Orac GmbH & Co KG, VIENNA
Canada	LexisNexis Butterworths, MARKHAM, Ontario
Chile	LexisNexis Chile Ltda, SANTIAGO DE CHILE
Czech Republic	Nakladatelství Orac sro, PRAGUE
France	Editions du Juris-Classeur SA, PARIS
Hong Kong	LexisNexis Butterworths, HONG KONG
Hungary	HVG-Orac, BUDAPEST
India	LexisNexis Butterworths, NEW DELHI
Ireland	Butterworths (Ireland) Ltd, DUBLIN
Italy	Giuffrè Editore, MILAN
Malaysia	Malayan Law Journal Sdn Bhd, KUALA LUMPUR
New Zealand	LexisNexis Butterworths, WELLINGTON
Poland	Wydawnictwo Prawnicze LexisNexis, WARSAW
Singapore	LexisNexis Butterworths, SINGAPORE
South Africa	Butterworths SA, DURBAN
Switzerland	Stämpfli Verlag AG, BERNE
USA	LexisNexis, DAYTON, Ohio

© Reed Elsevier (UK) Ltd 2002

All rights reserved. No part of this publication may be reproduced in any material form (including photocopying or storing it in any medium by electronic means and whether or not transiently or incidentally to some other use of this publication) without the written permission of the copyright owner except in accordance with the provisions of the Copyright, Designs and Patents Act 1988 or under the terms of a licence issued by the Copyright Licensing Agency Ltd, 90 Tottenham Court Road, London, England W1T 4LP. Applications for the copyright owner's written permission to reproduce any part of this publication should be addressed to the publisher.

Warning: The doing of an unauthorised act in relation to a copyright work may result in both a civil claim for damages and criminal prosecution.

Crown copyright material is reproduced with the permission of the Controller of HMSO and the Queen's Printer for Scotland. Any European material in this work which has been reproduced from EUR-lex, the official European Communities legislation website, is European Communities copyright.

A CIP Catalogue record for this book is available from the British Library.

ISBN 0 406 94677 9

Printed and bound in Great Britain by Thomson Litho Ltd, East Kilbride, Scotland

Visit Butterworths LexisNexis *direct* at www.butterworths.com

Preface

At the beginning of 2002, mental health law and policy is in a state of flux. This uncertainty has been brought about by the use of outmoded legislation, which struggles to meet the needs of patients and fails to reflect contemporary psychiatric practice. The Mental Health Act 1983, which is still currently in force, albeit in an amended form, derives most of its provisions from the Mental Health Act 1959 and the work of the 'Percy' Commission which reported its findings in 1957. It is, therefore, hardly surprising that demands for law reform have been heard since the mid-1980s.

Mental health law and policy was centred largely on the 'institution' and hospital-based psychiatric care right up until the 1960s. This view gradually shifted as it was realised that a less restrictive environment had greater therapeutic value. Combined with this, funding for inpatient facilities was cut with the introduction of Enoch Powell's Hospital Plan in 1962, improvements in pharmacology occurred and the publication of Erving Goffman's *Asylums* in 1961 informed people about the negative impact of long-term hospitalisation.[1] The adoption of the community care policy was a natural response and has existed in one form or another since the late 1970s. Yet, in recent years, the policy has been subject to mounting criticism, as patients, psychiatrists and the public have become increasingly disillusioned with the care approach. Despite this loss of enthusiasm, the current Labour Government continues to support the policy and in 1998 outlined the 'third way', which aims to combine greater

---

1 Goffman, E *Asylums: Essays on the Social Situation of Mental Patients and Other Inmates* (1961) Anchor/Doubleday, New York.

efforts to support patients with ensuring the protection of the public.[2] The publication of the White Paper *Reforming the Mental Health Act* in December 2000 reflected the current position in the reform process. The White Paper is divided into two parts. The first part sets out a new legal framework for how and when care and treatment should be provided without the consent of the patient, and the second part focuses on strengthening laws and services to protect the public from the risk posed by those with dangerous and severe personality disorders. Two significant departures from the current legal position have been introduced in the White Paper: the extension of powers to care and treat in the community environment; and the emphasis on risk assessment as a determinant of indefinite detention for those deemed to pose the greatest risk. The recommendations within the White Paper are simply the latest impetus for the reform of mental health law in England and Wales. Proponents of a strong framework of legal intrusion and judicial safeguards continue to argue against those who favour a welfarist approach, which focuses upon prompt treatment and therapeutic intervention by the medical profession. Those in favour of strong legalist intervention argue that a framework of legal rules is essential for the protection of patients, while advocates of medicalism insist that such tightly woven legal rules prevent the use of highly trained medical judgment being used effectively, thereby threatening therapeutic endeavour. The attempt to find a balance between these two perspectives remains a key objective in mental health law reform. However, achieving this balance has proved elusive. As such, the White Paper has courted controversy and many who work within the psychiatric care system and are in receipt of such services remain unconvinced by the proposals. Expectations that a new Bill would be included in the Queen's Speech in June 2001 were not met and, therefore, at the time of writing this book, the White Paper's future is uncertain.

Mental health law as a separate field of legal study has a relatively recent history. Its consideration has frequently been amalgamated with medical law. Consequently, books focusing on this area have been rather scarce although this is gradually changing. Brenda Hoggett's *Mental Health Law*,[3] which is currently in its fourth edition, provides an excellent starting point while Richard Jones' *Mental Health Act Manual*,[4] provides all the technical details associated with a practitioner guide. Most recently, the publication of Peter Bartlett and Ralph Sandland's *Mental Health Law*

---

2   Department of Health Press Release 98/311, 1998 and 98/580, 1988. Department of Health *Modernising Mental Health Services: Safe, Sound and Supportive* (1998) HMSO, London.
3   Hoggett, B *Mental Health Law* (4th edn, 1996) Sweet & Maxwell, London.
4   Jones, R *Mental Health Act Manual* (6th edn, 1999) Sweet & Maxwell, London.

Policy and Practice,[5] provides mental health law students with an accessible and user-friendly text. All of these books have much to commend them, whether it be the detailed analysis of the legal provisions or the provision of a more general exposition with students in mind. This book explores the way in which the law has responded to psychiatric provision and considers the impact of social, political and clinical trends on its development. It is important to recognise that context is a key consideration to understanding the nature and objective of mental health law. Many people are directly affected by the way in which it operates – both as users and providers of the psychiatric system. The law provides a group of individuals with wide powers over another (usually vulnerable) group. It enables the use of coercive powers of detention and treatment against the will of the individual. The operation of this power is not dependent on the criminal activities of individuals but rather as a result of their mental status. It is this that makes the application of mental health law and its social acceptance so contentious. Moreover, as mental health provision within the legal framework is multidisciplinary in nature, it is inevitable that tensions between the legal rules, psychiatric care practices, patient, and professional preferences constantly surface. This book endeavours to place these issues at the heart of its analysis.

These tensions, most notably the struggle between establishing a protective legal framework, which provides both suitable safeguards yet simultaneously allows sufficient flexibility in the use of medical discretion, are constantly present. Since the enactment of the Lunacy Act 1890 and in subsequent legislation throughout the twentieth century, solving these conflicting objectives has proved difficult, as will be illustrated in Chapter 1. Chapter 1 further considers the historical origins of modern day mental health law and considers the impact of major clinical, pharmacological and social developments on the gradual shift away from institution-centred psychiatric provision to community-based care. Chapter 2 analyses the current legislative provision: the Mental Health Act 1983. Despite revolutionary advances in science and a growth in psychological therapies during the 1950s and 1960s, pessimism regarding the power vested in psychiatrists began to creep back into the social consciousness. Growing awareness of human rights and the intensive work of the National Association for Mental Health (MIND), which promoted patient rights and the reassertion of a formalised legal framework, caused the Mental Health Act 1983 to act rather as a legal backlash against previous reliance on medical discretion. Chapter 2 evaluates the Mental Health Act 1983 and considers both its positive attributes and its limitations. Chapter 3 examines the way in which

5   Bartlett, P & Sandland, R *Mental Health Law: Policy and Practice* (2000) Blackstone Press, London.

community care as a care policy began to have an increasingly prominent role in psychiatric provision throughout the 1980s. Consideration is given to how this changing policy moulded the primary legislation (the Mental Health Act 1983), in order to counteract the new challenges facing psychiatry. Inevitably, as reliance was placed on a piece of legislation, which had not been drafted with the community care approach in mind, many difficulties existed during this period of 'unofficial' community care, not least the limited provision for community services and the lack of legal safeguards protecting patients. Chapter 4 considers the impact that re-orienting psychiatric support to the community has had in terms of making decisions on behalf of those who cannot make their own decisions. This chapter looks at the role of the common law in ascertaining capacity and considers the position of the informal hospitalised patient as highlighted in the decision of the House of Lords: *R v Bournewood Community and Mental Health NHS Trust, ex p L*. The Law Commission proposals on mental incapacity, the more recent Government reform proposals and the suggestion of a generic Mental Incapacity Bill are also analysed in Chapter 4.

Chapter 5 evaluates the official response to the changes in psychiatric practice and policy and examines the suggested community treatment orders in the late 1980s and the introduction of supervised discharge under the Mental Health (Patients in the Community) Act 1995. Chapter 6 examines the period of disillusionment that followed the implementation of community care and examines the basis for this disenchantment. Official inquiries into community care failures, such as *The Report into the Care and Treatment of Christopher Clunis*, regularly highlight the lack of practical provision supporting the community care ideology. Chapter 6 focuses on two of these practical needs – the provision of suitable housing and the therapeutic role of occupational activities – and assesses the effectiveness of the current system in meeting these needs. Chapter 7 examines the particular difficulties associated with mentally disordered offenders and considers the mechanisms that exist to divert such individuals out of the criminal justice system and into the healthcare system, primarily under the Mental Health Act 1983. Chapter 7 proceeds to illustrate how the system of diversion has not been fully effective and how a high number of mentally disordered offenders continue to find their way inappropriately into the penal system. Finally, Chapter 8 examines the recent policy initiatives, primarily the White Paper, which outlines the Government's forthcoming reform plans. These plans attempt to respond to some of the inherent problems of the current system. It is questioned within Chapter 8 whether these proposals will, in fact, meet the recognised inadequacies, whether they will be compatible with the Human Rights Act 1998 and whether they will be suitably financed.

In writing this book, I am indebted to a variety of people and would like to express my thanks to them. The initial work for this book is based upon research conducted for my PhD, which was awarded by the University of Manchester. I am grateful to my former PhD supervisor, Professor Margot Brazier, for her unstinting support, advice and direction during my three years at the University of Manchester. I would also like to express my appreciation to my PhD examiner, Professor Michael Gunn, for his input. I must also thank Mr Martin Davey and Mrs Caroline Bridge at the University of Manchester for reading and commenting on parts of my thesis. I thank Dr Faye Boland, Mr Warren Barr and Mrs Amanda Warren-Jones at the University of Liverpool for reading parts of the work and providing helpful comments. Finally, I must offer my greatest thanks to my husband, Dr Robert Thomas, who has provided tremendous support, both academic and emotional in nature, throughout the writing of this book.

N.G.T.

Liverpool, March 2002

Contents

Preface   v
Table of statutes   xvii
List of cases   xxi

Chapter 1

Historical trends in the development of mental health and law   1

1   Introduction   1
2   Early Reactions to Insanity   3
3   The Rise of the Asylum   5
4   The Growing Lunacy Trade   6
5   Influences of the Asylum   7
6   The Rising Fear of Abuse   11
7   Reform and Resistance   14
8   The Rise and Fall of the New Profession   16
9   The Lunacy Act 1890   16
10   The Mental Treatment Act 1930   19
11   The Mental Health Act 1959   22

Chapter 2

The Mental Health Act 1983   27

1   Introduction   27
2   The Revival of Legalism   29
3   The Emergence of a 'New' Legalism   32

xii *Contents*

4   The Functions of Legal Regulation in the Mental Health Act 1983   34
5   Voluntary Admission to Hospital   36
6   Civil Commitment and the Promotion of Legal Safeguards   41
     (a) Guiding principles: the four categories of mental disorder   41
     (b) Mental illness   42
     (c) Mental impairment and severe mental impairment   43
     (d) Psychopathic disorder   44
     (e) Any other disorder or disability of mind   46
     (f) Further threshold criteria   47
7   The Detention Provisions   48
8   The Role of Mental Health Review Tribunals   52
9   Treatment Provisions   54
10   Protective Legal Mechanisms for Staff and Patients   59
11   Conclusion   62

Chapter 3
Re-orienting psychiatric support   65

1   Introduction   65
2   The Development of Community Care   67
3   The Modern Impetus for Change   71
4   Guardianship   73
     (a) The history of guardianship   73
     (b) The guardian's powers   74
     (c) Difficulties associated with guardianship   78
5   Leave of Absence   80
     (a) Application of leave of absence   80
     (b) The objective of extended leave   82
     (c) The Hallstrom decision   83
6   Greater Reliance on Pharmacology   85
7   The Provision of After-Care Services   86
8   Conclusion   94

Chapter 4
Decision-making on behalf of the mentally incapacitated   97

1   Introduction   97
2   Establishing Incapacity   99
3   Providing Non-Consensual Treatment for Physical Conditions   102

4 Bournewood and the Informal Patient 108
5 Law Reform and the Mentally Incapacitated 110
  (a) Reform 110
  (b) Mental capacity 112
  (c) Best interests 113
  (d) General authority to act reasonably 114
  (e) Continuing powers of attorney 115
  (f) A new Court of Protection 116
6 Conclusion 119

Chapter 5
Community care: law and policy 121

1 Introduction 121
2 Community Treatment Orders 123
3 International Influences 128
  (a) Introduction 128
  (b) Community treatment models 128
  (c) Criticisms surrounding community treatment orders 130
4 The Position in England and Wales 132
  (a) Introduction 132
  (b) The Ten-Point Plan and supervision registers 132
  (c) The Mental Health (Patients in the Community) Act 1995 134
5 Conclusion 143

Chapter 6
Community care: the road to disillusionment 145

1 Introduction 145
2 Inter-Agency Co-operation 147
3 The National Health Service and Community Care Act 1990 148
4 The Role of Housing 150
  (a) Background 150
  (b) Types of housing provision 151
  (c) Homelessness 155
  (d) The link between mental health problems and homelessness 157
  (e) The duty to provide adequate housing 159
  (f) Duties to the homeless 161
5 Establishing Financial Security 162

    (a) Employment   162
    (b) Alternative employment opportunities   170
6 Conclusion   171

Chapter 7
Mentally disordered offenders   173

1 Introduction   173
2 Diversion from the Criminal Justice System   173
3 The Role of the Mental Health Act 1983   176
4 Early Diversion   177
    (a) The police   177
    (b) The appropriate adult scheme   179
5 Diversion Before Sentencing   182
    (a) Proceeding with the prosecution   182
    (b) Bail   182
    (c) Remand to hospital for report or treatment   183
    (d) Other criminal law provisions   185
        (i) Unfitness to stand trial   185
        (ii) Insanity: the special verdict   186
6 Diversion at Sentencing Stage   187
    (a) Medical and pre-sentence reports   187
    (b) Therapeutic disposals   188
        (i) Hospital order   188
        (ii) The psychiatric probation order   189
        (iii) Guardianship order   190
        (iv) Interim hospital order   191
        (v) Restriction order   193
        (vi) Hospital direction   194
7 The Transfer of Prisoners to Hospital   197
    (a) Introduction   197
    (b) Transfer of sentenced prisoners   197
    (c) Transfer of unsentenced prisoners   198
8 Difficulties with the Diversion Policy   199

Chapter 8
Mental health law and policy: future directions   203

1 Introduction   203
2 The White Paper   205
    (a) The reform plans   205
    (b) The definition of mental disorder   207

         (c) A new care and treatment order   208
         (d) Increased public protection   211
    3   Future Moves   215

Chapter 9
Conclusion   219

Index   225

Table of statutes

	PAGE
Bail Act 1976	
s 3(6)	183
4(1)	182
Sch 1	
Pt I	183
Chronically Sick and Disabled Persons Act 1970	149
County Asylums Act 1808	6, 10
Crime (Sentences) Act 1997	194, 195, 201
s 46	195
47	195
49	192
Criminal Justice Act 1991	187
s 3	187
27(1)	191
Criminal Justice and Public Order Act 1994	182
s 25, 26	182
Criminal Procedure (Insanity) Act 1964	186
Criminal Procedure (Insanity and Unfitness to Plead) Act 1991	186, 187
s 2	185
3	185
4(5)	185
5	185
Disability Discrimination Act 1995	134, 147, 163, 164, 166, 167, 172
s 1(1)	164

	PAGE
Disability Discrimination Act 1995—*contd*	
s 2(1)	166
4	165
5(1)	165
(2)	165
(b)	165
(3)-(5)	165
6(1)(a)	165
(b)	166
(4)	166
7	163
8	166
11	165
(2)	165
Sch 1	
para 1-4	164
Sch 2	164
Sch 3	166
Disabled Persons (Employment) Act 1944	163
Disabled Persons (Employment) Act 1958	149, 163
Disabled Persons (Services, Consultation and Representation) Act 1986	149
Enduring Powers of Attorney Act 1985	115
Health and Social Services and Social Security Adjudications Act 1983	90
s 17	90

xviii Table of statutes

Health Services and Public Health Act
  1968
  s 45 92
Housing Act 1985
  Pt III (ss 58-78) 156
Housing Act 1988 .... 153, 154, 156
Housing Act 1996 .... 154, 156, 160
  s 175 156
  189 159
    (1)(c) 159
  191 159
Housing (Homelessness Persons) Act
  1977 .... 156, 159
  s 175 156
Human Rights Act 1998 .viii, 45, 206,
  214
  s 3, 19 206
Local Government and Housing Act
  1989 .... 153, 154
Lunacy Act 1890 ...... 3, 12, 16, 18,
    19, 20, 21, 22, 24,
    25, 29, 32, 36,
    209, 219, 220
  s 2 18
  29(1) 18
  30, 45 18
Lunacy Acts (Amendment) Act
  1889 .... 12, 18
Lunatics Act 1845 .... 12, 15, 16
Lunatics Act 1857 17
Madhouses Act 1774 .... 3, 7, 14
Madhouses Act 1828 15
Medical Registration Act 1858 14
Mental Deficiency Act
  1913 .... 66, 69, 70, 73, 94
Mental Health Act 1959 .... v, 3, 22,
    25, 26, 27, 28, 29,
    30, 31, 32, 33, 36,
    46, 47, 51, 52, 54,
    55, 59, 62, 66, 70,
    71, 74, 75, 76, 77,
    87, 95, 173
  s 1 59
  34 78
Mental Health Act 1983 ... v, vii, viii,
    1, 27, 28, 29, 34, 35,
    36, 37, 38, 41, 42, 44,
    46, 47, 53, 54, 55, 60,
    67, 97, 132, 144, 146, 173,
    176, 187, 203, 204, 207,
    208, 212, 215, 220
  s 1 ...... 43, 44, 61, 77, 196, 198
    (1)-(3) 41

Mental Health Act 1983—contd
  Pt II (ss 2-34) 35, 38, 39, 87
  s 2 .... 38, 40, 48, 49, 51,
    53, 80, 87, 109
    (2) 49
      (a), (b) 48
  3 .... 38, 40, 49, 51, 53,
    58, 80, 85, 87,
    109, 136, 139, 184
    (2)(b) 47
  4 .... 50, 51, 87
  5 ....39, 40, 140
    (2), (4) 39, 40
    (7) 39
  6 77
  7 .... 76, 191
  8 ....77, 78, 191
  9(3)(c) 77
  11(1) 49, 76
    (4) 49, 77
    (5) 76
  12 135
  16 .... 49, 58
  17 .... 47, 80, 82, 85, 87
    (4) 85
  18(3),(4) 78
  19 82
  20 58
    (1) 49
    (2) 83
  23 .... 39, 51
    (2) 51
      (a) 49
  25 49
  25A 134, 135
    (1) 135
    (4) 136
      (b) 136
  25B, 25C 134, 135
  25D 134, 135
    (4) 137
  25E 134, 135, 140
    (2) 140
    (4)(a) 140
  25F 134, 135
  25G 134, 135
    (2)(a), (b) 139
    (3)(a), (b) 139, 140
  25H-25J 134, 135
  29 77
  Pt III (ss 35-55) 176
  s 35 .... 183, 184, 185
    (2)(b) 184

Mental Health Act 1983—contd
s 35(5) 184
    (7) 183, 184
  36 .... 183, 184, 185
    (4) 184
    (6) 183, 184
  37 .... 188, 189, 190, 195
    (2)(a) 188
  38 191
    (1), (4) 192
  39 .... 189, 192
  39A 191
  41 .... 193, 196
    (1) 193
    (3), (6) 194
  45A 195, 196
    (3)(a) 195
    (10) 195
  45B 195
  46 195
  47 .... 196, 197, 198, 199
    (3) 198
  48 .... 196, 197, 198, 199
    (1) 198
  49 197
  50(1) 195
  Pt IV (ss 56-64) 55, 56, 78,
                  80, 81, 86, 97,
                  102, 139, 192
  s 56(1) 56
    (b) 178, 184
    (2) 57
  57 .... 56, 57, 59, 102
    (1)(a) 56
    (2)(a) 56
  58 .... 57, 86, 102
  62 .... 57, 58
    (1)(a)-(d) 58
  63 .... 56, 102, 103, 104
  66 142
  68 51
  71(1) 90
  72(1)(a), (b) 53
    (2)(b) 53
  73 54
    (1)(b) 54
    (2) 54, 88
  117 .... 35, 86, 88, 90,
                  91, 92, 93, 94, 96,
                  129, 134, 140
    (2) 91
  118 176
  121(2) 62

Mental Health Act 1983—contd
s 126 61
  127 61
    (1) 61
  129 78
  131(1) 36
  135 179
  135(6) 177
  136 .... 177, 178, 179, 181
  137 137
  139 .... 59, 60
  145 ....50, 58, 103
    (1) 47, 103, 177
Mental Health (Amendment) Act
  1982 .... 29, 37, 86
  s 62(2) 37
  Sch 2 37
Mental Health (Patients in the
  Community) Act 1995 ..... viii,
                121, 123, 134, 135,
                139, 141, 142, 143,
                145, 221
Mental Treatment Act 1930 ...3, 19,
                22, 24, 36, 66,
                70, 74, 95
National Assistance Act
  1948 .... 22, 177
  Pt III (ss 21-36) 92
National Health Service Act 1946 ..22
National Health Service Act
  1977 .... 87, 93
  s 21 92
  Sch 8 92
    para 2(1) 87
National Health Service and
  Community Care Act
  1990 .... 92, 96, 110,
                148, 149, 150, 157
  Pt III (ss 42-50) 92, 149
  s 46(3) 92
  47 .... 92, 93
    (1), (8) 92
  50 93
National Insurance Act 1946 22
Police and Criminal Evidence
  Act 1984
  s 11 133
  66 .... 177, 179, 180
  76 180
    (2)(a), (b) 180
  77 180
    (1) 180
  78 180

Police and Criminal Evidence
Act 1984—*contd*
  s 78(1) 180
Powers of Attorney Act 1971 ... 115
Powers of Criminal Courts Act 1973
  s 3(5), (6) 190
  Sch 1
    para 4 190
Rent Act 1965 153
Rent Act 1977 .... 153, 154
  s 70(1) 153
Representation of the People Act
  1949 37
  s 7(2)-(9) 37
Trial of Lunatics Act 1883
  s 2 186
Tribunals and Inquiries Act 1958 ...52
Vagrancy Act 1744 4
  s 20 4

List of cases

A

PAGE

A (medical treatment: male sterilisation), Re (2000), CA 107
Airedale National Health Service Trust v Bland (1993), HL 99, 113, 117
Application 7215/75: X v United Kingdom (1981), ECtHR 52, 138, 194
Application 10801/84: L v Sweden (1988) 81

B

B (a minor) (wardship: sterilisation), Re (1987); affd (1987), CA; on appeal
   (1988), HL 107
B v Barking Havering and Brentwood Community Healthcare NHS Trust
   (1999), CA 51, 82, 85, 86
B v Croydon Health Authority (1995), CA 103
Bolam v Friern Hospital Management Committee (1957) 106

C

C (adult: refusal of medical treatment), Re (1994) 59, 101
Campbell v Secretary of State for the Home Department (1988), HL 89
Clunis v Camden and Islington Health Authority (1998), CA 88
Cobham v Forest Healthcare NHS Trust (1995) 166

D

Din v Wandsworth London Borough Council (1983), HL 156
Dlodlo v Mental Health Review Tribunal for South Thames Region (1996),
   CA 184

E

E (a minor) (medical treatment), Re (1991) 107

F

F (mental patient: sterilisation), Re (1990), CA; affd (1990),
  HL 98, 105, 106, 113
Fox, ex p. See R v Ealing District Health Authority, ex p Fox

G

GF, Re (1992) 107

J

J v C (1970), HL 76
James v Mayors and Burgesses of the London Borough of Havering (1992),
  CA 60
Johnson v United Kingdom (1997), ECtHR 89

K

KB (adult) (mental patient: medical treatment), Re (1994) 103
Kynaston v Secretary of State for Home Affairs (1981), CA 44, 51

L

L v Sweden (Application 10801/84) (1988) 81
Lewis v North Devon District Council (1981) 160
Lubert v Italy (1984) 138

M

MB (an adult: medical treatment), Re (1997), CA 100, 105
M'Naghten Case. See R v McMaughton
Mason v Skilling (1974), HL 154
Metropolitan Property Holdings Ltd v Finegold (1975) 153

P

Palmer v Peabody Trust (1975) 153
Pountney v Griffiths (1976), HL 59, 60
Practice Note (Official Solicitor: sterilisation) (1996) 106

R

R (a minor) (wardship: consent to treatment), Re (1991), CA 59
R v Birch (1989), CA 188, 193
R v Bournewood Community and Mental Health NHS Trust, ex p L (1999),
    CA; revsd (1999), HL 37, 38, 39, 49,
                                                        98, 105, 108, 209
R v Bracknell Justices, ex p Griffiths. See Pountney v Griffiths
R v Brent London Borough Council, ex p Awua (1995), HL 156
R v Brent London Borough Council, ex p Gunning (1985) 141
R v Broadmoor Special Hospital Authority, ex p S (1998), CA 61
R v Cambridge District Health Authority, ex p B (1995), CA 93
R v Canons Park Mental Health Review Tribunal, ex p A (1995),
    CA 47, 49, 58, 76, 103
R v Central London County Court (1997) 77
R v Collins (Dr James Donald) and Ashworth Hospital Health Authority, ex p
    Brady (Ian Stewart) (2000) 104
R v Courtney (1987), CA 193
R v Crown Court at Cardiff, ex p Kellam (1993) 133
R v Ealing District Health Authority, ex p Fox (1993) 88, 90
R v Ealing London Borough Council, ex p Sidhu (1983) 156
R v Eastleigh Borough Council, ex p Beattie (No 2) (1984) 160
R v Gardiner (1967), CA 193
R v Gardner, ex p L (1986) 47, 49, 82, 83
R v Gloucestershire County Council, ex p Barry (1995); revsd (1996), CA;
    affd (1997), HL 90, 93
R v Gloucestershire County Council, ex p Mahfood (1995) 93
R v Gordon (June Christina) (1981) 189
R v Gunnell (1966), CCA 188
R v Hall (1988), CA 43
R v Hallstrom, ex p W (1986) 47, 49, 51, 78,
                                                        82, 83, 84, 88
R v Hertfordshire County Council, ex p Three Rivers District Council (1992) .. 93
R v Higginbotham (1961), CCA 188
R v Holmes (1979) 61
R v Inner London Education Authority, ex p Ali (1990) 90
R v Islington London Borough Council, ex p McMillan (1995) 90, 93
R v Kirklees Metropolitan Borough Council, ex p C (a minor) (1993), CA 48
R v London Borough of Harrow, ex p Cobham (1999) 91
R v London Borough of Richmond, ex p Watson (1999) 91
R v McFarlane (1975) 189
R v McNaughton (1843), HL 186
R v Managers of Gordon Hospital, ex p AX london (1997) 77
R v Manchester City Council, ex p Stennett (1999) 91
R v Mental Health Act Commission, ex p X (1988) 42, 56, 59, 103
R v Mental Health Review Tribunal, ex p Clatworthy (1985) 42
R v Merseyside Mental Health Review Tribunal, ex p K (1990), CA 54
R v Newham London Borough Council, ex p Campbell (1995) 160
R v Newington (1990), CA 61
R v North Devon District Council, ex p Lewis. See Lewis v North Devon District
    Council
R v North West London Mental Health NHS Trust, ex p S (1998), CA 184
R v Officer (1976) 189

xxiv List of cases

PAGE

R v Oxford Regional Mental Health Review Tribunal, ex p Secretary of State for the Home Department. See Campbell v Secretary of State for the Home Department
R v Pritchard (1836) 185
R v Redcar & Cleveland Borough Council, ex p Armstrong (1999) 91
R v Salford City Council, ex p Devenport (1983), CA 159
R v Secretary of State for Education and Employment, ex p Morris (1995); affd (1995), CA 142
R v Secretary of State for Scotland (1998), Ct of Sess; revsd (1998) 50
R v Secretary of State for Social Services, ex p Association of Metropolitan Authorities (1986) 141
R v Tower Hamlets NHS Trust, ex p Appleby (1997) 89
R v Wandsworth Borough Council, ex p Banbury (1986) 159
R v Waveney District Council, ex p Bowers (1983), CA 159
Reid v Secretary of State for Scotland (1999), HL 47
Rochdale Healthcare (NHS) Trust v C (1997) 105

S

S-C (mental patient: habeas corpus), Re (1996), CA 77
St George's Healthcare NHS Trust v S (1999), CA 104

T

T (adult: refusal of treatment), Re (1993), CA 59, 112
T v T (1988) 78
Tameside and Glossop Acute Services Trust v CH (1996) 104
Tower Boot Co Ltd v Jones (1995), EAT 166

W

W v L (1974), CA 42, 43
Waldron, ex p (1986), CA 60
Winch v Jones (1985), CA 60
Winterwerp v Netherlands (1979), ECtHR 137, 138, 214

X

X v United Kingdom (Application 7215/75) (1981), ECtHR 52, 138, 194

Chapter 1
Historical trends in the development of mental health and law

1 Introduction

People have always been susceptible to attacks of insanity and chronic mental illness. Indeed, we may all be subject to mental illness at some time in our lives. Therefore, the question of how to deal with mental illness and the provision of appropriate care has, throughout history, been the subject of significant inquiry and a source of debate. This is not only a problem for the individual, as it affects society as a whole. It has been estimated that one adult in every seven suffers from depression, anxiety, or some other form of mental disorder.[1] Recent Department of Health figures have estimated that one adult in four will suffer from some form of mental illness at some stage in his life.[2] Consequently, mental ill-health is not a small problem, nor should it be regarded as one.

The intention of this chapter is to map out in broad terms the legislative developments of mental health law up to the current legislation, the Mental Health Act 1983. It is vital to bring to light the historical trends in the development of mental health law, for only if we realise the past can we confront and evaluate the present challenges facing mental health law. These developments have been characterised by the shifting emphasis between a patient's rights and interests and the treatment of his needs as someone classified by society as suffering from mental illness, and the increasing demands for public protection.

1 Randall Kropp, P et al 'The perceptions of correctional officers towards mentally disordered offenders' *International Journal of Law and Psychiatry* 1989, Vol 12, p 181, at p 187.
2 Department of Health Press Release 98/126, 2 April 1998. See also Department of Health *Modernising Mental Health Services: Safe, Sound and Supportive* (1988) HMSO, London.

2   *Historical trends in the development of mental health and law*

The discussion has largely focused on the conflict between the patient and his individual needs and how such decisions regarding the patient should be made and by whom? It is a basic theme in this chapter that this discussion has been conducted between the two viewpoints of legalism (or liberalism) and medicalism (or welfarism). Proponents of legalism view the construction of a framework of legal rules as being essential for the protection of patients. They argue that the interests of the patient and psychiatrist are essentially incompatible. The psychiatrist wants to control the patient and the patient wants to be free from any control. Without formalised rules laying down the rights and responsibilities of patient and psychiatrist alike, the more vulnerable party (the patient) will be disadvantaged. Unless legal controls are formulated, there is no assurance that the psychiatrist will use the compulsory powers in the patient's best interests. The legalist perceives the provision of mental health care as offering an opportunity where one person can force their view upon another unless a structured legal regime exists. 'Legalism focuses on the coercive aspects of psychiatry such as detention, forcible treatment and restraint, and seeks to regulate them by imposing due process safeguards.'[3] Advocates of medicalism insist that such tightly-woven legal rules prevent the use of highly-trained medical judgment from being used effectively, thereby threatening therapeutic endeavour. Medicalism seeks to encourage the view that the medical practitioner is in the best position to make decisions regarding treatment and care programmes and that the administration of such programmes should be a matter for professional discretion. This viewpoint encourages trust to be placed in the psychiatric profession. Jones believes that those favouring legal regulation to promote the rights of patients are adherents of 'resuscitated Diceyism',[4] which reduces the opportunity for the improvement of patient welfare. Legal rules are inappropriate because treatment consists of the exercise of clinical judgment and the best people to judge how the patient's needs can be most effectively fulfilled are those with the professional training and expertise. Medicalists believe that mental health care provision is an intervention allowing many patients to be liberated from the confines of mental illness from which they can regain control of their lives. The psychiatrist is viewed as acting for the best interests of the patient with the aim of improving the patient's condition, a goal that is ultimately shared by the patient.

This struggle between legalism and medicalism is shown throughout the history of mental health legislation in England and Wales. The policy

---

3   Fennell, P *Treatment Without Consent: Law, Psychiatry and the Treatment of Mentally Disordered People Since 1845* (1996) Routledge, London, p 10.
4   Jones, K 'The limitations of the legal approach to mental health' *International Journal of Law and Psychiatry* 1980, Vol 3, p 1, at p 10.

underpinning the Lunacy Act 1890 reflected a legalist reaction to the unstructured and exploitative provision of care for the insane. The adoption of a formalised legal structure in the Act revealed a pessimistic attitude towards medical judgment and the fear that the sane might also be subjected to wrongful confinement. Yet by 1930, when the Mental Treatment Act 1930 was passed, the political, medical and legal mood had again shifted. In the 40 years since the Lunacy Act 1890 confidence in the medical profession had been re-established. The Mental Treatment Act 1930 rejected legalism in favour of placing greater power in the hands of the medical professional; a support which continued in the Mental Health Act 1959. The development of mental health legislation over the last 150 years has therefore seen the pendulum swing from one view to the other. Medicalism and legalism represent these two points of view. At any given time, the favoured conception has been dependent on the social and political mood, the current attitudes of society and contemporary psychiatric practice. These factors have regularly influenced the shift in policy and, consequently, the law.

This chapter will examine the development of mental health legislation up until the mid-1960s. It will focus upon the political and social conditions that initiated the process of legal reform, and how the concerns and goals of all those involved with the provision of psychiatric care have revealed themselves to be cyclical in nature. The retracing of these statutes is vital in understanding what the motivations for mental health law reform were and continue to be to this day.

2 Early Reactions to Insanity

The passing of the Madhouses Act 1774 marked the beginning of a new era of lunacy legislation. The Act introduced a system for inspecting madhouses and required licences for the first time. It was recognised that the insane, as a group, were different from other unfortunate individuals and had separate needs. Prior to this, 'madmen were assimilated into the much larger, more amorphous class of the morally disreputable, the poor and the impotent'.[5] No public support was offered to the insane or their families; instead they struggled along relying on haphazard charitable handouts and various forms of parochial relief. Lunatics were still just one group among the many relying upon this parish aid, with the result that many received very little support. Up until the end of the seventeenth century, the vast majority of those thought to be mentally unstable were

---

5   Scull, A *The Most Solitary of Afflictions: Madness and Society in Britain, 1700 - 1900* (1993) Yale University Press, New Haven, p 1.

cared for by their families within the confines of their local, often isolated, communities.

However, by the turn of the eighteenth century interest in controlling and 'hiding' the indigent and deviant began to grow. Many institutions sprang up; some privately owned and some publicly funded. Those institutions which already existed, such as Bethlam Hospital, expanded considerably. Isolating such individuals from the rest of society in large institutions was increasingly approved.[6] Hospitals and workhouses were built in many of the cities and large market towns in the first-half of the eighteenth century, and between 1719 and 1751 seven new hospitals alone were added to the foundations of St Bartholomew's, St Thomas' and Bethlem. These purpose-built institutions became places for the socially undesirable and discarded. The existence of these large, imposing buildings provided the necessary foundation for the Vagrancy Act 1744 from which the law relating to the control of people with mental disorder originates. This Act was designed to protect property owners from those who did not own property and were perceived to be of the lower social order. It aimed at preventing those who 'wander abroad', such as gypsies and beggars, from damaging and stealing from others, and specifically included reference to the insane. The Vagrancy Act 1774, s 20 stated: 'there are sometimes persons, who by Lunacy, or otherwise, are furiously mad or are so far disordered in their senses that they may be dangerous to be permitted to go abroad'.[7] Upon finding such an individual in a public place, two or more justices of the peace were provided with the power to direct a public official, such as a constable or churchwarden, to escort the individual to a secure place where, if necessary, he could be chained up.

Despite the Vagrancy Act 1774 with its power to remove undesirables wandering abroad and to conceal lunatics from public view, many individuals remained in the care of their families. Such care required the constant presence of a family member or friend and as the eighteenth century ended this became more and more difficult to fulfil. Some have argued that the rise of the institution came into being as a direct result of the Industrial Revolution, when the 'family', as a social-base, changed in response to the growing demands of the market.[8] An increasingly mobile population meant that social relationships became more transient and the informal support structure, upon which many vulnerable people relied, disappeared. Families who did stay together found it gradually more difficult to support an unproductive relative, as each member of the family

6 This was founded in 1247 as the Priory of the Order of St Mary of Bethlehem.
7 The Vagrancy Act 1744, s 20. See also, Unsworth, C *The Politics of Mental Health Legislation* Oxford University Press, Oxford, p 53.
8 Mechanic, D *Mental Health and Social Policy* (1969) Prentice Hall, Englewood Cliffs, New Jersey.

was expected to work. Caring for a mentally unstable relative within the home became an unrealistic option in practice as urban poverty became a growing problem. Scull has further argued that instead of there being a simple correlation between the institution and the growth of large industrial cities, the rise of the asylum was brought about by the emerging capitalist market economy and capitalist ideology, which led to a change in the attitudes of people towards the vulnerable.[9] Capitalism dominated the lives of urban and rural populations, which in turn left little room for the provision of humanitarian relief.

3 The Rise of the Asylum

Greater urbanisation following the Industrial Revolution shifted attitudes away from localised community relief towards more efficient and specialised systems dealing with the poor, the insane and other groups. The capitalist ideology encouraged organised efficiency, which the makeshift system of relief did not reflect. Consequently, throughout the nineteenth century, the mentally disordered were rapidly despatched to asylums. Past experience of confining the mentally disordered in workhouses and gaols had proved troublesome, as neither institution was suitably equipped to deal with these demanding inmates.

The large indefinable group which represented the needy and disreputable classes included the insane, the poor, petty criminals and physically disabled. Of course, those who were mentally unstable could clearly be differentiated from the rest, yet serious attempts to house them in separate facilities were not made until the mid-nineteenth century. The establishment of the market economy prompted the need to distinguish between insanity and other deviant behaviour. Those who were insane were unproductive and could not work, whereas the poor and petty criminals could be made to contribute to the economy. The provision of parochial relief in the form of workhouses and charitable aid interfered with this as it was thought to encourage idleness and lassitude. At the height of the Industrial Revolution the population was looked upon as an industrial labour force and all those who could work were expected to obtain remunerative employment. A distinction was thereby established between those who could work and those who could not. Setting up asylums for the insane segregated them from the general public while, at the same time, measures to force the able-bodied to work could also be carried out.

---

9   Scull, A 'The Most Solitary of Afflictions: Madness and Society in Britain, 1700 1900' (1993) Yale University Press, New Haven, p 29.

4 The Growing Lunacy Trade

However, the charitable institutions were unable to provide for all of those who needed help. At this time barely any consideration was given to the possibility of curing 'madness' and therefore treating the insane therapeutically was considered futile. 'Mechanical restraint' by way of shackles, cages and straitjackets, was a common method of controlling the insane and as such, treatment did not require experienced medical supervision. Owing to the entrepreneurial atmosphere of the nineteenth century, the provision of insanity 'relief' emerged as a growing trade.[10] The demand to house the insane was increasing and up-and-coming capitalists were quick to provide supply. Throughout England and Wales, private madhouses were established with the primary aim of profit-making. Keepers of madhouses were frequently able to secure large fees for their services. Many of those who managed charitable concerns also owned and ran private asylums. For example, William Battie, who founded St Luke's in London, often spoke of the maniac's plight and society's indifference, yet he used patients of St Luke's to populate his own private institutions in Islington and Clerkenwell.[11] Setting up a private madhouse was not difficult. There were no licensing laws to contend with and few asked any questions about the care being offered to the inmates. As competition grew, many establishments advertised their services and often made claims about the frequency of 'cure', yet many madhouses were without proper medical supervision. However, few relatives or friends of affluent inmates investigated or complained because the key benefit associated with the madhouse was its discretion. Individuals could enter the asylum and effectively cease to exist. During this period, anxieties about the heirs of large estates being removed to an institution by another family member were relatively common.

The cumulative effect of this growth in the number of private madhouses and the increase of rate-funded county asylums since the County Asylums Act 1808 led to a re-orientation of how the mentally disordered were cared for. Caring for the individual within the home was no longer considered a feasible option and many ended up in an institution. Yet few private madhouses were purpose-built, most being cheaply-converted houses, and as no legal restraints were placed on prospective keepers, inmates often suffered abusive treatment. Owning and running a madhouse was a financial enterprise. Attendants were not trained in caring for the insane and, owing to this, reliance on restraint by way of chains and manacles

10   Parry-Jones, W *The Trade in Lunacy* (1972) Routledge and Kegan Paul, London.
11   Battie, W *A Treatise on Madness* (1758) Whiston & White, London. See also, Andrews, J 'A respectable mad-doctor? Dr Richard Hale, F. R. S. (1670 – 1728)' *Notes and Records of the Royal Society of London* 1990, Vol 44, p 169.

was commonplace. Yet not all private madhouses were run primarily for profit. Some made every effort to provide a safe and comfortable environment for their inmates.[12] However, these attempts were rarely noticed as more reports of harsh and uncaring treatment were published.[13] Towards the middle of the eighteenth century, calls to investigate the lunacy trade became more vocal. In 1763, a half-hearted Parliamentary investigation of private London madhouses was carried out. The investigation uncovered many examples of inadequate care yet attempts to legislate were vehemently opposed by the Royal College of Physicians as many of its members, like William Battie, were benefiting from the trade. Eleven years after the 1763 investigation was undertaken, the Madhouses Act 1774 was enacted. The aim of this legislation was to protect the rights of wealthy, private patients and to ensure the running and maintenance of private madhouses to a certain standard. However, the Madhouses Act 1774 was completely ineffectual. Although paupers far outnumbered private patients, they were not covered by the Act. Moreover, while it became compulsory for each madhouse to be licensed, the licensing board had no powers to reject a licensing application and if, upon inspection, a madhouse was found guilty of incompetence or ill-treatment the inspectors could visit no sanctions upon it.

5 Influences of the Asylum

It was not until King George III (1760–1820) began to experience psychiatric problems in 1788 that medical interest in mental illness began to emerge and the volume of medical writings in the area expanded.[14] However, treatment remained focused on the body rather than the mind. As Scull observed, if doctors had treated the mind separately from the body, this would have questioned the foundations of Christianity and opened up the field to the services of the spiritualist.[15] Francis Willis' treatment of George III typifies this approach.

12 See for example, Smith, L D 'Eighteenth century madhouse practice: The Prouds of Bilston' *History of Psychiatry* 1992, Vol 3, p 45.
13 'The idea of a mad-house is apt to excite ... the strongest emotions of horror and alarm ...', per Pargeter, W in 1792 as quoted in Scull, A *The Most Solitary of Afflictions: Madness and Society in Britain, 1700 - 1900* (1993) Yale University Press, New Haven, p 24.
14 For example, the inception of the Association of Medical Officers of Asylums and Hospitals in 1841, which later became the Medico-Psychological Association in 1865, and then finally the Royal College of Psychiatrists in 1925, produced its first journal, *Asylum Journal*, in 1853, which became the *British Journal of Psychiatry* in 1962. See further, Jones, K *Lunacy, Law, and Conscience 1744 – 1845* (1955) Routledge and Kegan Paul, London, p 26.
15 Scull, A 'From Madness to Mental Illness: Medical Men as Moral Entrepreneurs' *European Journal of Sociology* 1975, Vol 16, p 219.

'[The King] ... was no longer treated as a human being. His body was ... encased in a machine which left it no liberty of motion. He was sometimes chained to a stake. He was frequently beaten and starved, and at best he was kept in subjection by menacing and violent language.'[16]

Blisters, seatons, cupping and scarifying were all common methods of the time, which involved invasive physical treatment such as the burning of skin or the opening of a vein. Such treatments would today be viewed with repugnance as methods of torture. Yet, during this same period, there was a newly developing method of treatment called 'moral therapy', which has proved to be one of the most important vehicles in the progression of modern psychiatry. 'Moral therapy' adopted a pragmatic approach to the care of the insane. Advocates of this method believed that rather than treating a lunatic like an animal, his standing as a 'moral subject' should be recognised. 'Lunatics are not devoid of understanding, nor should they be treated as if they were; on the contrary, they should be treated as rational beings.'[17] 'Moral therapy' included therapeutic techniques such as offering 'pleasant pastimes ... [such as painting and basket weaving] ... [which] served as diversions from painful thoughts or obsessive chains of ideas',[18] which were designed to affect the patient's psychology.[19] It incorporated a more humane and sensitive approach to caring for the mentally disordered, recognising that the use of fear, brutality and restraint would be ineffective.[20] A leading pioneer of this approach was William Tuke, a Quaker philanthropist, who founded the York Retreat in 1792.

The York Retreat and its practice of moral therapy was immortalised by Samuel Tuke's book *Description of the Retreat*, published in 1813 and dedicated to his grandfather, William Tuke.[21] The book laid down the objectives of moral therapy and the particular approach adopted by the York Retreat. Details of the Retreat's accounts, treatment regimes, staff and management were also outlined. The book was significant in allowing

16 Jones, K *Lunacy, Law and Conscience 1744 - 1845* (1955) Routledge and Kegan Paul, London, pp 41-42. See also, MacAlpine, I & Hunter, R *George III and the Mad-Business* (1969) Allen Lane, London.
17 Bakewell, T *The Domestic Guide in Cases of Insanity* (1805) privately published, Stafford, pp 55–56.
18 Digby, A *Madness, Morality and Medicine* (1985) Cambridge University Press, Cambridge, p 34.
19 Carlson, E & Dain, N 'The Psychotherapy That Was Moral Treatment' *American Journal of Psychiatry* 1960, Vol 117, p 519
20 Sanbourne Bockoven, J 'Moral Treatment in American Psychiatry' *Journal of Nervous and Mental Diseases* 1956, Vol 124, p 167.
21 Tuke, S *Description of the Retreat* (1813; reprinted, introduced and annotated by R Hunter and I MacAlpine (1964) London, Dawson).

the theory of moral therapy to be disseminated to a wider audience. Contrasted with the activities of the York Asylum, the Retreat offered inmates kindness and respect. It adopted fully the methods of moral therapy and was managed by laypersons. Moral therapy offered little room for medical intervention and its success affirmed the growing doubts about the role of medicine in the care of the insane. In contrast, the York Asylum was seen to follow a medical model and was presided over by a physician. Patients were not treated with dignity, the vast majority of them being chained to the floor and left to survive in gloomy, crowded cells. The Asylum was bedevilled by stories of mismanagement and alleged abuse and simply could not compete with the glowing reputation of the Retreat. The success of moral therapy and the apparent failure of medicine threatened the role of medicine in the management of the insane.

'The Victorian age [also] saw the transformation of the madhouse into the asylum [and then] into the mental hospital.'[22] As moral therapy emerged as the primary source of treatment, the asylum began to play a more prominent role. Alienists (madhouse owners), who administered moral treatment to the insane, saw the asylum as a crucial therapeutic instrument. The environment of care became a chief factor in the potential for success. Henry Maudsley wrote in 1868 that:

> '[t]o remove the patient from the midst of those circumstances under which insanity has been produced must be the first aim of treatment ... . An entire change in the surroundings will sometimes of itself lead to his recovery.'[23]

Unlike the madhouses of the eighteenth century, the asylums of the nineteenth century were purpose-built. Thought was given to the architecture and design of these buildings, with the aim of maximising the possibilities for cure. Indeed, William Tuke and his son Henry drew up the first plans for the York Retreat after visiting St Luke's and forming an idea of the essential elements needed for the Retreat's structure.[24] Previously, madhouses had only been concerned with the provision of secure and safe confinement of the insane. Therefore the physical structure of the asylum became more significant throughout the nineteenth century and from this grew the culture of institutionalism.

22 Scull, A 'Psychiatry in the Victorian Era' in Scull, A (ed) *Madhouses, Mad-Doctors and Madmen* (1981) The Athlone Press, London.
23 As quoted in Busfield, J *Managing Madness: Changing Ideas and Practice* (1986) Hutchinson, London. Also quoted in Bean, P & Mounser, P *Discharged From Mental Hospital* (1993) Macmillan in Association with MIND Publications, London, p 4.
24 Digby, A *Madness, Morality and Medicine* (1985) Cambridge University Press, London, p 18.

10 *Historical trends in the development of mental health and law*

In the nineteenth century, superintendents used the design of their private asylums to attract wealthy patients. The legitimacy of psychiatry and of those practising the art relied heavily upon the public's response. Those asylums that could not attract the 'right' clientele either became establishments for pauper and criminal lunatics or closed. Public asylums did not have this particular concern. Indeed, public asylums often became the haven for a variety of people, from those who were suffering mental disease to vagrants and paupers who failed to find relief elsewhere. Overcrowding became a major problem. Lancaster Asylum was one of the first built under the County Asylums Act 1808. In its early days the treatment regime consisted of coercion and restraint. By the time moral therapy arrived, the asylum contained over twice as many inmates as the early reformers had envisaged for a curative institution. In 1827 there were, on average, 116 inmates per asylum. By 1850 there were 297 inmates per asylum and by 1890 there were 802 inmates per asylum.[25] Such overcrowding became a standard feature of pauper and criminal lunatic asylums in the nineteenth century. For example, at Warburton's White House, 170 male lunatics were often cared for by only two attendants and many relied on convalescing inmates for their meals and the little care they did receive.[26]

Overcrowding was not the only problem associated with the institution. The asylum, in its many guises of hospital, prison and workhouse, featured prominently in Victorian Britain, by which time concerns about the negative impact of institutionalism were beginning to surface. The asylum had been used as a panacea to the social problems of the day, but this approach was beginning to attract heavy criticism.[27] Towards the end of the nineteenth century the overcrowding signified the asylum's inability to treat effectively or cure the patient. The notion that the asylum offered a curative environment was no longer accepted. Many leading protagonists in the mental health field were asked to report before the 1877 Parliamentary Select Committee on Lunacy Law as to their view on institutional care for the mentally disordered.[28] Sir James Coxe, a Medical Commissioner of the Scottish Board of Lunacy, and Dr Joseph Mortimer Granville, who chaired *The Lancet's* inquiry in 1877 into 'The Care and Cure of the Insane', both suggested that life in an asylum could lead to the further deterioration of many patients. Reference was made to the

25 Skultans, V *English Madness* (1979) Routledge and Kegan Paul, London, p 122.
26 House of Commons *Report from the Select Committee on Pauper Lunatics in the County of Middlesex* 1827, p 3, 120–1, 124– 6.
27 Granville, JM *The Care and Cure of the Insane* (1877) Hardwicke and Bogue, London, Vol 1, p 8.
28 House of Commons *Report from the House of Commons Select Committee on Lunacy Law* 1877.

frequency of patients falling into a kind of 'dementia' when living in groups of large numbers under a regimented system.

Therefore by 1877 it was already recognised that patients living in such an environment could suffer from institutionalism, preventing many from living in the community again. Those inmates that might have coped with the outside world were also prevented from doing so because as John Connolly pointed out in 1830, '[o]nce confined, the very confinement is admitted as the strongest of all proofs that a man must be mad'.[29] The stigma of being an inmate of an asylum was almost impossible to shake off. Calls to eradicate the asylum and to replace it with non-institutional methods were made throughout the second-half of Queen Victoria's reign, yet these arguments fell on deaf ears. The issue of whether additional control should be introduced to ensure decisions to detain individuals in asylums were made correctly continued to be raised.[30] Institutionalism had bred its own kind of mental disorder. Whatever abilities patients might have possessed when they entered the asylum were soon lost and by the end of the nineteenth century huge populations of asylum inmates were condemned to spending the rest of their lives in the asylum.

6 The Rising Fear of Abuse

Most of the inmates in these institutions were deserted and left to their bleak futures. Meanwhile, the treatment of the insane was exposed to inspection.[31] Many visitors found the inmates living in dank, foul smelling cells with little ventilation; few were fully clothed and many were chained to the walls of their cell. Edward Wakefield, a land agent and leading parliamentary reformer observed that '[t]he nakedness of [the inmates was] covered by a blanket gown only ... many unfortunate women were locked up in their cells, naked and chained on straw'.[32] Few inmates ever received regular treatment for their mental conditions and despite many institutions having a resident apothecary, many of the inmates' physical ailments were also neglected. Desperately low levels of staffing meant that most asylums were forced to rely on mechanical restraint.

---

29 Connolly, J *An Inquiry Concerning the Indications of Insanity* (1830) Taylor, London, pp 4–5.
30 As found for example, in the case of Mrs Georgiana Weldon in (1884) Times, 18 March to 2 April.
31 House of Commons *Report of the Select Committee on Madhouses* 1815.
32 Wakefield, E 'Extracts from the Report of the Committee employed to visit houses and hospitals for the confinement of insane persons' *The Medical and Physical Journal* 1814, Vol 32, p 122.

Lunacy reformers continued to call for the establishment of a system of public asylums, which would be subject to a national inspectorate. By the 1840s, the possibility of having these demands fulfilled became increasingly likely as the abusive treatment of inmates was gradually more publicised. The problems associated with the current asylum system were well known but it was also accepted that the scale of the trouble could not be fully calculated without a more comprehensive inspection of the country's asylums and madhouses. In 1842, Lord Granville Somerset, the chair of the Metropolitan Commissioners, which was employed to carry out the inspection, required the process to be extended for three years. The *Report of the Metropolitan Commissioners in Lunacy* was completed before the close of the 1844 Parliamentary session.[33] It was observed that the real problem associated with the 37 madhouses in the Metropolitan area was a common evasion of the law rather than cruelty and neglect of the patients. The recommendations of the report had two objectives: to establish a unified system of administration over asylums and madhouses; and to extend the lunacy laws to cover all types of institution. The result of this report was the enactment of two Lunatics Acts in 1845. The first Lunacy Act (8 & 9 Victoria c 100) established a permanent national Lunacy Commission, an independent body which had powers to monitor standards and govern private madhouses, county asylums and hospitals. The second Lunacy Act (8 & 9 Victoria c 126) made the erection of county and borough asylums to house pauper lunatics compulsory.

The conditions of the insane in institutions were not the only public concerns. As more asylums were built and faith in the institution continued to gain pace, the fear that sane people might also be locked away began to sweep the country. This concern was generated by the rising levels of detention and is reflected in the literature of the time, which described experiences of unjust confinement. In Wilkie Collins' *The Woman in White*, Lady Glyde was incarcerated by her husband in a private madhouse for the 'clear gain of thirty thousand pounds'.[34] Likewise, stories of abuse within the lunatic asylum such as that depicted in Charles Reade's novel *Hard Cash*[35] and Henry Cockton's *The Life and Adventures of Valentine Vox the Ventriliquist,*[36] fuelled the fears of the public. Such tales added to the growing public concern that many were being wrongfully confined. The public supported the idea of placing the mentally unstable in the secure environment of an asylum, yet the fear of false imprisonment

33 *Report of the Metropolitan Commissioners in Lunacy to the Lord Chancellor* (1844) Bradbury and Evans, London.
34 Collins, W *The Woman in White* (1994) Penguin Popular Classics, London, p 388. This book was serialised in *All the Year Round* in 1859/60.
35 Reade, C *Hard Cash* (1863) Sampson Low, Son & Marston, London.
36 Cockton, H *The Life and Adventures of Valentine Vox the Ventriliquist* (1840) Robert Tyas, London.

lingered. The petition to acquire further legal safeguards to protect the innocent persevered. The thresholds for justifiable medical coercion needed to be defined and established.

However, the clarity of these thresholds depended greatly on the meaning of madness. Early on madness was understood as being a fearsome state of affairs, where the individual became uncontrollable and little more than an animal. There were often conflicting feelings of sympathy for the insane and their families and fear, because the condition represented a real threat to the social order and placed huge costs on society: '[t]heir behaviour imperilled the fundamental principles of social life: household and hierarchy'.[37] Up to the late eighteenth century, insanity was thought to be incurable. Providing for the individual's basic daily needs and ensuring his safety and the safety of others was all that could be done. Yet after the apparent cure of King George III by Francis Willis, medical theories and debate about the treatment and cure of the insane began to emerge. With the advent of the 'asylum' as a purpose-built institutional system for the care and treatment of the insane, a need was created for the establishment of a professional class whose responsibility it was to cater for and control this group. This period saw the steady rise of psychiatry as a profession in its own right. At this time, the medical profession consisted of three categories: the physician, the surgeon and the apothecary. The physician was the doctor of the well to do, who possessed a degree in medicine and was a member of the Royal College of Physicians. The surgeon gained his skills by undergoing an apprenticeship and his reputation was inextricably linked with gruesome surgical procedures. The lower-middle and working classes employed the apothecary, who also learned his trade under an apprenticeship. The profession was not regulated so it was good fortune if a high-quality doctor was found and in the battle against insanity few others could be relied upon. Doctors already controlled the treatment of most physical ailments, and expanding this reliance to cover disorders of the mind provided many patients and their families with some comfort. By exploiting this to the full, doctors managed to justify their claims of exclusivity over treating the insane.

Doctors working within the lunacy field soon realised that it offered a number of advantages over more acceptable specialisms. The growing lunacy trade made the running of a private madhouse a highly lucrative enterprise. For the first time, doctors were guaranteed a secure source of income and as the field began to gain some respectability this profit continued. Increasingly, links between medicine and insanity were being made, and with the arrival of medical books, which focused on the

---

37 MacDonald, M *Mystical Bedlam: Madness, Anxiety, and Healing in Seventeenth Century England* (1981) Cambridge University Press, Cambridge, pp 147–48.

treatment of insanity, this connection was strengthened.[38] The medical profession also quickly recognised that dominating the lunacy market would increase its status. Still attached to the lunacy trade were connotations of profiteering and 'quackery' but gradually, as doctors gained more control, psychiatry became recognised as a separate field of medicine. As the emphasis continued to shift towards providing the insane with its own asylums, the medical profession was able to acquire a large stake in this new market. Since the Madhouses Act 1774, the law had given doctors the power of patient certification and the presence of an asylum in each borough for the insane poor provided the scope for expanding this discipline.[39] Frequently doctors disagreed over an individual's diagnosis and, by stretching the popular conception of insanity, the medical profession manoeuvred itself in order to act as the moral arbiter; mental normalcy being commonly equated with socially agreeable behaviour, which was derived from Victorian codes of acceptability.

The profession faced difficulty in its argument for exclusive control over the insane. Although doctors relied on medicinal rhetoric, their approach remained firmly committed to the use of mechanical restraint and other 'physical' treatments. By asserting their special medical knowledge, doctors were claiming the role of the healer. Yet the experience of inmates suggested that this was false. As the nineteenth century progressed and moral treatment, innovated by laymen, gradually became the preferred approach, medicine's claim was further undermined when William Tuke managed to achieve something doctors had not – the reconciliation of the conflicting roles of healer and gaoler.

7 Reform and Resistance

Under the Medical Registration Act 1858 the medical professions of physician, surgeon and apothecary, for the first time, began to acquire a common identity. The Act required the establishment of uniform standards for entry into the medical profession. Also by this time effective forums for medical discussion and debate had been established, medical journals were regularly published and by 1841 the Association of Medical Officers of Asylums and Hospitals had been founded. Yet despite the apparent authority of the medical profession and its role in treating the insane,

38 For example, Cullen, W *First Lines of the Practice of Physic* (1808) (2 Vols) Bell and Bradfute, Edinburgh.
39 See Defoe, D 'Demand for Public Control of Madhouses (1728)' reprinted in R Hunter (ed) *Three Hundred Years of Psychiatry 1535 - 1860* (1963) Oxford University Press, London.

doubts about the use of coercion and potential for wrongful confinement continued to surface.

The nineteenth century witnessed a growing volume of lunacy legislation but the introduction of each Act of Parliament provoked criticism from the medical profession of the day. It had not welcomed the Select Committee's findings in 1815–16, which had suggested that a Board of Inspection, consisting of county Magistrates, be established. This would have given power to laymen whom the medical profession were seeking to weaken. The Bills of 1815, 1816 and 1819 which followed all failed in the House of Lords, but the attempt to invoke such powers of inspection was enough to frighten doctors into affirming their role in the treatment of lunatics. During this period numerous books and articles on the treatment of insanity were published and, for the first time, it was included in formal medical training.[40]

The profession decided that attack was the best form of defence and set about publicising their work and lobbying for the right to maintain control. The 1827 Select Committee's findings were the basis for further legislative reform in 1828 and rather than wait for this, medical men published pamphlets and gave lectures to encourage people to preserve their confidence and belief in the profession. As public fears about false and unjust imprisonment had not been dispelled, it was recognised by the medical profession that calls for increased inspection would continue to be made. The medical profession, therefore, took the approach that self-regulation would be preferable to outside inspection. The Madhouses Act 1828 reconstituted the Metropolitan Commissioners and increased their number to fifteen, five of which were physicians. While campaigning to sustain this control, the profession also sought to counter the growing threat that moral therapy posed to medicine. Furthermore, the profession responded by demonstrating that moral therapy had little theoretical basis. Doctors argued that insanity was caused by physical abnormalities, which could be proved,[41] whereas the doctrine that insanity arose predominantly from the mind was condemned as an absurdity. This approach was effective and eventually the methods of moral therapy, which were originally adopted by the likes of Tuke, were subsumed into ordinary psychiatric medicine. By the time of the Lunatics Act 1845, the medical profession successfully dominated the field and with the introduction of the Lunacy Commission, which had a heavy medical contingent, the role of the layman in managing the insane virtually disappeared.

40 Hunter, R A & MacAlpine, I *Three Hundred Years of Psychiatry* (1963) Oxford University Press, London, pp 305–309.
41 However, proving that physical lesions on the brain existed was often difficult. See, Halliday, A *A General View of the Present State of Lunatics and Lunatic Asylums* (1828) Underwood, London.

8 The Rise and Fall of the New Profession

The Lunatics Act 1845 had placed the medical profession in a strong position. A great deal of effort had brought the desired reward. The profession managed to secure powerful support in the fight to be recognised and approved as having the central role in the treatment of the insane. This monopoly allowed doctors to go about their business without hindrance and, with the 1845 Act providing legislative backing, the profession sought to consolidate its position.

Yet, this success was relatively short-lived. The basis for their control was founded on the premise that insanity stemmed from physical abnormality. The profession acquired support because it was claimed that such disorders could, within a period, be cured. Yet, as the years went by it gradually became clear that such cures were not materialising. This depressing performance was blamed on the difficulty in obtaining inmates at a time when their mental condition was still receptive to treatment. By the mid-1870s, the asylum had begun the transition from curative institution to 'dumping ground' for the old, vulnerable and sick. The possibility of curing the insane was gradually diminishing as each year passed and once the asylum superintendent stopped the pretence that such cures were likely, all attempts to treat the inmates vanished. An essentially custodial institution rapidly replaced the curative one. By the end of the nineteenth century the asylum's population had swollen to huge proportions; the composition of inmates having shifted to include the socially undesirable as well as the insane. A sufficient amount of medical gloss was painted to legitimate these changes on a superficial level. Yet what the asylum amounted to by this time was nothing more than a method of social control. The role of medicine was crumbling away and it became clear that steps to improve the legal framework of civil commitment to mental asylums needed to be taken.

9 The Lunacy Act 1890

The clash between the medical profession and the layman had been won and with the enactment of the Lunatics Act 1845 the doctor's position had been strengthened. Yet, although the 1845 Act recognised the doctor as the primary protagonist in the treatment of the insane, it also represented a great victory for the reformists who desired greater legal control of the detention process.[42] However, in order to achieve these reforms, the widely

---

42 Most notably, Lord Ashley, later Seventh Earl of Shaftesbury (1801–85), who was the first and best known chairman of the Lunacy Commission, which was established by the Lunatics Act 1845.

held beliefs of the public concerning the plight of the insane were manipulated, stirring up sympathy for these unfortunates. The conditions of the asylums were shocking and the possibility of abuse seemed very real. Such abuse exposed the latent risk that the sane might also be detained in an asylum; the wealthy seemed the most likely victims. By the mid-nineteenth century followers of the reform programme demanded that measures be adopted that centred on protecting the liberty of the subject, restricting the role of the private madhouse (as this was thought to pose the greatest threat) and curbing medical discretion.

However, the demand to protect the rights of individuals to their liberty was not complete. While there were fears that the wealthy were being bundled off to the asylum for the financial gain of others, the State was also concerned with maintaining social order. The interpretation of insanity had gradually been widened throughout the nineteenth century to include many of society's disadvantaged; the changing role of the asylum fuelled public agitation regarding the protection of free will of rational individuals. The sane attracted the same liberties, while the insane, whose condition was thought clearly to prevent rational thought, justified paternalistic intervention. Lunacy reform reflected these concerns. The demands to protect the (wealthy) sane from malevolent and self-interested relatives called for the reassertion of the rule of law and the restriction of medical hegemony, a step that satisfied the lunacy reformists.

Medical claims that insanity could be cured and that only doctors could achieve this were increasingly vilified. Asylums had become sizeable over the nineteenth century because few inmates were actually restored to health. Owing to this, most regarded insanity with some pessimism and the medical profession with mounting repugnance. In response to these concerns, a Select Committee was established in 1877 to consider the lunacy legislation and the provisions for protecting the liberty of individuals.[43] This entailed a large-scale review of the lunacy system and considered the views of many of those involved in insanity provision. Consideration was also given to a number of different systems, which operated elsewhere, such as those in Scotland and Ireland. The Scottish system, which was introduced by the Lunatics Act 1857, raised much interest as emphasis was placed on the role of the sheriff to order confinement. Such an order was granted if two medical certificates in favour of detention were available. At first glance, this system displayed fundamental legalist principles. This legislative provision emphasised the role of the non-medical professional. The decision to interfere in an individual's life and to remove liberty seemed to be influenced by judicial rather than solely medical considerations. However, in reality, the sheriff

43 House of Commons *Report of the Select Committee on Lunacy Law* 1877.

acted in his administrative capacity rather than in his judicial one, because he merely validated the due completion of the insanity certificates. The original concern that the operation of private madhouses needed to be restricted became sidelined as attention turned to reforming the lunacy law in more general terms. The Select Committee concluded that some further legal intervention in the provision of care for the insane would be beneficial and that all inmates, whether private or pauper, should be processed through the same system.

The Select Committee suggested that an application to detain an individual in an asylum should be accompanied by two medical certificates, with the order being signed by the nearest relative. Regular monthly reports about the inmate's condition were also suggested to prevent unnecessarily protracted detention. The protection of the individual's liberty was to be brought about by the implementation of a system of frequent review and where no evidence of continuing insanity could be produced, the Lunacy Commission could discharge the inmate. The Committee finally suggested that, where possible, care should be carried out at home or in a less restrictive environment. The open-door system, where patients stayed in hospital but were allowed to go out daily, and the use of occupational therapy in the asylum was explicitly approved.

This major review of the lunacy laws resulted in the enactment of the Lunacy Acts (Amendment) Act 1889 and the consolidating Lunacy Act 1890. Clarity in the detention process was brought to bear by including detailed information about the medical certificate under the Lunacy Act 1890, s 30 and the use of monthly reports under the Lunacy Act 1890, s 29(1). Certification of inmates was now a legal reality. Treatment approaches were also regulated.[44] Legalist principles were most evident in the Lunacy Act 1890, s 2, which provided that all applications to incarcerate private patients (apart from emergency cases or individuals found insane by inquisition) required judicial authority.[45] Original petitions for detention had, where possible, to be made by the individual's spouse or another relative.

The Lunacy Acts 1889 – 1890 represented a high water mark in legalism. The role of medicine had been superseded by legal rules and judicial, rather than medical, sanction. Advocates of legalism claimed that the provision of a clear legal framework ensured the protection of individual freedom; the law was painted as the saviour of individual liberties. In practice, application of the Lunacy Act 1890 was often left to the justice

---

44   The Lunacy Act 1890, s 45 required a medical certificate every time mechanical restraint was to be used.
45   Judicial authority could be gained from a county court judge, a stipendiary, a Metropolitan Police magistrate or a justice of the peace.

of the peace; but the legal profession were keen to shore up concerns about the medical profession and its role in insanity relief. In the prevailing years, the medical profession had to accept that emphasis had shifted to legal interventionism. However, by using the legal framework to its advantage the medical profession managed to re-acquire some of its legitimacy.

10 The Mental Treatment Act 1930

The passing of the Lunacy Act 1890 had represented a true blow to the medical profession. Decisions to detain an individual in an asylum were to be made by a justice of the peace rather than a doctor. Powers to detain patients had been withdrawn from the medical profession and handed over to the legal profession. Yet, over time, medical professionals managed to regain some of their former power. The re-establishment of its position was exemplified by the enactment of the Mental Treatment Act in 1930. After 40 years of legalistic dominance, medicalism, and the importance of medical discretion in the care of the mentally disordered, emerged once again.

Throughout the 1920s, while the law was despised because of its apparent failure to reduce levels of hospitalisation and protect the rights of individuals, the modern age of psychiatry was beginning to flourish. The medical profession had been galvanised into action with the arrival of new theories and approaches to caring for the mentally unstable. Psychological treatment for the mentally unstable had been launched in the early 1920s, and advocated a complex system of inpatient and outpatient treatment; while the founding of the National Council for Mental Hygiene in 1922 brought together psychiatrists, psychologists and social workers in a united attempt to improve the system. The significance of social welfare in the battle against mental instability was also properly recognised for the first time. However, the most striking development was the emphasis placed on early diagnosis and treatment. As progress in treating the chronic psychiatric patient had so far proved illusive, preventative intervention became popular, an approach which had some success. These developments encouraged those who practised in this field to distinguish themselves from other medical professionals. The emergence of psychiatry, as a recognised and respected profession, had fully commenced.

Faith in psychiatric practice had been gaining pace but the outbreak of World War I assured respect for the psychiatric profession once again. Many 'shell-shocked' soldiers returned from the front, presented an opportunity for the profession to re-assert its influence. Thousands of men had been affected by this condition and their status as 'protectors of the Empire' meant that effective treatment had to be developed. The work, which was carried out on the 'shell-shock' cases, substantiated claims that the lunacy laws should be amended. The need to certify a patient before he could be admitted to hospital was disliked by the profession and increasingly by the country as a whole. The stigma, which accompanied certification, was therefore deemed inappropriate for those who had fought for King and country.

This shift in legislative policy was brought about by a combination of several factors. In the 1890s medical dominance had led to fears of abusive practices to both the sane and insane, while legal regulation represented more consistency and impartiality. Yet this optimism in the law was gradually dissipated as it became clear the system adopted in the Lunacy Act 1890 had done little to improve the protection of individual liberty. The main source for this reversal in legislative opinion can be located in the 1926 MacMillan Report. The tide had turned and reform of the lunacy laws was only a matter of time. In 1924 the Government announced its decision to appoint a Royal Commission on the question of reform.[46] This Royal Commission was set up to examine the law and administrative machinery in England and Wales relating to the certification, detention and care of persons of unsound mind. The main thrust of the report was the argument that a clear demarcation between mental and physical illness could not be established. The Report suggested that when justices of the peace were faced with an application to detain an individual in a psychiatric facility, they should rely on medical opinion and seek clarification from one or more of the certifying doctors. This shift towards reliance on medical discretion cannot be explained by a successful therapeutic revolution prior to 1930. Recovery rates were still low; many patients remained in 'hospital' for much of their lives and the developments in psychiatric treatment had proved disappointing. Therefore, the main reason for the rejection of legalism must have been the ostensibly poor role that the law played. The justice's role in the admission procedure failed to act as an effective safeguard because many felt ill-equipped to make a judgment about a seemingly medical issue.[47] Owing to this, many justices bowed to medical opinion.

The legal profession was heavily represented on the Commission and psychiatrists were pessimistic about the Commission's likely recommendations. The medical profession did not foresee any possibility that its discretion would be extended or that legal safeguards would be

46 The Macmillan Report: *Report of the Royal Commission on Lunacy and Mental Disorder* 1924-26, Cm 2700.
47 *Royal Commission on Lunacy and Mental Disorder: Minutes of Evidence, I* Question 7187.

relaxed. Yet the Commission did go further than expected, a fact that pleased the medical profession. It was recommended that existing certification procedures should be overhauled and that treatment without certification be introduced. Certification still needed the recommendation of two medical professionals, but this was extended to both private and pauper patients. This uniformity of approach was designed to protect pauper patients whose detention had, up until then, not required such recommendations. The voluntary admission of patients was also suggested. Such admission would not require the accompanying medical recommendation and the patient would be free to leave the hospital after providing 72 hours' notice. Such patients could not be treated without their consent. The Provisional Treatment Order was, unlike voluntary admission, a compulsory provision. Yet this new compulsory power would also not require certification. As the patient was not certified under the order, it was not necessary to show that he 'was of unsound mind and a fit person to be detained'; instead, such treatment, care and observation would have to be appropriate. Detention was authorised initially for one month but could be renewed for a maximum of five months. This Provisional Treatment Order was designed with the 'early case' in mind. The provision clearly reflected the new focus in psychiatric care practice towards preventative treatment of the acute patient, rather than ongoing care of the chronically ill. It was considered that people who had recently become mentally ill would particularly benefit as they would not be burdened with the stigma of having been certified and could re-establish their lives in the outside world.

The Mental Treatment Bill was finally introduced into Parliament and by November 1929 it had reached the House of Lords. The tone of the MacMillan Report had been retained in the Bill but the radical approach, had to some extent, been tamed. The Bill aimed to reduce the level of stigma associated with psychiatric treatment, which had been created by extensive judicial participation since the Lunacy Act 1890. The Bill authorised voluntary admission to hospital but the patient had to apply formally in writing and his admission had to be reported to the Board of Control. The Bill also followed the Commission's recommendation to require 72 hours' notice before the voluntary patient could discharge himself. The other innovation was the inclusion of a 'Temporary Treatment Order' under (what became) section 5, which would apply to those patients who were incompetent and could neither assent nor dissent to temporary treatment. A second medical opinion would be enough to justify the use of this provision. This measure was included in the Bill as a replacement for the Royal Commission's recommendation of a Provisional Treatment Order, which was scrapped as being too near judicial certification. The 'Temporary Treatment Order' and the introduction of voluntary admission ratified the role of the medical profession. Both measures abandoned the need for a justice of the peace to order admission to hospital, a step that clearly reflected the growing confidence in the medical profession. The final endorsement of psychiatry over law was the terminological changes used in the 1930 Bill. For example, 'asylum', which had underpinned the provision of insanity care for the last 130 years, was exchanged for 'mental hospital'. The use of the word 'hospital' demonstrated a distinctive re-orientation towards therapeutic relief instead of coercion and restraint.

The Mental Treatment Act of 1930 represented a recognition that the care and treatment of the mentally ill had resoundingly shifted. Sinister undertones were no longer associated with psychiatric theory or practice, having been replaced with liberal progressiveness. The law's involvement was significantly limited in the Mental Treatment Act 1930, a clear reflection that legalism was no longer a favoured approach in mental health legislation. This position was further confirmed with the enactment of the Mental Health Act 1959.

11 The Mental Health Act 1959

The Mental Treatment Act 1930 only managed a restrained anti-legalist response to the Lunacy Act 1890, while the Mental Health Act 1959 moved substantially closer towards greater emphasis on the decision-making of the medical practitioners. The ideology behind the Act aimed at de-stigmatising mental health care by adopting a more inclusive health care approach where the distinction between mental and physical illness was, to some extent, lessened. Confidence in medical discretion and the interventionist approach of treating mental disorder as one, among many, social problems, was at an all time high. The Mental Health Act 1959 was an attempt to provide a modern comprehensive mental health service, which accorded to the other major social welfare reforms of the post-war period, such as the National Health Service Act 1946.[48] Attitudes towards the provision of mental health care had been exposed to some fundamental shifts in the years since the Lunacy Act 1890 and as the Mental Treatment Act 1930 did not sufficiently satisfy the demands for change, further reform was expected. With the enactment of the National Health Service Act 1946 came further pressure to transform the mental health legislation so that it echoed changing psychiatric policy and practice. While the Lunacy Act 1890 was still in force, mental health services were, for the first time, incorporated into the rest of the health services. It was envisaged that integration would encourage the adoption of universally high

48 Those being the: National Health Service Act 1946, National Assistance Act 1948, and National Insurance Act 1946.

standards and promote parity between mental and other health services thereby leading to a reduction in stigma. This equality was not achieved and stigma was still associated with mental illness, yet the 1946 Act remains important for it proved the final catalyst towards reforming the law.[49]

Psychiatry's social standing had improved dramatically by the 1950s with the emergence of some major therapeutic innovations. Convulsive therapy and insulin coma therapy were developed in the 1930s and 1940s but the largest breakthrough came in the 1950s with the arrival of tranquillisers and other drug therapies. These developments had a huge impact upon the perceived role of the psychiatrist. Prior to these advances, psychiatrists had to battle with the image of 'gaoler', as most patients entered hospital to be restrained rather than formally treated.

> '[The psychiatrist] found himself working in a place where many patients did not get better; he had to endorse many things – such as straight jackets, padded cells, forced feeding – which he did not like and which conflicted with his picture of himself as a beneficent healer'.[50]

Yet, after the introduction of these drugs, psychiatrists could make a 'more passable imitation of conventional medical practice'.[51]

This therapeutic optimism was an essential component in the decision to reform the law, which the Royal Commission on the Law relating to Mental Illness and Mental Deficiency (the 'Percy' Commission), was set up to consider.[52] The Commission convened at a time of great change: the National Health Service was still in its infancy and medical professionals and the public still felt tremendously positive about what it could offer. The Commission was required to consider ways of modernising the legislation relating to the care and treatment of the mentally disordered so that the mental health services, as opposed to the legal system, was afforded greater power. The role of the law was to be limited to the provision of safeguards to those who were subject to the mental health legislation.

The Commission's report, which outlined its final recommendations, was published in May 1957. The emphasis leant clearly towards the

49 Butler. T *Mental Health, Social Policy and the Law* (1985) Macmillan, London, p 125.
50 Clark, D H *Administrative Therapy* (1964) Tavistock, London, p 4.
51 Scull, A *Decarceration: Community Treatment and the Deviant – A Radical View* (2nd edn 1984) Polity Press, Cambridge, p 79.
52 The 'Percy' Commission: *Royal Commission on the Law Relating to Mental Illness and Mental Deficiency 1954–1957,* Cm 169.

empowerment of the medical profession. The Commission recommended the use of informal admission to hospital, as the move towards voluntary admission since the Mental Treatment Act 1930 had been a notable success and the use of coercion had diminished considerably. Indeed, by 1957 75% of all admissions to psychiatric hospital were on a voluntary basis. This widespread appeal of voluntary admission stemmed from the fact that certification made the patient and his family feel ashamed and conspicuous; feelings that were not viewed as particularly beneficial in the treatment process. The move towards voluntarism reflected the greater reliance, which was placed in medical judgment and supported the view that both patient and doctor wanted to achieve the same goal: treatment and cure. The legalist principles, which provided the foundation for the Lunacy Act 1890, were no longer considered appropriate in an age of therapeutic and medical optimism. The rise of voluntarism and reliance on medical opinion shifted policy away from legal coercion to a more informal and flexible approach. The Commission recognised the benefits of voluntary admission but also realised that some patients who might benefit from such admission were not eligible. For a patient to admit himself to hospital under the Mental Treatment Act 1930, he had to make a formal written application, and notice of his admission had to be supplied to the Board of Control. These formalities restricted voluntary admission to those who were capable of completing a written application: those who were not either had to be certified or did not receive hospital care and treatment. Owing to this the Commission recommended that informal admission should be made available to those who were able to express willingness to accept treatment and to those who did not dissent. Compulsory powers were to be retained but it was emphasised that they should only be used in cases of last resort.

Judicial involvement was further restricted by the Commission's proposals. It suggested that where formal admission was necessary the decision to detain would become an entirely medical one. The application to admit a patient into hospital would be made to the receiving hospital. This application would be made by the nearest relative or the mental welfare officer and would be supported by two medical recommendations, while the role of the magistrate in the whole decision-making process would be abolished. This recommendation was the most radical of the report. Its inclusion demonstrated the growing conviction that medicalism should be encouraged.

However, the reduction of legal involvement, which was reflected in the removal of magisterial control, was tempered by the introduction of the Mental Health Review Tribunal. This Tribunal had the power to review the application of all compulsory powers. It also had the power to discharge a patient if the admission criteria were no longer in existence and it meant that patients had a forum where they could seek review of their position. Despite this apparent retention of some legalist principle, the Mental Health Review Tribunal did not resemble a typical judicial forum. The Percy Commission recommended the creation of locally-based tribunals, which would consist of one or more medical members and non-medical members who would have legal and/or administrative experience and a legally-qualified chairman. The style of the tribunal was to be much more relaxed and less adversarial in nature, thereby emphasising the multi-disciplinary, therapeutic objectives of the tribunal. To counter any possibility of the tribunal appearing to be court-like, application to the Mental Health Review Tribunal was not to be a legal appeal where the merits of the original decision was considered. Rather the tribunal was to consider the applicant's mental fitness for release at the time of the hearing.

The release of patients into the community where possible was greatly endorsed by the medical profession at this time. The influx of pharmacological developments meant that more options to treat and care for patients in a less restrictive environment became available. Furthermore, while drug therapies were emerging, other therapies such as industrial therapy and the 'shift' system where patients either stayed at hospital during the day or night had come to the fore. The importance of social care in treating the mentally disordered gained pace. The idea of the 'therapeutic community' where the social environment was a critical factor in the recovery of the patient became a more established psychiatric theory.[53] Community care encouraged the patient to maintain the skills he would need to cope in society while the institution had gradually been regarded as an anathema to recovery from mental instability.

The Mental Health Act 1959 was passed at a time of psychiatric enlightenment. This statute, unlike previous statutes, had for the first time fully reflected contemporary mental health practice. It recognised the need for increased flexibility in the provision of mental health care and also readily accepted and endorsed the augmented role of medical discretion. While the influence of legalism was over, lawyers had been mollified by the introduction of Mental Health Review Tribunals to afford patient rights some protection.

The arrival of the Mental Health Act 1959 provided a striking contrast to the Lunacy Act 1890, which had been enacted nearly 70 years before. The Lunacy Act 1890 had attempted to reflect the concerns of the time, which had predominantly focused on the potential for false confinement of the sane, and the lack of safeguards to ensure appropriate detention. Psychiatry as a distinct medical field was still in its infancy and its claims of offering a therapeutic contribution were given little credence. Yet by

---

53 Rapoport, R N *Community as Doctor* (1961) Tavistock, London.

the end of the 1950s great strides had been made in psychiatry and confidence in medical judgment was high. Psychiatry had become a therapeutic tool, which enabled people to receive treatment that allowed them to get on with their lives. Admission to hospital was no longer expected to be a long-term event. Patients would hopefully enter hospital voluntarily, receive the necessary treatment and then be released into the less restrictive environment of the community where ongoing support could be given. The Mental Health Act 1959 reflected a period of great medical optimism, yet this confidence was short lived and by the mid-1960s disillusionment and criticisms had again begun to resurface.

Chapter 2
The Mental Health Act 1983

1 Introduction

The Mental Health Act 1959 reflected the high watermark of medical influence over the treatment of psychiatric patients. The 1950s had seen the development of revolutionary pharmacological and psychological therapies and periods of in-hospital care were becoming shorter. Immense optimism in the ability of the psychiatric profession to treat psychiatric illness enabled proponents of medicalism to argue successfully for greater professional freedom and a retraction of legal controls. Yet by the 1960s pessimism towards psychiatrists' coercive powers over patients had gradually crept back into the social consciousness. A growing perception of rights emerged during the 1960s. Individuals were recognised as being bearers of rights regardless of their status as psychiatric patients. Changing social trends saw the rise of feminism and women's rights and by the 1970s public awareness of the European Convention on Human Rights as a source of rights protection had grown. Moreover, the role of the legal system was increasingly recognised as having a significant role to play in maintaining and enhancing individual rights. The anti-psychiatry movement is exemplified by the writings of Thomas Szasz[1], R D Laing[2], Erving Goffman[3] and Thomas Scheff[4] and the work of each compounded the rising concerns about the position of the psychiatric patient.[5]

1 Szasz, T *The Myth of Mental Illness: Foundations of a Theory of Personal Conduct* (1961) Harper and Row, New York; Szasz, T *Law, Liberty and Psychiatry* (1963) Macmillan, New York.
2 Laing, R D *The Divided Self* (1959) Tavistock, London.
3 Goffman, E *Asylums: Essays on the Social Situation of Mental Patients and Other Inmates* (1961) Anchor/Doubleday, New York.
4 Scheff, T *Being Mentally Ill: A Sociological Theory* (3rd edn, 1999) Aldine de Gruyter.
5 See also the work of Michel Foucault *Madness and Civilisation: A History of Insanity in the Age of Reason* (1989) Routledge, London. See generally, Ingleby,

'The expression "mental illness" is a metaphor that we have come to mistake for a fact. We call people physically ill when their body-functioning violates certain anatomical and physiological norms; similarly, we call people mentally ill when their personal conduct violates certain ethical, political and social norms. This explains why many historical figures, from Jesus to Castro, and from Job to Hitler, have been diagnosed as suffering from this or that psychiatric malady.'[6]

The anti-psychiatric approach, as depicted by Szasz, believed mental illness to be a myth constructed for the purpose of social control. This approach also believes that *all* psychiatry is an agency for social control.

'Most of the legal and social applications of psychiatry, undertaken in the name of psychiatric liberalism, are actually instances of despotism. To be sure, this type of despotism is based on health values, but it is despotism nonetheless. Why? Because the promoters of mental health do not eschew coercive methods but, on the contrary, eagerly embrace them.'[7]

Furthermore, by the mid-1970s the National Association for Mental Health (MIND) had galvanised its campaign to promote patient rights and to re-assert a formalised legal framework for decision-making governing the care and treatment of psychiatric patients. MIND argued that by establishing such a framework the opportunities for oppressing the vulnerable would be substantially reduced because legally enforceable rights would be conferred upon patients. Scepticism towards medicalism was once again on the increase.

Consensus was growing that professional power over patients should be subject to control. The Mental Health Act 1983 (hereafter referred to as the MHA 1983) was the product of over 20 years of opposition to medicalism. In 1975 a review of the operation of the Mental Health Act 1959 was undertaken. The interdepartmental Committee, which undertook the review, laid down its recommendations in a consultation document.[8] After further periods of consultation and a change in government in 1979, the White Paper *Reform of Mental Health Legislation*, along with the Bill

---

D (ed) *Critical Psychiatry: The Politics of Mental Health* (1981) Penguin, London for an anthology on the anti-psychiatry movement and academic viewpoint.
6 Szasz, T *Ideology and Insanity: Essays on the Psychiatric Dehumanisation of Man* (1970) Penguin, Harmondsworth, p 23.
7 Szasz, T *Law, Liberty and Psychiatry* (1963) Macmillan, New York, p xvii.
8 DHSS *Review of the Mental Health Act 1959* (1976) HMSO, London.

embodying the Government's reform proposals, was introduced.[9] The Bill was enacted in October 1982 as the Mental Health (Amendment) Act 1982. It made a number of substantial changes to the 1959 Act by introducing new powers to treat patients and to discharge mentally disordered patients. In the White Paper, the Government made clear its intention to consolidate the Mental Health Act 1959 and the Mental Health (Amendment) Act 1982. By the end of October 1984 the whole of the MHA 1983 was in force.

The purpose of this chapter is to examine the provisions of the MHA 1983 with reference to the social context, which directs the way in which the legislation is interpreted and applied. This Act is the primary piece of legislation governing the care and treatment of psychiatric patients and represents the contemporary legal response to psychiatric care provision. This chapter will also consider the political and legal reaction to changing social trends towards the protection of individual rights. The MHA 1983 rejected the idea of giving the medical profession too much power over decision-making such as existed in the Mental Health Act 1959 and re-embraced a formalistic legal framework. It will further be demonstrated that the 1983 Act added a new dimension to the traditional conception of legalism as epitomised by the Lunacy Act 1890. In contrast with the 1890 Act, the purpose of which was to protect the sane from unjust detention, the MHA 1983 has sought to protect the rights of the mentally disordered while subject to detention by introducing formalised legal safeguards.

2 The Revival of Legalism

The enactment of the Mental Health Act 1959 reflected a period of great optimism in psychiatry. The antagonism towards the psychiatric profession had largely been dispelled leaving a newly found trust, which allowed the reduction of legal controls to be fully endorsed. Proponents of the 1959 Act had warmly embraced medicalism as a legislative strategy because they believed legal controls would inhibit psychiatrists from utilising the huge scientific and psychosocial developments that were beginning to emerge in the 1950s. The legalism, which stemmed from the Lunacy Act 1890, was the result of a widespread fear that the sane were being wrongfully confined. The 1890 Act had been motivated by the intense wish to curb psychiatric authority. However, by the 1950s restricting the profession's power was no longer considered a viable option as modern medicine was claiming the psychiatric field as its own, thereby demanding the same level of support. In an age where drug treatment and

9   DHSS et al *Reform of Mental Health Legislation* (1981) Cm 8405, HMSO, London.

other therapies were increasingly available, psychiatrists were no longer regarded as gaolers; they now had an extensive pharmacopoeia upon which to rely thus legitimating their services. These advances were the means by which public opinion had shifted towards the support of psychiatric hegemony. Yet despite these developments the enthusiasm and sanguinity that was generated was brief.

Unlike the successes of the 1950s (such as pharmacological developments) which were principally owed to the developments in psychiatric practice, the 1960s and 1970s proved to be an anti-climax, as psychiatrists consolidated their current knowledge and pharmaceutical companies reaped the profits yielded by the established drugs. This apparent inactivity caused some pessimism to enter the social consciousness and an increasing level of complaint began to be directed at the Mental Health Act 1959. The 1959 Act was supposed to represent 'a new era of enlightened mental health provision', yet many considered the highly liberal approach threatened public safety.[10] The emphasis upon medical discretion had gone too far with the result that some patients, who in the past would have been considered too dangerous, were being released into the community. This looser approach to legal provision was supposed to provide psychiatric practitioners with the flexibility they claimed necessary to carry out their duties. Yet, it engendered strident criticism by lobbyists in favour of reintroducing a strong legal framework, as it was thought that public safety was being compromised by decisions taken by psychiatrists to release unsuitable patients into society. An attempt to balance the rights of the patient with the needs of the wider community had, once again, proved elusive.

At the heart of the ideology behind the Mental Health Act 1959 had been the attempt to de-stigmatise psychiatric patients, to prevent patient institutionalisation and to reduce the debilitating effects of mental illness. These objectives were to be achieved by the introduction of community care. Where possible patients would enter hospital on a voluntary basis and then be released into the community with appropriate support. However, the financial burden of this support had not been fully anticipated and local authority mental health services were left under resourced. Consequently, many patients remained in hospital because the community services were not available.

While this problem raised some disapproval of the Mental Health Act 1959, it was the retraction of legal regulation that prompted the main criticism. Despite appearances to the contrary, confidence in liberalism

---

10 Unsworth, C *The Politics of Mental Health Legislation* (1987) Oxford University Press, Oxford, p 313.

and medical discretion was diminishing by the beginning of the 1960s. It became clear that the Mental Health Act 1959 had only briefly managed to reflect the social mood before becoming outmoded. This change of attitude resulted largely from the improved dissemination of data. More information was placed in the public domain and people's knowledge about mental illness was enhanced. With the emphasis shifting towards short patient-stays in hospital and community care, more of the public had some contact with the mentally ill. Fears about the long-term impact of institutional care and reliance on medical discretion were also increasing. Szasz's work in the 1960s confirmed many of these fears. He suggested that the notion of mental illness was a socially constructed concept used to provide a justifiable basis for coercive social control.[11] 'Much of what passes for "medical ethics" is a set of paternalistic rules the net effect of which is the persistent infantalization and domination of the patient by the physician'.[12] Szasz argued that psychiatry was merely used to extend the powers of the state and coercive measures were a means of oppression.[13] Goffman's work on the pathology of institutional life also added to the argument to move away from hospital-based psychiatric provision. The 'total institution' stripped the patient of his own identity, subjected him to physical and mental assault and stigmatised him for life. In Goffman's view, the institution is for the benefit of relatives, psychiatrists and other professionals while the patient gains little from the hospital experience except feelings of isolation, injustice and alienation.[14] Goffman states that the patient suffers these injustices because of his stay in a 'total institution' while Scheff considers the labelling of people as being mentally ill causes them to be perceived by others as mentally ill and therefore a potential threat. The labelling process is self-prophesising.[15]

Larry Gostin, the Legal and Welfare Rights Officer at MIND during the 1970s, spearheaded MIND's campaign to highlight the shortcomings of

---

11 See more recently the work of Rose, N 'Law, rights and psychiatry' in Rose, N & Miller, P *The Power of Psychiatry* (1988) Polity Press, Cambridge: 'psychiatrists were engaged in a moral enterprise of social control, rationalised and legitimised through the appeal to a specialist body of esoteric knowledge' (p 179).
12 Szasz, T *The Myth of Mental Illness: Foundations of a Theory of Personal Conduct* (1961) Harper and Row, New York, p 174.
13 Szasz, T *Law, Liberty and Psychiatry* (1963) Macmillan, New York, and Szasz, T *The Manufacture of Madness: A Comparative Study of the Inquisition and the Mental Health Movement* (1971) Routledge and Kegan Paul, London.
14 Goffman, E *Asylums: Essays on the Social Situation of Mental Patients and Other Inmates* (1961) Anchor/Doubleday, New York.
15 Scheff, T *Being Mentally Ill: A Sociological Theory* (3rd edn, 1999) Aldine de Gruyter, pp 58-60.

the Mental Health Act 1959. In his work *A Human Condition*[16] he gave details of MIND's objectives and laid down the organisation's demand to restore formal legal safeguards. The call to re-embrace legalism challenged the Act's liberal stance in two ways. First, MIND's campaign centred on the protection of patient rights because by the 1970s a rights culture had become truly entrenched in social thinking. Second, other calls were made to re-introduce strict legal regulation to protect the wider community. Although some fears about released psychiatric patients representing a threat to the public was vocalised,[17] MIND's campaign managed to orientate the argument for reform towards patient protection and the role of law in the provision of paternalistic care. The law could be used to strengthen and enhance the position of the patient by injecting more legal control over psychiatric intervention. It could confer enforceable legal rights to patients. Stricter criteria for compulsory admission; greater legal emphasis within the review procedure; the strengthening of patients' rights to resist unwanted treatment; the protection of informal patients' rights; and the setting up of an independent advocacy structure were all MIND's objectives. The support that was generated for this campaign to adopt a clearer legal structure for psychiatric care provision demonstrated a considerable resurgence in legalism.

3 The Emergence of a 'New' Legalism

The call to re-assert legal control within psychiatry had developed since the beginning of the 1960s. Disillusionment with medicalism and reliance on medical discretion had quickly followed the enactment of the Mental Health Act 1959. However, the resurgence of legalism during this period differed significantly from that which developed during the nineteenth century and which influenced the Lunacy Act 1890. The traditional conception of legalism reflected in the 1890 Act was founded upon the notion of segregation. The mentally ill were distinguished from the more amorphous group of social misfits and admitted to county asylums. Yet the fear of wrongful confinement brought about the need to establish a clear and efficient legal framework for civil commitment. The old legalism

16   Gostin, L *A Human Condition Volume 1: The Mental Health Act from 1959 to 1975: observations, analysis and proposals for reform* (1975) MIND, London.
     Gostin, L *A Human Condition Volume 2: the law relating to mentally disordered offenders: observations, analysis and proposals for reform* (1977) MIND, London.
17   At the Annual Conference of the National Council of Women, the liberal ideology of the proposed Mental Health Act was criticised for jeopardising the welfare of the population as a whole for the 'benefit of the mentally disordered', *The Times*, 25 October 1957.

was therefore concerned with the protection of third parties and the establishment of social order. Patient rights were not high on the agenda, as insane people were not thought to bear rights. Although legal control was significant, it was used to protect the public from being 'contaminated'. By the end of the nineteenth century the psychiatric profession had lost a considerable amount of power, yet the notion of mental illness had been medicalised sufficiently to ensure that the general public believed themselves to be at risk of contracting the condition by being in close proximity with the insane. Therefore, if the mentally unstable were removed from society, risk of contagion was reduced. As the civil commitment criteria were introduced to protect the sane from erroneous confinement, those who were deemed sufficiently unstable for admission to an asylum were viewed as deserving of such treatment.

The new legalism that emerged after the Mental Health Act 1959 was somewhat different.[18] Principally, the law was to be used to protect the rights of detained patients. Psychiatric provision was no longer to be left to medical discretion; instead psychiatric coercion was to be assessed by legal criteria. This shift in the concept of legalism was partly inspired by the work of the anti-psychiatry movement as exemplified by Thomas Szasz. Szasz had argued that mental illness was essentially a myth,[19] which had been created as a label for 'problems in living'.[20] He claimed that the 'ideology of insanity which underlie[d] psychiatry ... [was] ... fundamentally totalitarian ... [as it served] ... the socio-economic interests of the state and legitimise[d] confinement in mental hospital'.[21] The anti-psychiatry movement argued that psychiatric practice should be subject to rigorous legal examination. In response, legal academics and practitioners acquired a greater involvement and these combined factors nourished the revival of legalism and a gradual increase in public uncertainty regarding psychiatry surfaced.

---

18 Carson, D 'Mental Processes: The MHA 1983' (1984) *Journal of Social Welfare Law* p 195. Gostin, L *A Human Condition Volume 1: The Mental Health Act from 1959 to 1975: observations, analysis and proposals for reform* (1975) MIND, London, at p 16 and Unsworth, C *The Politics of Mental Health Legislation* (1987) Oxford University Press, Oxford, at p 341.
19 Szasz, T *The Myth of Mental Illness: Foundations of a Theory of Personal Conduct* (1961) Harper and Row, New York; Szasz, T *Law, Liberty and Psychiatry* (1963) Macmillan, New York.
20 Szasz, T *Law, Liberty and Psychiatry* (1963) Macmillan, New York, p 13.
21 Unsworth, C *The Politics of Mental Health Legislation* (1987) Oxford University Press, Oxford, p 346. See also Szasz, T *Ideology and Insanity* (1974) Penguin, Harmondsworth, p 48.

4 The Functions of Legal Regulation in the MHA 1983

The roles of law and medicine appear, at times, to be naturally antipathetic rather than supportive. Since the inception of the early mental health legislation, this conflict and strain between the two disciplines has been particularly evident.[22] The objectives and ideologies of law and medicine are at odds. For medicine, the goal is to achieve therapeutic success above all else while the law attempts to limit the actions of the medical professional in the interests of protecting the patient's rights. The strain between the two professions can be traced by the rise and fall of legalism within mental health law over the past hundred years. These shifts have reflected the social and political 'mood' of the time. After the substantial retraction of legal control in the Mental Health Act 1959, the 1970s witnessed increasing demands for the re-establishment of legal intervention in order to protect the rights of patients. Before the MHA 1983 is considered in more detail it is necessary to understand the reasoning behind the calls for greater legal control in the new legislation. This additional legal control serves a number of functions.

The most apparent function of the law in psychiatry is the control of the professional's power over the patient. Mental health law faces a predicament: how to ensure the application of the legislation is not characterised as being wholly arbitrary and oppressive. A person is detained due to his mental condition, rather than his illegal activities, thereby providing the potential for compromising individual autonomy. To avoid this possible abuse the law is used to establish a formal framework in which decisions are made. This framework provides a mechanism for inspecting the validity of decisions to detain and treat individuals. Such decisions need to be justified because once they have been legitimated for therapeutic purposes it becomes increasingly difficult to establish oppressive activity. Psychiatric practice must be seen to be subject to social, moral and political control. Legal scrutiny provides the final opportunity to protect patient rights. Clearly, the law acts as a mechanism of control because it establishes a framework in which care decisions are made and incorporates legal safeguards surrounding detention, treatment and other coercive aspects of the legislation. The formation of these safeguards protects both the patient and those working within the psychiatric field. They legitimate psychiatric practices because they ensure the decisions are made in a procedurally sound way. Where decisions have been made in adherence to the safeguards, public acceptance invariably follows. The existence of a formal legal framework

---

22 Jones, K *A History of Mental Health Services* (1972) Routledge and Kegan Paul, London.

allows the public to accept decisions, which overtly remove rights from individuals. The need for psychiatrists to seek second medical opinions and to obtain opinions from other professionals allows psychiatric practice to be seen as accountable and legitimate.

While the MHA 1983 adopted the new legalism to establish more control over psychiatrists, it also established a legislative framework for a 'therapeutic division of labour.'[23] This is thought to encourage a more efficient care system and establish a hierarchy of professional authority. The endowment of greater legal control over professional activities under the 1983 Act has allowed more scrutiny over care decisions, thereby ensuring such decisions are appropriately made. Furthermore, the professional's responsibility is clarified. The 1983 Act has accorded new roles and responsibilities to other professions working within the mental health service. The role of nurses, social workers and psychologists are equally as valuable as psychiatrists in the provision of care. By acknowledging the vital input of these other professions their status has been enhanced and consequently elevated in the eyes of the public.

The legal regulation of psychiatric services has enabled the establishment of additional services. The MHA 1983 not only recognises the right of a patient to object to certain forms of treatment (such as non-reversible and hazardous treatments like psychosurgery), but also encourages informal care, thereby placing more responsibility on the patient himself. For example, owing to the MHA 1983 emphasis on voluntary hospitalisation and care within the 'least restrictive environment',[24] it incorporated a new duty upon health authorities and local social services authorities to provide after-care services under the MHA 1983, s 117.[25] This innovative step reflects an expanding legal obligation to provide the necessary support services in the community to ensure therapeutic success.

Finally, law in the psychiatric field seeks to define the legal status of the patient. By establishing a definition, the scope of a patient's right to make certain decisions can be evaluated. The classification of a patient as either a detained patient, a voluntary patient or a restricted patient influences the amount of control he has over the direction of his care and treatment. In the past, psychiatric patients have, on the basis of their status, been

---

23 Gostin, L *A Human Condition Volume 1: The Mental Health Act from 1959 to 1975: observations, analysis and proposals for reform* (1975) MIND, London, p 7.
24 Gostin, L 'Contemporary Social Historical Perspectives on Mental Health Reform' (1983) *Journal of Law and Society* Vol 10, p 50.
25 This section imposes a duty on health and social services authorities to provide after-care services for certain categories of psychiatric patient who have ceased to be detained in hospital under the MHA 1983, Pt II.

prevented from holding other rights such as property rights, voting rights, access to the courts and a variety of other rights. Where patient rights were restricted, this was accepted because medical opinion dictated such action. It is only with the MHA 1983 that the above rights have remained with the patient after admission to hospital. Their social and civil status has been elevated because their rights have not automatically been reduced once the legislation is invoked. The MHA 1983 has played a significant role in reducing the level of discrimination, which dominated mental health law in the past.

5 Voluntary Admission to Hospital

It is clear that the role of law in psychiatry is fundamental in protecting detained patients. However, the vast majority of hospitalised psychiatric patients are in that environment because they have chosen to seek help freely. Therefore, the MHA 1983 and its civil commitment provisions are not invoked. Voluntary care and treatment where the patient receives care and treatment willingly without use of coercion has become increasingly important, despite the struggle to re-establish a legalist strategy during the 1970s. It was not until the Mental Treatment Act 1930 that informal hospital care and treatment was given a statutory footing. Since then voluntary admission has been increasingly relied on and represents the primary basis upon which hospital care is now provided. The basic principle of voluntary admission to hospital was re-affirmed in the Mental Health Act 1959 and can now be found in the MHA 1983, s 131(1). This section provides that a patient can either enter hospital for treatment for mental disorder on an informal basis, or remain in hospital on an informal basis once the authority for his original detention has ceased. The importance of this provision is that it recognises that an individual may seek hospital care for psychiatric difficulties in the same way as one would for a physical disorder. Resort to the coercive measures contained within the MHA 1983 is viewed with ambivalence by many psychiatrists and on occasion by the courts as social stigma is still commonly associated with being 'sectioned' under the Act. It is judged that being subjected to formal detention under the Act brings with it an inescapable social stigma. Therefore, where an individual is willing to enter hospital voluntarily, this should be encouraged. The incorporation of voluntary admission in the Mental Health Act 1959 was a reaction against the highly legalistic and institutionally oriented tradition, which was laid down in the Lunacy Act 1890. Reliance upon formal statutory criteria for hospital care was considered too restrictive. Encouraging individuals to take a more pro-active role in improving their position was thought to offer considerable benefits to both the mental health system and patients alike. These benefits continued to be recognised under the MHA 1983.

Patients who voluntarily enter a psychiatric hospital are considered to enjoy a number of legal rights, which are denied to the formally detained patient. A voluntary patient may leave the hospital whenever he so wishes. He has elected to become a patient and therefore he may cease to be a patient when he chooses to. The voluntary patient may also refuse treatment that is offered to him. As a voluntary patient the individual retains most, if not all, of his rights. Unlike the formally detained patient, the voluntary patient may register to vote. The Representation of the People Act 1949 excluded patients in mental institutions from using the hospital's address as their address for electoral purposes. However, the Mental Health (Amendment) Act 1982 allowed voluntary patients to use their last or alternative non-hospital address for electoral purposes.[26] The voluntary patient also enjoys other rights such as easy access to the courts and freedom from censorship. All of these rights provide the voluntary patient with one overriding benefit: a reduction in the social stigma associated with the application of the mental health legislation.

The different types of psychiatric patient that are not subject to formal detention under the MHA 1983 was highlighted in the House of Lords decision in *R v Bournewood Community and Mental Health NHS Trust, ex p L*.[27] Such patients include those who have voluntarily chosen to enter hospital and those who are deemed to be informal patients. Whilst attending a day centre, L (an individual requiring 24-hour care) became agitated and hurt himself. His carers who were able to deal with his 'tantrums' could not be contacted and as a result, he was sedated and taken to hospital. L seemed compliant and did not resist admission so no further steps were taken to detain him formally under the MHA 1983. L's carers were not satisfied with the motives of the Trust and thought it necessary to have the legal position clarified. The Court of Appeal found that the MHA 1983 removed any common law jurisdiction but the hospital trust appealed to the House of Lords. The House of Lords regarded the Court of Appeal's reasoning to be erroneous and it confirmed that informal admission for patients like L, who could neither consent nor dissent to such admission, was acceptable practice. The House of Lords thought L's best interests had been served by hospitalising him without reference to the MHA 1983. The House of Lords also endorsed the common law

---

26 See the Mental Health (Amendment) Act 1982, s 62(2) and Sch 2. This provision is now contained in the Representation of the People Act 1983, s 7(2)-(9) .
27 [1999] 1 AC 458. See also Glover, N '*L v Bournewood* Community and Mental Health NHS Trust' *Journal of Social Welfare and Family Law* 1999, Vol 21, No 2, p 151.

doctrine of necessity and concluded that this common law principle justified any interference with L's civil liberties.[28]

Therefore, the House of Lords clearly rejected the Court of Appeal's decision that informal patients like L, who were unable to consent to admission to hospital but who did not show any positive dissent, could not be admitted and effectively detained, unless the admission provisions within the MHA 1983 were used. The Court of Appeal's decision would have overturned accepted psychiatric practice, creating huge practical difficulties across the country. Every patient, like L, would have had to be formally detained in hospital thereby invoking the machinery of the mental health legislation and increasing the time needed to provide care for these vulnerable individuals. The House of Lords considered the Court of Appeal's reasoning to be flawed and informal admission for those who are unable to consent but who do not object, was reinstated.

There are those patients who, having the capacity to consent to the admission, do consent and are classified as 'voluntary' patients and those who, though lacking capacity to consent to the admission do not object and are classified as 'informal' patients. Only those patients who understand the need to enter hospital and accept treatment for their conditions can truly be regarded as 'voluntary' as they freely submit to medical intervention. Those groups of patients that are not able to provide such consent are regarded as 'informal' patients. The *Bournewood*[29] decision confirmed that where patients lack any real understanding of their situation owing to learning disability, brain damage or senility, and they object to being in hospital, consideration should be given to invoking the compulsory measures under the MHA 1983, Pt II. However, the House of Lords do not consider this step to be mandatory. Recent figures suggest that the *Bournewood* decision has led to an increase in the MHA 1983, s 2 (admission for assessment and followed by treatment) and the MHA 1983, s 3 (admission for treatment) applications to convert informal patients into formally detained patients. In 1993-94, 3,000 informal patients were subsequently admitted under section 3; in 1998-99, this figure rose to 5,000.[30] These increases in admission figures suggest that despite the House of Lords fully endorsing the practice of informal admission, some professionals are now more wary of relying on this informal approach and regard formal admission as a safer option for both the patient and themselves. Where the individual does not object to his

28 [1999] 1 AC 458.
29 See Glover, N '*L v Bournewood* Community and Mental Health NHS Trust' *Journal of Social Welfare and Family Law* 1999, Vol 21, No 2, p 151.
30 Department of Health *Statistical Bulletin* 1999, Vol 25, p 7.

detention and it is in his best interests to be admitted to hospital, the confinement can be justified on the basis of the common law doctrine of necessity.[31]

All voluntary or informal patients have the right to leave hospital at any time. However, 'for many ... [patients] ... this right remains purely theoretical since there is nowhere else for them to go ... [or] ... because they lack the capacity to express an informed desire to leave'.[32] Voluntary patients who are capable of making the decision to leave hospital may also stay and accept the treatment even when they would rather not because they believe they could otherwise be forced to stay. The availability of coercive powers may effectively negate any choice the voluntary patient might have. Voluntary patients may be prevented from leaving hospital when formal procedures within the MHA 1983 are activated, during which time an application can be made to admit the patient for either assessment or for treatment. To prevent the patient from leaving hospital, he may be detained for a short period under the MHA 1983, s 5, which provides doctors and nurses with short-term holding powers over the patient. Therefore, the spectre of compulsion remains clearly visible even for those who have submitted themselves to voluntary hospitalisation.

The MHA 1983, s 5 provides that compulsory detention can be carried out in respect of mentally disordered patients who are already receiving treatment as voluntary patients in hospital. The MHA 1983, s 5(2) enables a voluntary patient to be held for up to three days if the medical officer in charge believes an application under the MHA 1983, Pt II[33] is appropriate, although no particular grounds for the activation of the procedures for formal admission are required.[34] Nurses have also been granted a holding power, which is valid for six hours when the appropriate medical officer is unavailable.[35] During this time, it is for the medical officer in charge to

---

31 [1999] 1 AC 458.
32 Fennell, P 'Informal compulsion: the psychiatric treatment of juveniles under common law' *Journal of Social Welfare and Family Law* 1992, p 311.
33 The MHA 1983, Pt II includes MHA 1983, s 2, which authorises compulsory admission to hospital for assessment (or for assessment followed by treatment) and MHA 1983, s 23, which authorises compulsory admission of a patient to hospital for treatment.
34 This provision is only applicable to patients who are inpatients. The MHA 1983, s 5(2) can be invoked even if the patient is receiving treatment for a physical illness, but the MHA 1983, s 5(4) can only be invoked if the patient is being treated for a mental disorder.
35 The MHA 1983, s 5(4). The nurse must be of the prescribed class: the MHA 1983, s 5(7).

apply his own power to detain the patient.[36] Therefore, the MHA 1983, s 5 provides medical professionals with a means of preventing voluntary patients from leaving hospital if it is considered necessary and it is thought that a formal application under the MHA 1983, ss 2 or 3 is warranted.

The MHA 1983, s 5 creates a natural strain on the relationship between the voluntary patient, the medical officer and the nominated nurses. The professional's image is transformed from that of a carer into that of a keeper. The patient enters hospital in the hope that he and the psychiatric staff have a common goal. The removal of his decision-making powers may have a negative influence on the way he perceives the professionals involved in his care. The use of the MHA 1983, s 5(4)[37] creates a particularly difficult and compromising position for nurses because they provide the day-to-day care.[38] In the past, nurses have been reluctant to use the MHA 1983, s 5(4) as they prefer to 'use powers of persuasion and common law for detention, until the arrival of the doctor'.[39] The threat of using formal provisions against voluntary patients may jeopardise the delicate relationship between the professional and patient thereby reducing the therapeutic usefulness of voluntary care. This power has been used sparingly and is seen as an emergency provision invoked when no doctor is available. Despite the apparent reluctance to invoke the MHA 1983, s 5, the voluntary patient's status and the retention of the rights outlined above seem dependent upon his willingness to co-operate. When he does not co-operate coercion is available to the professionals involved

---

36 The MHA 1983, s 5 provisions have been more frequently used since the *Bournewood* decision in 1998: section the MHA 1983, s 5(2) was applied 7,400 times in 1993-94 and 10,200 times in 1998-99; the MHA 1983, s 5(4) was used 1,200 times in 1993-94 and 1,700 times in 1998-99, an increase of around 42% (Department of Health *Statistical Bulletin* 1999, Vol 25, p 7).

37 Cooper, S A & Harper, R 'Section 5(2): who acts as the consultant's nominated deputy' *Psychiatric Bulletin* 1992, Vol 16, p 759.

38 In a recent study of the use of the MHA 1983, s 5(4) and the factors influencing the medical response times following 180 section 5(4) applications over a 16-year period, findings showed an overall mean medical response time of 122 minutes. Medical response times varied over the 24-hour period, and were shorter on weekends compared to weekdays. Annual mean medical response times decreased significantly over the 16-year period. For further details see, Ajetunmobi, O 'Detaining patients: A study of nurses' holding powers' *Nursing Times* 1 February 2001. See also, Ashmore, R 'Medical response time to section 5(4)' *Psychiatric Care* 1995, Vol 1, No 6, p 228; Blower, A 'Section 5(4)' *Psychiatric Bulletin* 1993, Vol 17, p 147; Lavelle, K, Gray, R & Thomas, B 'The use of nurses' holding power in a large psychiatric hospital' *Nursing Standard* 1998, Vol 12, No 43, p 40; Salib, E 'Audit of the use of nurses' holding power under section 5(4)' *Medicine Science and the Law* 1998, Vol 38, No 3, p 227.

39 Cooper, S and Harper, R 'Section 5(2): who acts as the consultant's nominated deputy' *Psychiatric Bulletin* 1992, Vol 16, pp 759, 760.

in his care. However, the importance of maintaining an effective relationship with the patient seems to have taken priority so far.

6 Civil Commitment and the Promotion of Legal Safeguards

(a) Guiding principles: the four categories of mental disorder

The espousal of this new form of legalism in the MHA 1983 has led to some interesting practical changes; the most obvious of which is the ascendancy of patient rights. Although voluntary patients constitute the largest section of the patient population, there remain those patients who require formal detention. It is on these patients that the restoration of formal legal safeguards has had the greatest impact. The MHA 1983 reflects many of the reform proposals suggested by Larry Gostin in the 1970s[40] which called for the creation of stricter legal criteria for compulsory detention to psychiatric facilities, thereby ensuring a more rigorous and robust framework to protect civil freedoms. Sir Thomas Bingham MR has observed:

> 'no adult citizen of the United Kingdom is liable to be confined in any institution against his will, save by the authority of law ... [Psychiatric patients] ... present a special problem since they may be liable ... [to detention] ... as a result of mental illness'.[41]

The psychiatric patient raises the distinct problem of justifying compulsory detention without evidence of criminal activity. Therefore, the exceptional circumstances that surrounds such detention means that ensuring its legality is vital.

The MHA 1983 applies to those who suffer from a mental disorder.[42] The term is defined by four specific categories: 'mental illness'; 'mental impairment' and 'severe mental impairment' which are broadly grouped together as 'arrested or incomplete development of mind'; 'psychopathic disorder'; and 'any other disorder or disability of mind'.[43] The definition of these categories is broad, enabling many conditions and behaviours to fall within the scope of 'mental disorder'. However, the MHA 1983, s 1(3) excludes some behaviours and activities from the definition. A person

---

40 Gostin, L *A Human Condition Volume 1: The Mental Health Act from 1959 to 1975: observations, analysis and proposals for reform* (1975) MIND, London. Gostin, L *A Human Condition Volume 2: the law relating to mentally disordered offenders: observations, analysis and proposals for reform* (1977) MIND, London.
41 *Re S-C (Mental Patient: Habeas Corpus)* [1996] 2 WLR 146, at p 148F-H and 149A.
42 MHA 1983, s 1(1).
43 MHA 1983, s 1(2).

cannot be classified as mentally disordered for the purposes of the MHA 1983 solely 'by reason only of promiscuity or other immoral conduct, sexual deviancy or dependence on alcohol or drugs'.[44]

(b) Mental illness

Despite 'mental illness' being the most prevalently used classification, it remains undefined in the legislation. It is commonly assumed that 'mental illness' simply refers to 'whatever disorders are left once the various forms of handicap and psychopathic disorder are subtracted'.[45] The broad scope of this classification means that the threshold of detention is more flexible thereby increasing the possibility of jeopardising civil freedoms. An attempt was made by the Department of Health to define the term but it was found that there had been little 'evidence that the present lack of definition of mental illness ... [had led] ... to any particular problems'.[46] The Butler Committee suggested in 1975 that the term should not include mental impairment or personality disorders because, unlike these conditions, mental illness 'denotes a disorder which has not always existed in the patient but has developed as a condition overlaying the sufferer's usual personality'.[47] The Butler Committee recommended the use of broad terms instead of trying to 'describe medical conditions in detail'.[48] During the passage of the MHA 1983, Parliament noted that mental illness was notoriously difficult to define accurately and that trying to establish a definition that 'would be likely to stand the test of time' was unlikely to succeed.[49] The meaning of the term within the MHA 1983 was left deliberately vague in order to allow enough flexibility.[50] When an opportunity arose for the courts to define 'mental illness' in *W v L*, Lawton LJ found that the term had neither a specific medical nor a legal significance and, therefore, the words should be understood as a layperson would construe them.[51] Lawton LJ noted that an 'ordinary sensible person'

44 Such behaviour must be supported by independent medical evidence. In *R v Mental Health Review Tribunal, ex p Clatworthy* [1985] 3 All ER 699, persistent sexual deviancy as evidence of mental disorder was not sufficient for the patient to be classified as suffering from a psychopathic disorder. See also *R v Mental Health Act Commission, ex p W* (1988) 9 BMLR 77.
45 Hoggett, B *Mental Health Law* (4th edn, 1996) Sweet & Maxwell, London, p 31.
46 *Review of the Mental Health Act 1959* Cm 7320 (1978) HMSO, London, para 1.17.
47 Butler, Lord *Report of the Committee on Mentally Abnormal Offenders* Cm 6244 (1975) HMSO, London.
48 Laing, J *Care or Custody? Mentally Disordered Offenders in the Criminal Justice System* (1999) Oxford University Press, Oxford, p 6.
49 Session 1982–83, Vol XI, Col 213 Special Standing Committee Mental Health (Amendment) Bill per M Thomas MP.
50 Memorandum of Guidance for the 1983 Act (1983) DHS.
51 [1974] QB 711.

would judge the individual's conduct to result from his mental illness.[52] The court assumed that a layperson would clearly understand the intricacies of mental illness and would be able to differentiate behavioural types. This approach has been severely criticised because depending on the abilities and understanding of ordinary sensible people to decide whether an individual is mentally ill or not is unsatisfactory when that patient's liberty is at stake.[53] Such views have done little to encourage a clear understanding of the threshold criteria for formal detention and calls for official guidance have been frequently made.[54] However, no such guidance has been issued. The *Code of Practice*, which was published in 1993, does not refer to the question of how mental illness should be defined. In 1998 the Department of Health issued a revised Memorandum to the Act but it merely states that the 'operational definition and usage is a matter for clinical judgment in each case'.[55]

(c) Mental impairment and severe mental impairment

Under the MHA 1983, s 1, mental impairment and severe mental impairment have been distinguished. When an individual is classified as having a mental impairment, their impairment has a *significant* impact on their life. Where an individual is classified as severely mentally impaired, their limited intelligence and/or social functioning are thought to have an *overwhelming and severe* impact on their life. As in the case of *W v L* where mental illness was to be construed as a layperson would construe it, likewise in the case of *R v Hall*, it was held that mental impairment and severe mental impairment should be interpreted in the way an ordinary person would interpret them.[56] Similar problems and criticisms exist with this approach as they do in relation to mental illness. Clearly relying on the understanding of laypersons to judge whether mental impairment or severe mental impairment is evident opens up

---

52 [1974] QB 711 at 719A-C per Lawton LJ looked to the judgment of Lord Reid in *Cozens v Brutus*, who said that such words should be construed as a layman would construe them. Such a test has been described by Hoggett as the 'man-must-be-mad-test' (*Mental Health Law* (4th edn, 1996) Sweet & Maxwell, London, p 32).
53 Cavadino, M 'Mental illness and neo-polonianism' *Journal of Forensic Psychiatry* 1991, Vol 2, p 295.
54 Cavadino, M 'Mental illness and neo-polonianism' *Journal of Forensic Psychiatry* 1991, Vol 2, p 295.
55 Department of Health/Welsh Office *MHA 1983: Memorandum on Parts I to VI, VIII and X* (1998) HMSO, London, para 8.
56 (1988) 86 Cr App R 159. The *Code of Practice* notes that the decision as to whether an individual is mentally impaired or severely mentally impaired will lie with clinicians: DoH/Welsh Office *MHA 1983, Revised Code of Practice* (1999) HMSO, London, para 30.5.

opportunities for inconsistencies in approach and broad interpretations to be made.

Prior to the enactment of the MHA 1983, a campaign was launched to remove learning disabilities and other mental impairments from the Act altogether. MENCAP, MIND and the Royal College of Psychiatrists vigorously denounced the inclusion of the mentally impaired in the new Mental Health Act. It was argued that those with some form of mental impairment would be confused with those who suffered from a mental illness with the result that they would be alienated and excluded from society.[57] In addition to this, it was argued that mental impairment was rarely thought to benefit from active therapeutic techniques. The mentally impaired frequently suffer from birth and do so for the rest of their lives. Cure is rarely an option and therefore, detention in a psychiatric hospital has little benefit to offer the patient while at the same time removes him from family and familiar surroundings.

A compromise was reached during the Act's passage through Parliament. Mental impairment and severe mental impairment would remain in the Act but in order for the legislation to apply to such people, a behavioural criterion would need to be satisfied. The individual has to display 'abnormally aggressive or seriously irresponsible conduct' which is associated with the impairment in mental functioning. This criterion looks to the social repercussions of being aggressive or irresponsible due to mental impairment, thereby shifting the focus from a medical perspective to a legal one. Where socially unacceptable conduct is threatened, compulsory detention is justified, although the behavioural criterion has ensured that mental impairment is no longer grouped together with mental illness or other mental disorders.[58]

(d) Psychopathic disorder

In the MHA 1983, s 1, psychopathic disorder is defined as 'a persistent disorder or disease of the mind, which results in abnormally aggressive or seriously irresponsible conduct on the part of the person concerned'. This definition is vague and unhelpful to those who have to apply it. In 1959, Baroness Wootton observed that the category was tautological[59] as '[t]he

---

57   Session 1981–82, vol XI, col 63 Special Standing Committee Mental Health (Amendment) Bill cols 143 and 144, 27 April 1982.
58   Where no mental disorder is found, a patient cannot be detained: *Kynaston v Secretary of State for Home Affairs* (1981) 73 Cr App R 281.
59   Wootton, B (assisted by Seal, V G & Chambers, R) *Social Science and Social Pathology* (1959) Allen and Unwin, London.

psychopath's mental disorder is inferred from his anti-social behaviour while the anti-social behaviour is explained by mental disorder'.[60] The psychopathic classification within the mental health legislation has engendered the most criticism. Much still needs to be understood about the condition(s) and while knowledge is still sketchy, it has been argued that the psychopath should not be denied the opportunity of a therapeutic disposal when appropriate. The psychopathic disorder category has been the source of much debate not only as a result of the lack of scientific knowledge about the condition but also because some would argue that some criminal offenders are being singled out for special treatment owing to the label of psychopath being attached to them. Yet, despite this, there have been no plans to dispense with the category for, although there is some argument that such individuals are not treatable, it is thought that there are enough individuals 'who can be helped by detention in hospital'.[61]

The current Labour Government has recently re-considered the position with regard to the psychopathic individual.[62] The Government issued a consultation paper, *Managing Dangerous People With Severe Personality Disorder – Proposals for Policy Development* in July 1999.[63] The paper's proposals followed the announcement of the then Home Secretary, Jack Straw MP, in February 1999 to introduce powers to detain indefinitely people with personality disorders who represent a danger to the public.[64] It was acknowledged that the current means of dealing with dangerous and severely personality disordered (DSPD) individuals via the criminal justice system and/or under the mental health legislation has failed to meet their particular needs. It is envisaged that these powers will be applicable to those who are thought to represent a risk to the public irrespective of whether the individual concerned has been convicted of a criminal offence. Furthermore, the new proposals could apply to those who have not had any past contact with the criminal justice system, as the proposals are hinged on the role of risk assessment and its management. Although risk assessment and management will play a crucial role in the implementation of the consultation paper's proposals, undoubtedly there

---

60 Wootton, B *Crime and the Criminal Law* (1981) Stevens & Sons, London, p 90.
61 DHSS *Reform of the Mental Health Legislation* Cm 8405 (1981) HMSO, London, para 12.
62 Department of Health *Modernising Mental Health Services: Safe, Sound and Supportive* (1998) HMSO, London, paras 4.31–34.
63 Home Office/Department of Health *Managing Dangerous People With Severe Personality Disorder - Proposals for Policy Development* (1999) TSO, London.
64 HO Press Release 056/00 'New measures to protect the public from dangerous people' Session 1998–99 HC Debs, 15 February 1999. '

are some human rights concerns. Since the enactment of the Human Rights Act 1998, any new statutory provisions must comply with the European Convention on Human Rights. Owing to these new provisions, a further period of consultation (in conjunction with the wide-ranging review of the mental health legislation) was to be conducted before the proposals ended up on the statute book. This review ended when the Government's White Paper,[65] which emphasised the importance of upholding and endorsing the aim of public protection, was published in December 2000. New criteria for compulsory treatment under the new mental health legislation will form a key part. Clear authority will be given for the detention for assessment and treatment of all those who pose a significant risk of serious harm to others as a result of mental disorder or severe personality disorder. The criteria will separate out those who need treatment because it is in their own best interests and those who will receive treatment because of the risk they pose to others. 'Treatability' is no longer necessary. For these people, their rights are to be superseded by the need to minimise risk. It is clear that in all high-risk cases, 'management' of the consequences of the disorder will take precedence over 'therapeutic' endeavour and 'treatment' itself will become something of a misnomer.[66]

(e) Any other disorder or disability of mind

This final category remains without a definition in the MHA 1983. It is a residual category, which allows for the use of short-term powers up to 28 days detention. During the passage of the Mental Health Act 1959, parliamentary debates indicated that the category would be used to cover 'the sort of disorders and disabilities, which would not be covered by any of the other categories'.[67] It was envisaged that brain damage as a result of injury or disease would fall within the ambit of this classification. Once again, commentators berate the wide scope of this category as it opens up the possibilities of abuse.[68] In practice it is thought that clinicians will label a patient as 'having any other disorder or disability of mind' if the patient's condition has been recognised and documented in standard psychiatric textbooks.

65 *Reforming the Mental Health Act* Cm. 5016–I (December 2000) TSO, London, Part Two.
66 The recent White Paper *Reforming the Mental Health Act* Cm. 5016–I (December 2000) TSO, London, will be explored in more detail in Ch 8.
67 HC Deb vol 4, cols 65-6, 12 February 1959 (Derek Walker Smith MP).
68 Hoggett, B *Mental Health Law* (4th edn, 1996), Sweet & Maxwell, London, p 40.

(f) Further threshold criteria

It is necessary to satisfy the threshold criteria in order to gain access to the civil commitment provisions. In 1957 the Percy Commission recommended using a number of guiding principles when invoking compulsory care.[69] The first principle is the 'appropriateness' of inpatient care and treatment. It must be shown that treatment in a hospital environment is apposite owing to the type and severity of the individual's condition.[70] There must be evidence that treatment in hospital is necessary and cannot be provided in any other environment. However, the definition of medical treatment under the MHA 1983, s 145(1) firmly opens the door to an extensive interpretation of hospital care to be made because it includes 'nursing care, habilitation and rehabilitation under medical supervision'. In *Reid v Secretary of State for Scotland*[71] the House of Lords found that a patient's anger management improved when he was in the structured setting of a hospital, thereby satisfying the definition of 'medical treatment'.

The second principle suggested by the Percy Commission was the 'treatability' test. Under the Mental Health Act 1959, the mentally impaired and psychopathically disordered had to require or be susceptible to medical treatment. Under the MHA 1983, this condition must be satisfied in order to admit compulsorily an individual for treatment under the MHA 1983, s 3(2)(b). It must be demonstrated that treatment 'is likely to alleviate or prevent a deterioration of [the patient's] condition'. The purpose of the 'treatability' test is to ensure detention has a therapeutic rather than a custodial basis. However, problems arise in relation to conditions that are not thought to improve by conventional and even unconventional means. Personality disorders are providing the challenge to the current understanding of 'treatability'.[72] Such disorders are not considered to be treatable, thereby making inpatient hospital care inappropriate. Clearly, however, many individuals with these disorders need help. Other treatment regimes such as psychotherapy, which require the co-operation of the patient, will also satisfy the 'treatability' test even where the patient does not comply.[73]

69 The 'Percy' Commission: Royal Commission on the Law Relating to Mental Illness and Mental Deficiency 1954 1957, Cm 169.
70 In *R v Hallstrom, ex p W (No 2); R v Gardner, ex p L* [1986] 2 All ER 306, McCullough J found that it was not appropriate to admit a patient to hospital with the intention of granting immediate leave of absence under the MHA 1983, s 17.
71 [1999] 1 All ER 481.
72 Home Office/Department of Health *Managing Dangerous People With Severe Personality Disorder - Proposals for Policy Development* (1999) TSO, London.
73 *R v Canons Park Mental Health Review Tribunal, ex p A* [1995] QB 60. See Glover, N 'Treatability: its scope and application' *Journal of Forensic Psychiatry* 1996, Vol 7, No 2, p 353.

48 The Mental Health Act 1983

The final principle is based on the protection of both the patient and other persons. Inpatient treatment must be shown to be in the interests of the patient's own health and safety and for the protection of others. The 'safety' requirement is relatively easy to satisfy, as it will follow that if detention is appropriate then it will be necessary for the patient's health. The decision as to whether detention is necessary for the protection of other people remains one for the medical practitioners involved in the patient's care. The consideration of safety issues requires reflection on the perceived risk posed by the patient. As assessing risk is notoriously difficult, psychiatrists tend to err on the side of caution. These three principles have been incorporated into the MHA 1983 to ensure decisions to detain are subject to rigorous scrutiny.

7 The Detention Provisions

Once the threshold criteria have been satisfied a decision as to the type of detention has to be made. The MHA 1983, s 2 authorises compulsory admission to hospital for assessment. This is an interim measure, which enables a thorough assessment of the patient's mental condition in a 28-day period. For the MHA 1983, s 2 to apply the patient must be suffering from a mental disorder that necessitates detention in hospital for assessment[74] and that detention is in the 'interests of the ... [patient's] ... own health or safety or ... [for] ... the protection of others'.[75] In *R v Kirklees Metropolitan Borough Council, ex p C*,[76] Lloyd LJ noted:

> 'there is ... power to admit a patient for assessment under section 2, if he appears to be suffering from mental disorder, on the ground that he or she is so suffering, even though it turns out on assessment that she or he is not. Any other construction would unnecessarily emasculate the beneficial power under section 2 and confine assessment to choice of treatment'.[77]

The MHA 1983 makes it clear that admission under the MHA 1983, s 2 is not limited to assessment alone. The MHA 1983, ss 2(2)(a) and 63 authorise the administration of treatment of a patient without his consent when the treatment is necessary. The MHA 1983, s 2 is procedurally weighted in favour of the wider community for the patient may be removed

---

74 MHA 1983, s 2(2)(a).
75 MHA 1983, s 2(2)(b).
76 [1993] 2 FLR 187.
77 [1993] 2 FLR 187 at 190.

from society for assessment even when the result proves negative.[78] Once the assessment period has ceased the patient may remain in hospital as a voluntary patient,[79] or he may be detained under the MHA 1983, s 3. The Act further provides that the patient may appeal to a Mental Health Review Tribunal within the first 14 days of his admission under the MHA 1983, s 2 to seek his discharge. The patient's nearest relative may also apply for his discharge[80] subject to the requirements set out in the MHA 1983, s 25.[81]

Under the MHA 1983, s 3 a patient may be compulsorily detained for up to six months where treatment will be administered.[82] The initial application for detention for treatment may be made by an approved social worker[83] or by the patient's nearest relative. If the approved social worker wishes to apply for the patient to be detained in hospital under the MHA 1983, s 3, but the nearest relative objects,[84] the application cannot continue. Detention under the MHA 1983, s 3 is only appropriate if the patient requires treatment in hospital. Under the MHA 1983 a patient cannot be detained for detention's sake. In *R v Hallstrom, ex p W (No 2)* and *R v Gardner, ex p L*,[85] McCullough J observed that 'admission for treatment has no applicability to those whom it is intended to admit and detain for a purely nominal period, during which ... [time] ... no necessary treatment will be given at all'.[86] However, once the criteria and procedure invoked in the MHA 1983, s 3 have been satisfied and the patient is detained, the treatment requirement no longer exists. In *R v Canons Park Mental Health Review Tribunal, ex p A*,[87] the applicant was detained in hospital under the MHA 1983, s 3 having been reclassified under the MHA 1983, s 16 as suffering from a psychopathic disorder. It was thought that the only effective therapy would be group therapy but the applicant had refused to co-operate. The applicant contended that because she had been reclassified as suffering from a psychopathic disorder and her condition

---

78 MHA 1983, s 2(2) provides that this power is restricted to cases where it is necessary to remove the patient from society. Memorandum of Guidance for the 1983 Act (1983) DHS para 23.
79 See *L v Bournewood Community and Mental Health NHS Trust* [1999] 1 AC 458.
80 MHA 1983, s 23(2)(a).
81 For a nearest relative to order discharge, he must first give written notice to the hospital managers at least 72 hours beforehand. If a report is furnished by the responsible medical officer that the patient is dangerous, this will prevent the nearest relative from exercising his power to order discharge.
82 MHA 1983, s 20(1).
83 MHA 1983, s 11(1).
84 MHA 1983, s 11(4).
85 [1986] 2 All ER 306.
86 Per McCullough J at 315b-c.
87 [1995] QB 60.

was not likely to respond to treatment in hospital, she should not continue to be detained. However, Roch LJ found that treatability extended beyond the 'narrow' view that treatment had to be likely to alleviate or prevent deterioration of the applicant's condition. Roch LJ's wider interpretation included consideration of:[88]

(i) the tribunal's duty to discharge the patient if the patient's detention in hospital was simply an 'attempt to coerce the patient into participating in group therapy';[89]
(ii) the 'treatability' test being satisfied if treatment in hospital is likely to prevent a deterioration of the patient's condition;
(iii) immediate alleviation is not required to satisfy the 'treatability' test;
(iv) the 'treatability' test may still be met if deterioration of the patient's condition occurs before it improves;
(v) the MHA 1983, s 145, which allows for medical treatment in hospital to cover nursing care and rehabilitation; and
(vi) nursing care which might lead to the patient's condition improving sufficiently for her to get an insight into her own condition.

This extended 'treatability test' was confirmed in *R v Secretary of State for Scotland*[90] and a further factor was identified, namely:

'that the patient's condition includes the symptoms or manifestations of it and behaviour caused by it, so that, if there was treatment likely to alleviate or prevent the deterioration of such symptoms, manifestations or behaviour, that would suffice to demonstrate treatability'.[91]

The *Canons Park* decision affirms the view that 'mere care' may be sufficient in the long-term rehabilitation of the patient.

Under the MHA 1983, s 4 a patient may be detained for 72 hours for emergency assessment. Fewer safeguards are in place owing to the necessity for swift action. The Royal Commission in 1957 expected emergency assessment to be rarely used yet it has proved a common form

---

88 Per Roch LJ at 81G-H-82A-C.
89 Per Roch LJ at 81H.
90 1998 SC 49, 2 Div.
91 Price notes that 'compulsory hospitalisation can be defended on *parens patriae* grounds only where the patient is treatable and legally incapable of making decisions concerning treatment and where the purpose of commitment is to prevent a deterioration, or effect an improvement in the person's health, and where hospitalisation is the least restrictive alternative in the circumstances': Price, D 'Civil commitment of the mentally ill' *Medical Law Review* 1994, p 321, at pp 323-24. However, *Canons Park* prevents this situation occurring as the decision to detain and keep detained is based on other factors, like the possibility that remaining detained could lead to a possible recovery in the future.

of compulsory admission.[92] The provision is preferred because it is quicker, cheaper, easier to obtain and, as the period of detention is shorter, less likely to create unease in the patient. However, as there are minimal safeguards in place, the frequent use of the MHA 1983, s 4 certainly raises some concern. Although the period of detention is much shorter, the patient is deprived of additional psychiatric opinion, as only one medical recommendation for the detention is required, thereby increasing the risk of unnecessary detention. As the length of detention is much shorter than under the MHA 1983, s 2 or the MHA 1983, s 3, only the responsible medical officer (who is the doctor in charge of the patient's treatment) and hospital managers are able to grant the patient's discharge.[93] Therefore, on the basis of one medical opinion the patient may be admitted to hospital for assessment and will have no means of questioning or ending his detention for the full 72 hours.

The duration of detention periods under admission for treatment are an initial period of six months followed by a further period of six months and then renewed subsequently at yearly intervals. In *R v Hallstrom, ex p W (No 2)*,[94] McCullough J stressed that the renewal provision could only be used when the patient's mental condition requires detention within the controlled environment of a psychiatric hospital. This has since been overruled by the Court of Appeal in *B v Barking, Havering and Brentwood Community Healthcare NHS Trust*,[95] where it was held that a patient's detention could be renewed while the patient was on leave if the treatment required an 'inpatient element'. The Mental Health Act 1959 had longer periods of detention: one year in the first instance, followed by another year and then successive periods of two years. The shorter detention periods, which were introduced by the MHA 1983, have opened up greater opportunities for patients to apply to the Mental Health Review Tribunal for discharge. Patients have one right of access to the tribunal during each period of detention and where patients do not apply for their detention to be reviewed, the hospital manager is under a duty automatically to refer the case to the tribunal.[96] No specific requirements need to be satisfied when deciding whether discharge should be granted.[97] However, in *Kynaston v Secretary of State for Home Affairs*,[98] it was observed that once a mental disorder can no longer be found, the patient should be discharged.

92 The 'Percy' Commission: *Royal Commission on the Law Relating to Mental Illness and Mental Deficiency 1954–1957*, Cm 169, para 409.
93 MHA 1983, s 23.
94 [1986] 2 All ER 306.
95 [1999] 1 FLR 106.
96 MHA 1983, s 68.
97 MHA 1983, s 23(2).
98 (1981) 73 Cr App R 281.

8 The Role of Mental Health Review Tribunals

The introduction of Mental Health Review Tribunals under the Mental Health Act 1959 was a concession to legalists in an otherwise psychiatrist-friendly statute. The *Report of the Franks Committee on Tribunals and Inquiries*, which was implemented by the Tribunals and Inquiries Act 1958, recognised the importance of tribunals as offering opportunities of adjudicating appeals by individuals against public decisions.[99] Patients had the opportunity to apply to the tribunal once during every period of detention. However, if patients did not apply, no review of their position was made. The adoption of a new legalism in the MHA 1983 is reflected by the radical step of establishing automatic review by the tribunal. This ensures that all periods of detention are regularly reviewed irrespective of whether the patient has initiated it himself. The tribunal's role has been described as a 'safeguard for the liberty of the individual and to insure against unjustified detention in hospital'.[100] The tribunal preserves the legally structured threshold between civil detention and liberty by seeking to realise the right balance between patient liberty, third party protection and patient welfare. In *X v United Kingdom*, it was found that when a person is detained in hospital, this situation should be periodically reviewed to establish whether the detention is still appropriate. This case was important in establishing automatic tribunal review under the MHA 1983 in the event that the patient does not apply for review himself. It was also found that for detention to be lawful under Article 5 of the European Convention on Human Rights five requirements must be satisfied:
(i)   a true mental disorder must be established by objective medical advice;
(ii) the mental disorder must be of a 'kind or degree warranting compulsory confinement';
(iii) the disorder must be persistent;
(iv) the patient must have access to a judicial body independent of the executive with 'court like' attributes; and
(v)   a judicial hearing must be attached by certain basic guarantees.[101]

The tribunal has a legal role to play in that it protects the patient's right to be free from unjustified detention. 'The outcome sought is a legal one and the tribunal has to issue a legal decision: it must determine whether the patient's continued detention is lawful or unlawful'.[102]

99 The Franks Report, *Report of the Franks Committee on Tribunals and Inquiries*, Cm 218 (1957) HMSO, London.
100 The Aavold Report, *Report on the Review of Procedures for the Discharge and Supervision of Psychiatric Patients Subject to Special Restrictions*, Cm 5191 (1973) HMSO, London, para 35.
101 (1981) 4 EHRR 188.
102 Richardson, G & Machin, D 'Judicial review and tribunal decision-making: A study of the Mental Health Review Tribunal' *Public Law* 2000, p 500.

Applications for tribunal hearings have continued to increase since the enactment of the 1983 Act. In 1984 there were 3,558 applications in England and Wales. In 1994 this increased to 12,247 applications and by 1998 application levels further increased to 18,503.[103] The percentage of applications that reach hearing stage was 49% in 1998.[104] The increase in tribunal usage appears encouraging but this increase must be seen in light of soaring admission figures under the 1983 Act owing to many more patients becoming subject to the 'revolving door syndrome'.[105] This phenomenon has been brought about by the re-admission of those that have already been treated as inpatients and discharged from hospital. In 1984 there were 17,121 formal admissions to the NHS hospitals, special hospitals and nursing homes catering for the mentally disordered. However, by 1998 formal admissions to hospital rose to 27,100 the substantial majority of which were under section 2.[106]

The tribunal has to discharge the patient if the requirements for detaining him no longer exist. If the patient has been detained under the MHA 1983, s 2 for assessment, discharge is to be granted if the patient is 'not then suffering from a mental disorder or from a mental disorder of a nature or degree which warrants his detention'[107] or the detention cannot be justified on the basis of the patient's own safety or the safety of others.[108] Likewise, if the patient has been detained in hospital for treatment under the MHA 1983, s 3, the tribunal should grant the patient's discharge if there is no evidence in favour of continuing confinement because no further treatment is considered necessary. When the tribunal considers the patient's suitability for discharge, the MHA 1983, s 72(2)(b) requires the tribunal to consider whether the patient would be able to cope.[109] In 1981, Peay looked at the operation of the tribunal system and found alarming

---

103 DHS 'Mental Health Review Tribunals For England and Wales' Annual Report 1994, p 22 and DHS 'Mental Health Review Tribunals For England and Wales' Annual Report 1997-98, p 52.
104 Out of 18,503 applications, 9,057 cases were heard before a Mental Health Review Tribunal: DHS 'Mental Health Review Tribunals For England and Wales' Annual Report 1997-98, p 57.
105 See Payne, S 'The rationing of psychiatric beds: changing trends in sex-ratios in admission to psychiatric hospital' *Health and Social Care in the Community* 1995, Vol 3, p 289.
106 In 1984, there were 7,079 admissions under the MHA 1983, s 2; in 1992/3 this figure had risen to 11,550 admissions and by 1998, 89% of all admissions were under s 2.
107 MHA 1983, s 72(1)(a)(i).
108 MHA 1983, s 72(1)(a)(ii).
109 If the tribunal is unsure of this, it has discretion to refrain from granting discharge in relation to patients who have been classified as suffering from mental illness or severe mental impairment.

divergences in the attitude and knowledge of tribunal members.[110] The study illustrated that non-medical tribunal members held those medically trained in high regard and placed 'unnecessary reliance on medical integrity and a general emphasis on the medical approach'.[111] This is interesting because despite every effort during the 1970s to move away from the heavy emphasis on medical decision-making, the one legalist structure which was introduced in the Mental Health Act 1959 continued to adhere to medicalist principles.[112]

If satisfied that the patient is no longer suffering from any form of mental disorder, the tribunal must decide whether to grant a conditional or an absolute discharge.[113] If the tribunal is satisfied that it is 'not appropriate for the patient to remain liable to be recalled to hospital for further treatment',[114] an absolute discharge should be granted. If the tribunal cannot be satisfied about the above, the discharge must be conditional.[115] The tribunal system provides an additional review forum and, therefore, provides an important opportunity to inspect the validity of detention. If the patient is dissatisfied with the tribunal's decision he may instigate judicial review proceedings to challenge the decision. However, judicial review is used to challenge the legality of the decision rather than its merits.

9 Treatment Provisions

It is clear that the enactment of the MHA 1983 bolstered existing legal safeguards within the Mental Health Act 1959. However, at the time of the 1959 Act it was considered that mentally unstable patients were not able to make decisions about the form of treatment they received or indeed, whether to accept it. Those calling for legislative reform in the 1970s held

110 Peay, J 'Mental Health Review Tribunals - just or efficacious safeguards?' *Law and Human Behaviour* 1981, Vol 5, No 2/3, p 161.
111 Peay, J 'Mental Health Review Tribunals - just or efficacious safeguards?' *Law and Human Behaviour* 1981, Vol 5, No 2/3, p 170.
112 In the Mental Health Review Tribunal Annual Report 1998-99, it is clearly stated that the medical member of the tribunal should not give an opinion as to discharge in the pre-hearing meeting with the other tribunal members. DHS 'Mental Health Review Tribunals For England and Wales' Annual Report 1997-98, p 88.
113 MHA 1983, s 73.
114 MHA 1983, s 73(1)(b).
115 MHA 1983, s 73(2). In *R v Merseyside Mental Health Review Tribunal, ex p K* [1990] 1 All ER 694, the patient was no longer suffering from a mental disorder so he could not be subject to the provisions of the MHA 1983. Butler-Sloss LJ noted, however, that 'the tribunal are of the view that having regard to the period the ... [appellant] ... has been detained in hospital it was necessary to test the ... [appellant's] ... behaviour in the community and that therefore, he should be subject to recall'.

opposing views and argued for the new statute to incorporate consent to treatment provisions, which formally recognised the need for legal control over treatment decision-making. Despite the hospital setting being perceived as a therapeutic environment where psychiatric treatment would be administered, legalist appeasement required the introduction of a framework of formal safeguards. Clinical discretion would be restricted by these measures, yet the Mental Health Act 1959 treatment provisions would 'serve as a significant quid pro quo for the medical profession'.[116] The requirement of patient consent to treatment depends upon the type and gravity of treatment to be administered.[117] The purpose of the treatment provisions was to clarify the extent to which treatment for mental disorders could be imposed on a patient and to ensure patients were not detained without purpose. Prior to the MHA 1983 the Department of Health and Social Security was of the opinion that the Mental Health Act 1959 gave an inferred authority to treat, rendering patient consent unecessary.[118] However, this view was condemned by a number of committees owing to the possible exploitation of such a position.[119] In 1973 the Davies Committee observed that for voluntary patients, 'their remedy against receiving treatment to which they do not consent is the same as that of any patient in any kind of hospital, they can sue for assault,'[120] but it was acknowledged that voluntary patients who refused treatment were often threatened with being 'put on order'.[121] The Davies Committee recommended that a second medical opinion regime should be adopted to prevent such occurrences happening in the future.[122] The Butler Committee submitted a formula for treatment imposition: treatment (other than nursing care) should not be imposed on any patient if he is able to appreciate what is involved. However, three exceptions should be allowed where patient consent is not needed:

(a) where the treatment is not of a hazardous or irreversible nature and represents the minimum interference with the patient to prevent him from behaving violently or otherwise being a danger to himself or others;

---

116 Unsworth, C *The Politics of Mental Health Legislation* (1987) Oxford University Press, Oxford, p 324.
117 The MHA 1983, Pt IV.
118 Fennell, P *Treatment Without Consent: Law Psychiatry and the Treatment of Mentally Disordered People Since 1845* (1996) Routledge, London. See also Hansard HC Deb, vol 849, col 77 (23 January 1973).
119 Butler Committee, paras 3.57-3.59 and 'The Management of Violent or Potentially Violent Patients' CHOSE 1977.
120 The Davies Committee *Report of the Committee on Hospital Complaints Procedure* (1973) HMSO, London, para 7.35.
121 The voluntary patient was threatened with formal detention provision under the MHA 1983.
122 The Davies Committee *Report of the Committee on Hospital Complaints Procedure* (1973) HMSO, London, para 7.36.

(b) where it is necessary to save the patient's life; or
(c) where (not being irreversible) it is necessary to prevent him from deteriorating.[123]

The MHA 1983, Pt IV relates to the treatment of mental disorder and does not extend to treatment for physical problems.[124] The MHA 1983, s 63 provides that the:

> 'consent of the patient ... [is] ... not ... required for any medical treatment ... for the mental disorder from which he is suffering, not being treatment falling within ... [the safeguards provided under] ... section 57 and section 58.'

The MHA 1983, s 56(1) provides that the MHA 1983, s 63 applies to all detained patients. The consent to treatment provisions exist in order that a patient is not detained in hospital without being in receipt of some treatment.

The MHA 1983, s 57 applies to the most serious forms of treatment. Psychosurgery, which is defined as 'any surgical operation for destroying brain tissue or for destroying the functioning of brain tissue'[125] and surgical implantation of sexual suppressants can only be administered if the patient consents to the treatment. In *R v Mental Health Act Commission, ex p X*, Stuart-Smith LJ said that where a mentally disordered patient is sexually deviant 'it seems likely that the sexual problem will be *inextricably linked* with the mental disorder, so that the treatment for the one is treatment for the other'.[126] In the Divisional Court, the definition of 'surgical implantation' and 'hormone' were considered. The court viewed the term 'hormone' included synthetically produced hormones as well as naturally occurring hormones but did not include hormone analogues. With regard to 'surgical implant', the scope would depend upon a 'question of fact and degree'. In this case the Court was of the view that the use of a large-bore syringe could be distinguished from a surgical implant, as the deposit of the analogue did not require a surgical incision. For the consent to be valid, two independent people, one being a medical practitioner, must certify that the patient understands the information given about the treatment procedure and the consent given was a 'true choice'.[127] In *ex p W*, the patient consented to the administration of Goserelin, a hormone

---

123 The Davies Committee *Report of the Committee on Hospital Complaints Procedure* (1973) HMSO, London, para 3.54.
124 Treatment for physical problems, which is administered without the consent of the patient, will be subject to the common law.
125 MHA 1983, s 57(1)(a).
126 (1988) 9 BMLR 77.
127 MHA 1983, s 57(2)(a).

analogue, to suppress his sexual urges after having been informed of the procedure and the aim of the treatment. The consent of the patient was considered invalid because of the lack of independent medical opinion that the patient had the capability to understand the information given to him. The patient sought judicial review of the decision. As Goserelin was a hormone analogue and was injected rather than surgically implanted, the drug's administration did not fall within the MHA 1983, s 57 and, as such, the lack of independent medical opinion finding the patient's consent to be valid was irrelevant. If it is found that the consent given by the patient is not valid or the patient refuses to give consent, then the treatment cannot be administered. The Code of Practice identifies the 'basic principles' of consent as '[implying] the ability, given an explanation in simple terms to understand the nature, purpose and effect of the proposed treatment'. Efforts must also be made to ensure the patient is able to understand the implications of not undergoing the treatment.[128] This section also applies to voluntary patients[129] and persons who are not detained in hospital.

The MHA 1983, s 58 governs less serious (and reversible) treatments such as Electro-Convulsive Therapy (ECT) and drug therapy.[130] The patient must provide a valid consent and if he does not, a second medical opinion is required.[131] The validity of the patient's consent must be certified either by the responsible medical officer or by an independent medical practitioner. The responsible medical officer has three months in which to give treatment before he is under a duty to obtain the second medical opinion.

> 'Three months gives time for the psychiatrist to consider a treatment programme which suits the patient. Three months seems to fit in best with both clinical experience and clinical practice. It is long enough to allow a proper valuation and assessment of what, if any, long-term treatment may be needed. It is also short enough to ensure that patient consent, or a second medical opinion, is obtained before a long term course of drug treatment gets too far ahead.'[132]

The MHA 1983, s 62 provides that the procedural safeguards provided for in the MHA 1983, s 57 and the MHA 1983, s 58 shall not apply in an

128 The *Code of Practice* Cm 7320, paras 15.12 and 6.23.
129 MHA 1983, s 56(2).
130 See Mental Health (Hospital, Guardianship and Consent to Treatment) Regulations 1983, SI 1983/893, reg 16(2).
131 Paragraph 5 of the Advice to Second Opinion Appointed Doctors: 'It is not necessary that the treatment accord with the SOAD's personal practice providing that the SOAD feels that it is reasonable'.
132 Per Under-Secretary of State, Special Standing Committee, cols 769-846, 29 June 1982.

58 The Mental Health Act 1983

emergency. The Code of Practice advocates that the treatment given under this section has to be the responsibility of the responsible medical officer.[133] In the *Fifth Biennial Report*[134] it was noted that treatment given under the MHA 1983, s 62:

> '[fell] outside the consent to treatment provisions of the Act. Some treatment is described as being given under the provisions of section 62 when in fact the patient is either not detained or is held under the short-term holding powers of the Act to which section 62 does not apply'.

Treatment under the MHA 1983, s 62 must either be necessary to 'save the patient's life';[135] to prevent any further deterioration in the patient's condition;[136] to alleviate suffering;[137] or the treatment is necessary to 'prevent the patient behaving violently or being a danger to himself or to others'.[138] the MHA 1983, ss 3, 16 and 20 encompass the 'treatability test'.[139] As Ashworth and Gostin note[140] the treatment must 'effect some change in the ... [patient's] ... mental condition – in the sense either that the condition can be cured or remedied or that it can be prevented from getting worse'. In *R v Canons Park Mental Health Review Tribunal, ex p A*, it was recognised that medical treatment included nursing care and rehabilitation as laid down by the MHA 1983, s 145.[141] Medical treatment can range from intensive drug therapy, treatment preventing deterioration of mental state and nursing care, which allows the patient to gain insight into his condition thereby enabling him to co-operate.[142]

When considering the validity of the patient's consent, independent witnesses must examine the patient's understanding. The issue is whether it is the patient's 'actual understanding' of the treatment or the patient's 'capacity to understand' that is relevant. Such semantics have been

---

133 The *Code of Practice*, Cm 7320, para 16.18.
134 Mental Health Act Commission 1991-1993, para 7.12.
135 MHA 1983, s 62(1)(a).
136 MHA 1983, s 62(1)(b).
137 MHA 1983, s 62(1)(c).
138 MHA 1983, s 62(1)(d).
139 *R v Canons Park Mental Health Review Tribunal, ex p A* [1995] QB 60.
140 Ashworth, A & Gostin, L 'Mentally disordered offenders and the sentencing process', in Gostin, L (ed) *Secure Provision: A Review of Special Services for the Mentally Ill and Mentally Handicapped in England and Wales* (1985) Tavistock, London, p 215.
141 Per Roch LJ, at 81G-H and 82A-C.
142 Where the condition is physical but is closely connected to the psychiatric condition, difficulty is found in distinguishing whether the treatment can lawfully be given without the patient's consent.

difficult to clarify.[143] If actual understanding is required, the level of competence possessed by the patient may be subject to the amount of information passed on to him. The doctor could control the patient's level of competence by how much information he provides. However, the consent to treatment provisions endorse the 'capability to understand' approach. In *R v Mental Health Act Commission, ex p X*,[144] the test of capacity of the MHA 1983, s 57 was confirmed as 'the ... capacity and not actual understanding'.[145] In *Re T (adult: refusal of treatment)*,[146] it was noted that 'all adults are presumed to have ... [the] ... capacity ... [to consent] ... but it is a presumption which can be rebutted'.[147]

The consent to treatment provisions within the MHA 1983 was a significant step towards endorsing legalist principles. It was recognised that despite psychiatrists and patients having a common goal in bringing about therapeutic success, psychiatric treatment was capable of affecting the patient's behaviour and could produce many unpleasant side effects. The scrutiny of patient treatment programmes would thereby protect against any unnecessary infringement of patient rights.

10 Protective Legal Mechanisms for Staff and Patients

The new legalism is also reflected in the MHA 1983 by the reduction of immunities from litigation in respect of professional practice. Within the Mental Health Act 1959 significant levels of protection were afforded to staff. The Mental Health Act 1959, s 141 provided that no civil or criminal proceedings should lie against a member of staff unless the act complained of was done in bad faith or without reasonable care and that the plaintiff must apply to the High Court for leave to proceed. At this time, patients were perceived to be difficult to deal with and 'likely to harass those concerned with them by groundless charges and litigation'.[148] The MHA 1983 introduced a more rigorous system and staff were no longer free from the possibility of being subject to civil or criminal proceedings. The MHA 1983, s 139 protects members of staff from tortuous or criminal

---

143 In *Re R (a minor) (wardship: medical treatment)* [1991] 4 All ER 177 per Lord Donaldson, at 187e-g.
144 (1988) 9 BMLR 77.
145 (1988) 9 BMLR 77 per Stuart-Smith LJ at 85.
146 [1993] Fam 95, CA.
147 Per Lord Donaldson MR, at 664. In *Re C (adult: refusal of medical treatment)* [1994] 1 All ER 819, Thorpe J applied Lord Donaldson MR's dictum and held that in cases where a person is not incapacitated by virtue of RSC 1965, Ord 80, a rebuttable presumption of competence operates in favour of the patient, and regardless of their mental disorder.
148 *Pountney v Griffiths* [1976] AC 314, per Lord Simon at 329.

proceedings when they are acting under the auspices of the Act. In *R v Bracknell Justices, ex p Griffiths*,[149] Lord Edmund-Davies reiterated his stance taken in *Pountney v Griffiths*:[150]

> '[in] ... my judgment where a male nurse is on duty and exercising his functions of controlling the patients in the hospital, acts done in pursuance of such control, are acts within the scope of ... [the 1983 Act] ... and are thus, protected by the section'.[151]

The MHA 1983, s 139 is concerned only with the protection of individuals personally against the legal proceedings for alleged wrongs. The section does not, therefore, affect the right of a patient or his friends to apply to the High Court at any time for the dispensation of supervision by means of habeas corpus. Sir John Donaldson MR noted in *Winch v Jones*[152] that the MHA 1983, s 139 was intended to:

> 'strike a balance between the legitimate interests of the applicant to be allowed ... to seek the adjudication of the courts on any claim which is not frivolous, vexatious or an abuse of process and the equally legitimate interests of the respondent to such an application not to be subjected to the undoubted exceptional risk of being harassed by baseless claims by those who have been treated under the Mental Health Act 1983'.[153]

In *James v Mayors and Burgesses of the London Borough of Havering*, Farquharson LJ noted that the role of the MHA 1983, s 139 went beyond preventing frivolous claims but existed to protect members of staff who had made a wrong and misjudged decision.[154] However, where the patient or a third party instigate judicial review proceedings against public authorities, the MHA 1983, s 139 does not apply. In *Ex p Waldron*, Ackner LJ noted '[j]udicial review involves an *inquiry* into the decisions in this case whether there has been a plain excess of jurisdiction or not. The proceedings are not *an action against* the decision-maker'.[155] Therefore, as there are no recriminations in judicial review, the decision-maker should not need to be protected by the MHA 1983, s 139.

149 [1975] 3 WLR 140.
150 [1976] AC 314.
151 [1975] 3 WLR 140, per Lord Edmund-Davies at 147H.
152 [1985] 3 All ER 97.
153 [1985] 3 All ER 97 at 102h-j. As such, because there are no recriminations in judicial review, the decision-maker should not need to be protected by the MHA 1983, s 139.
154 (1992) 15 BMLR 1.
155 [1986] QB 824, per Ackner L, at 840D–E.

The MHA 1983, s 126 provides that staff are under a duty to ensure no false statements are made about a patient's mental state when making applications under the MHA 1983. The MHA 1983, s 127 creates two offences:
(i) staff in psychiatric hospitals are under a general duty not to ill-treat or wilfully neglect the patients in their care;[156] and
(ii) a guardian is under a duty not to ill-treat or wilfully neglect a mentally disordered person in the community.

Ill-treatment and wilful neglect are separate offences. If a patient is detained, care and/or treatment must follow. If a patient is wilfully neglected or ill-treated the spirit of the law to provide care and treatment is sadly lost. Ill-treatment and wilful neglect can amount to a single act such as a slap or smack.[157] In *R v Newington*,[158] it was found that three things had to be established in order to prove ill-treatment:
(i) deliberate conduct by the accused which could properly be described as ill-treatment irrespective of whether it damaged or threatened to damage the victim's health;
(ii) a guilty mind involving either an appreciation by the accused that she was inexcusably ill-treating the patient, or that she was reckless as to whether she was inexcusably acting in that way; and
(iii) that the victim was a mentally disordered person within the meaning of the MHA 1983, s 1.

Although better provision for patients to bring claims against their carers now exist, it remains very difficult for patients to prove that they have been ill-treated because the protection of staff and third parties continues to take priority. For example, in *R v Broadmoor Special Hospital Authority, ex p S*, it was found that where hospitals were detaining patients under the MHA 1983, there was a general power to authorise random and routine searches of patients without their consent and without cause, overriding, if necessary, medical opinion against its exercise.[159] Auld LJ observed that:

'[g]iven ... [the patients] ... mental condition and propensities requiring such treatment, it was obvious that, in the interests of all, in particular the need to ensure a safe therapeutic environment for patients and staff, that the express power of detention carried with it a power of control and discipline, including, where necessary, of search with or without cause and despite individual medical

---
156 The MHA 1983, s 127(1).
157 *R v Holmes* [1979] Crim LR 52.
158 (1990) 91 Cr App R 247.
159 [1998] COD 199.

objection ... . On occasion, an individual patient's treatment might have to give way to the wider interest'.

The final development in the MHA 1983, which reflects support for the new protective legalism is the introduction of the Mental Health Act Commission which establishes procedures to review treatment decisions under the MHA 1983, s 121(2). The Commission acts as an independent review mechanism and harnesses the knowledge and experience of a multi-disciplinary panel, which comprises doctors, lawyers, academics, psychologists and social workers. The functions of the Commission are:

(i) to keep under review the exercise of the powers and duties contained in the MHA 1983 which relate to detained patients;
(ii) to visit and interview patients detained under the MHA 1983;
(iii) to investigate complaints;
(iv) to appoint second medical opinion doctors;
(v) to receive and examine reports on treatment given under consent;
(vi) to submit proposals to revise the *Code of Practice*;
(vii) to review decisions of hospital managers; and
(viii) to publish a biennial report on its activities.

11 Conclusion

The ideology that shaped the MHA 1983 stemmed from a period prior to its enactment of immense unease about the current legislative provisions. Following the Mental Health Act 1959 support of medicalism and reliance on medical opinion had flagged. The fruitful years in therapeutic development preceding the 1959 Act had encouraged the view that psychiatrists knew what was best and that they should be given the flexibility necessary to carry out their duties effectively. However, throughout the 1960s and 1970s greater levels of scepticism emerged. Although the psychiatric profession continued to strengthen its current knowledge, it did not expand or establish new therapeutic techniques, neither did pharmaceutical companies develop more effective drugs. Instead they concentrated on making money from the established conventional drugs. The anti-psychiatry movement of this period compounded the view that legal control over psychiatric practice should be intensified. However, the seminal work of Larry Gostin at MIND had, perhaps, the biggest impact on the question of law reform. MIND's objective was to acquire greater legal safeguards over the detention process in order to protect patient rights. By the mid-1970s the new legalism emphasising the rights of patients rather than those of the wider community emerged. This concept supported the traditionally legalist approach of establishing a framework of social control, yet suggested that

Conclusion

psychiatric coercion had to be assessed on legal, social and moral grounds rather than on purely medical ones. The 1960s and 1970s were periods of great pessimism in psychiatry. In the opinion of Unsworth it is this which ultimately dictated the demand to re-embrace legalism.[160] Legalism enabled the introduction of a number of provisions within the MHA 1983, which bolstered the rights of patients. However, many of these safeguards do little more than consolidate medical hegemony in practice, the clearest example of which is the consent to treatment provisions. On the surface, these provisions appear to mollify demands to recognise that psychiatric patients should have a right to make personal treatment choices. Yet in reality, the MHA 1983 leaves essential decision-making powers in medical hands and legitimises their judgments.

The new legalism in the MHA 1983 has not been fully successful because it has failed to achieve an effective balancing strategy[161] between patient rights to liberty and autonomy, third party protection and patient welfare. Furthermore, although additional legal control has proved helpful in establishing negative rights such as rights against abuse, it has been less successful in instituting positive rights to services and support.[162] With the encouragement of voluntary treatment and a reduction in the use of civil detention, the psychiatric patient group that was not protected by the legislative safeguards expanded. Likewise, as civil detention reduced, a gradual move towards providing care in less restrictive environment increased. By the middle of the 1980s, the availability of hospital beds and facilities had diminished owing to the shift away from inpatient detention towards community care. The existing mental health services were beginning to show signs of strain and professionals had to find a 'new' care framework to supplement the existing one. Providing mental health care in a hospital environment was becoming more difficult as hospital facilities were shutting down. With mounting emphasis on community-based services, the struggle to offer adequate care intensified, leading practitioners to establish a way of maintaining contact with and control over mentally disordered people in the community.

---

160 Unsworth, C *The Politics of Mental Health Legislation* (1987) Oxford University Press, Oxford, p 351.
161 See generally, Veatch, R *Medical Ethics* (1989) Jones and Bartlett Publishers, Boston.
162 Jones, K *Asylums and After* (1993) Athlone Press, London, p 213.

Chapter 3
Re-orienting psychiatric support

1 Introduction

The struggle between legalism and medicalism over the level of legal control to be exercised over medical discretion persisted throughout the 1980s. While this conflict unfolded and gained pace during the twentieth century, a further matter for debate emerged: whether the provision of mental health care in the community was a more fitting alternative to institutional care, something upon which the psychiatric profession and, to some extent the public, had come to rely. By the early 1960s, institutional care was experiencing a media backlash as negative images of care provided in the hospital setting abounded. Patients were increasingly portrayed as individuals who were stripped of their dignity and their right to make personal choices. Simultaneously, a growing awareness of social rights and humanitarianism emerged, and with this the detention and restriction of individuals owing to illness was questioned.

Community care offered an alternative to the institution. By the 1960s, community care was understood as the provision of appropriate care and support (although not including the forcible administration of medication) outside the confines of the hospital. The purpose of community care was to offer vulnerable individuals the opportunity of living in the community, which would allow them to maintain relationships with relatives and friends, while also providing the social and psychiatric support they needed. Care within the community was no longer merely concerned with the distribution of food and shelter as it had been prior to the construction of the large, imposing asylums and workhouses during the nineteenth century. Rather it involved a more structured approach to care with the intention of enhancing the skills and independence of the mentally ill. The concept of community care had existed for a long time prior to the institutional era. While these institutions typified the Victorian values of placating a social conscience and at the same time exercising social control, before this the vulnerable were frequently cared for within a family setting. Indeed, the picture of the chained, incarcerated lunatic, as being the only method of care available at this time is a false representation of lunacy relief. The provision of food and shelter within the family home may for some fall outside the currently accepted notion of 'community care'; nevertheless this informal provision commonly characterised the nature of aid and established a foundation for the development of a formalised system of community care in the twentieth century.[1]

During the twentieth century statutory recognition of community care approached in two waves. The first emerged when the benefits associated with a less restrictive care environment for 'mental defectives' were acknowledged. The Mental Deficiency Act 1913 introduced two community-based measures: the guardianship order and supervision. The second wave occurred some time later, for developments in community care provision for the mentally ill took considerably longer because this group were thought to present a significantly larger risk to the public. Tentative steps towards the acceptance of mental health provision in a less restrictive environment were made in the Mental Treatment Act 1930 and the Mental Health Act 1959. Once voluntary admission to hospital had been embraced and it was realised that many of those with mental health problems were able to seek help for themselves, the perception of the uncontrollable, threatening 'crazies' diminished from the public consciousness. However, despite these steps, community care struggled to get off the ground owing to inadequate funding and planning.

Despite the problems associated with community care by the end of the 1950s, Enoch Powell, a Minister of Health, managed to revive the policy with the introduction of the Hospital Plan in 1961. The Plan led to a large-scale reduction of psychiatric hospital facilities for the mentally ill and impaired. At the same time, there was growing disillusionment with institutional provision, which was reflected in the work of the anti-psychiatry movement. Many of the movement's suppositions were anti-institutional rather than anti-psychiatry in nature.[2] The reduction of inpatient hospital facilities and the increasing mistrust of the institution

1   Walmsley, J, Atkinson, D & Rolph, S 'Community care and mental deficiency 1913 to 1945' in Bartlett, P & Wright, D (eds) *Outside the Walls of the Asylum* (1999) The Athlone Press, London, p 188.
2   Bartlett, P. & Wright, D 'Community care and its antecedents' in Bartlett, P & Wright, D (eds) *Outside the Walls of the Asylum* (1999) Athlone Press, London, p 2.

led to reliance on community-based professions such as social work and community psychiatric nursing. These combined events brought about a gradual restructuring of psychiatric practice and the emergence of an early community care framework. They provided the impetus for the creation of a modern notion of community care, yet despite these necessary changes in policy, legislative provision in the shape of the MHA 1983 left much to be desired. Community-based measures such as guardianship and leave of absence were somewhat limited in scope and practitioners were forced to develop these provisions in order to meet the current challenges within psychiatry.

The purpose of this chapter is to examine the nature of community care, a concept which came to play an increasingly prominent role in psychiatric provision. This chapter will consider the basis from which the modern idea of community care stemmed and why community care was embraced as the modern response to psychiatric need. It will further consider how the changing policy practice moulded the primary legislative document (the MHA 1983) in order to meet the new challenges facing psychiatry by the mid-1980s, and how successful these changes were.

2 The Development of Community Care

Until the mid–nineteenth century the vast majority of the mentally unstable were at large in the community.[3] The insane, as a group, were not singled out as requiring special provision: instead they were assimilated into a much larger class of 'morally disreputable' individuals.[4] The individual's family principally shouldered the responsibility of caring for the insane.[5] Families frequently provided shelter and food yet were unable to offer any assistance in improving the mental state of their unfortunate relative. These families were usually offered limited financial support by way of parish aid and charitable alms. However, by the mid-nineteenth century this traditional response to insanity had been somewhat replaced by the rise of the asylum and increasing support for the segregation of the mentally ill from the rest of society. From the mid-nineteenth century institutional provision became the foremost method of insanity relief, yet it cannot be said to be representative of psychiatric

---

3 Scull, A *Museums of Madness* (1979) Allen Lane, Penguin Books Ltd, London, p 14.
4 Scull, A *The Most Solitary of Afflictions: Madness and Society in Britain 1700 – 1900* (1993) Yale University Press, New Haven, p 1.
5 Porter, R 'Madness and its institutions', in Wear, A (ed) *Medicine and Society: Historical Essays* (1992) Cambridge University Press, Cambridge, pp 277–301.

provision throughout its history.[6] The notion of community care has existed for centuries. The insane, mentally impaired and elderly were frequently cared for in familiar, community settings. 'In the majority of cases, and in a notably larger proportion than others identified as "lunatics", the family was relied upon to provide.'[7] The emergence of the asylum in the 1850s did not lead to the automatic decline of community care. Rather, the community and institution as care environments operated symbiotically. Those mentally ill individuals who were fortunate enough to have relatives who remained willing to care for them continued to live in the community. However, by the end of the nineteenth century, asylums developed into 'warehouses' for the insane, as increasing emphasis was placed on social segregation and control.[8] As Walmsley, Atkinson and Rolph point out:

> 'contemporary rhetoric about care in the community tends to portray it as the semantic opposite to institutional care...[and there] remains a general belief amongst social policy commentators that it is a case of institutional care versus community care.'[9]

More accurately, community care continued to offer many individuals care and support after the emergence of the asylum; such care acted as an 'adjunct both to institutional care and to family care'.[10]

Until the twentieth century, aspects of community care, which involved the provision of food, shelter and familial support, were supplied on an informal basis. Early attempts to place community care on an official

6   Thomson, M 'Family, community and state: the micro politics of mental deficiency', in Digby, A & Wright, D (eds) *From Idiocy to Mental Deficiency* (1996) Routledge, London.

7   Andrews, J 'Identifying and providing for the mentally disabled in early modern London' in Digby, A & Wright, D (eds) *From Idiocy to Mental Deficiency* (1996) Routledge, London, pp 65–92.

8   Bartlett, P. & Wright, D 'Community care and its antecedents' in Bartlett, P & Wright, D (eds) *Outside the Walls of the Asylum* (1999) Athlone Press, London, p 303.

9   Walmsley, J, Atkinson, D & Rolph, S 'Community care and mental deficiency 1913 to 1945' in Bartlett, P & Wright, D (eds) *Outside the Walls of the Asylum* (1999) The Athlone Press, London, p 181. See also, Finch, J 'Community care: developing non-sexist alternatives' *Critical Social Policy* 1984, Vol 9, p 7. Thomson demonstrates that care provision was far more complex than this simplistic community/institution dichotomy and resoundingly refutes this misconception: Thomson, M 'The problem of mental deficiency in England and Wales 1913 – 1946' (1992) Unpublished D Phil Thesis, University of Oxford.

10 Walmsley, J, Atkinson, D & Rolph, S 'Community care and mental deficiency 1913 to 1945' in Bartlett, P & Wright, D (eds) *Outside the Walls of the Asylum* (1999) The Athlone Press, London, p 181.

footing were directed at 'mental defectives' rather than the 'mentally ill'. The term 'mental deficiency' (now commonly termed mental impairment), relates to those who have either been born with imperfect mental development leading to abnormally low intelligence or those who have suffered brain injury thereby reducing their mental abilities. By contrast, mental illness is a disorder of the mind, which does not necessarily affect the individual's intelligence or power of reasoning but prevents them from reacting to the world around them in a way which is considered 'normal'. After bodies like the Eugenics Education Society actively campaigned for mental defectives to be subject to more control, a Royal Commission, chaired by the Earl of Radnor, was set up in 1904 to consider how best this group should be dealt with. The Commission concluded that the mentally defective were abnormally fertile and owing to their inability to control themselves, far too many illegitimate children were being born and venereal disease was rife. The Commission found that mental deficiency was closely connected to hereditary tendency and therefore, mentally defective individuals had to receive greater levels of training and additional control over their activities was needed to ensure fewer pregnancies occurred. Despite this, the Commission was unwilling to condone non-consensual sterilisation of the defective 'insisting that the main criterion in certification should be the protection and happiness of the defective rather than the "purification of the race" '.[11] Despite the Radnor Commission's report in 1908, legislative recognition of the community as an effective care environment did not materialise until 1913 in the form of the Mental Deficiency Act 1913. This legislation focused specifically on the 'adult feeble minded' who were deemed a threat to the moral fibre of society. The main aim of the Mental Deficiency Act 1913 was to 'control the feeble minded through segregation'.[12] While the 1913 Act was directed towards the institutionalisation of the mentally impaired, it also introduced two community care techniques: guardianship orders and supervision. Significantly, the Mental Deficiency Act 1913 recognised the role of hospitalisation as a way of training and preparing the mentally impaired individual for community living rather than a means of permanent segregation. The Wood Report in 1929 noted 'the institution should no longer be a stagnant pool, but should become a flowing lake, always taking in and always sending out'.[13] At least for the

---

11   Jones, K *Mental Health and Social Policy 1845–1959* (1960) Routledge and Kegan Paul, London, p 53.
12   Andrews, J 'Identifying and providing for the mentally disabled in early modern London' in Digby, A & Wright, D (eds) *From Idiocy to Mental Deficiency* (1996) Routledge, London, p 184.
13   The Wood Report: *Interdepartmental Committee on Mental Deficiency, Part 3: The Adult Defective* (1929) HMSO, London, p 71.

mentally defective, the institution was regarded as a means to an end and care within the community represented that desired end.

Guardianship under the Mental Deficiency Act 1913 provided the guardian with extensive powers of control over the mental defective. These powers amounted to anything one could expect of a parent to a child below the age of 14 years. The guardian had to be a 'suitable' individual and invariably was a parent or relative. The local authority provided regular financial support to those acting as guardians to a mental defective. Local authorities were required to supervise mental defectives when neither institutional care nor guardianship was deemed appropriate. Supervision involved the overseeing of individuals in their own home by a variety of professionals such as social workers and health visitors. Regular reports to the local authority's Mental Deficiency Committee had to be made, outlining any unfulfilled needs of the individual and whether sufficient control was being exercised. Guardianship orders and supervision were designed to promote care of the mental defective in a less restrictive environment. The institution was viewed as providing the basis to prepare the individual for life in the community.

For the mental defective, community care has been a legislative reality since 1913. For the mentally ill, progress towards the establishment of community care has been more sporadic. Unlike the mentally impaired, the mentally ill have always had the problem of overcoming the social perception that such illness represents an immense risk towards others. However, by the end of the 1920s some progress had been made. The voluntary status of psychiatric patients had been established by 1930. The Maudsley Hospital in London had opened its doors to voluntary patients in 1923 and increasingly positive attitudes towards mental illness and to those who cared for and treated such illness were emerging. Acceptance of voluntarism was an important step towards the realisation that mental illness did not necessarily represent a threat to the public and that many sufferers were able to acknowledge their difficulties and seek help for themselves. The Mental Treatment Act 1930 improved the public perception of mental illness by encouraging the provision of psychiatric outpatient facilities and the use of community occupation centres. However, for the mentally ill, inpatient care always remained the final sanction if the patient refused to co-operate.

Despite these tentative steps towards the endorsement of greater flexibility in the care and treatment of the mentally ill, many consider the Mental Health Act 1959 provided the real basis for community care for such individuals. For instance, Jones states that 'the 1959 Act was a considerable legislative advance. It freed the mental hospital and most of their patients from separate designation, and greatly reduced stigmatising procedures'.[14] In 1958, it was noted by the Chief Medical Officer that 'the future of the mental health services depends on ... community services ... . [L]ong hospitalisation is out of fashion in mental medicine as it is in general medicine and surgery'.[15] The Mental Health Act 1959 fully embraced voluntary admission and the vast progress that had been made in pharmacology opened up the way for patients' symptoms to be controlled without the need for such a restrictive care environment. Furthermore, the Act endorsed guardianship as a means of providing care and control in the community. However, such provision was reliant upon adequate financial support. Under the Mental Health Act 1959 sufficient resources had not been made available, and for the next 20 years community care in practice floundered.

3 The Modern Impetus for Change

Recognition that the community could play a vital role in the care of vulnerable individuals gained momentum throughout the twentieth century. Progression towards the modern notion of community care as understood from the 1980s onwards was initiated by three factors: the closure of psychiatric inpatient facilities; shifting professional attitudes away from the institution; and the recognition of other professionals in the provision of mental health care. Community care support was reflected in the shift away from hospital care towards non-institutional care during the latter half of the twentieth century. The closure of inpatient psychiatric facilities gained considerable pace. In 1954, there were 152,000 beds and by 1994, only 43,000 beds were available for inpatient hospital care.[16] This state of affairs stemmed largely from the revival of the community care policy by Enoch Powell, when Minister of Health, in the early 1960s. Prior to Enoch Powell's intervention, the Mental Health Act 1959 had provided important legislative support for the provision of mental health care in a less restrictive environment by attempting to de-stigmatise psychiatric patients, preventing patient institutionalisation and reducing the debilitating effects of mental illness. Patients would enter hospital on a voluntary basis and then be released into the community with appropriate support. However, adequate financial backing had not been

14   Jones, K *A History of Mental Health Services* (1972) Routledge & Kegan Paul, London. See also, Jones, K *Asylums and After* (1993) Athlone Press, London, p 157.
15   Ministry of Health *On the State of the Public Health* (1958) HMSO, London, pp 123-24.
16   DHSS *Health and Personal Social Services Statistics for England and Wales* (1969) HMSO, London; Department of Health *Mental Health in England* (1995) HMSO, London.

forthcoming and consequently, community care provision at this time was rather haphazard. In 1962, Enoch Powell made known the Department of Health's plans for community care in the Hospital Plan.[17] It was proposed that a large reduction in hospital beds for the mentally ill and mentally impaired would be carried out concurrently with the development of community services.[18] In April 1963 the Department of Health's White Paper, *Health and Welfare*, recommended a ten-year plan for local authorities to employ more community-based staff such as social workers, provide additional training and resource centres for the mentally ill and make available more hostels and smaller, short-stay facilities for those in need. Although the White Paper collected information about current statistics pertaining to community care services it was neither able to outline estimated costs nor create a viable framework for community care. Yet, despite the White Paper's failings it continued to promote community care and opened up the debate for further developments in the policy.

During this period professional attitudes also shifted towards harnessing the community as an effective care environment. In 1968, the Seebohm report supplied the first major inspection of health and welfare services since the health and social care reforms of the 1940s. It acknowledged that psychiatrists were 'increasingly interested in the social context of mental health and supportive of community care'.[19] This attitudinal shift was partly a response to the mounting disillusionment about institutional care as promulgated by Erving Goffman's *Asylums* and the growing anti-psychiatry movement as depicted in the work of Thomas Szasz.[20] Increasingly, institutional care was thought to impede a full recovery as it removed many positive elements of the patient's personality during the treatment process. Goffman observed:

17 Department of Health *A Hospital Plan for England and Wales* Cm 1604 (1962) HMSO, London.
18 This position was not new. In September 1953 the World Health Organisation published *Report of Third Expert Committee on Mental Health*, which outlined a new model for the development of mental health services. The 'modern' system would use a variety of services, the hospital being just one such service and the 'balance of power would shift from the medical staff of the hospital to the medico-social team in the community': Jones, K *Asylums and After* (1993) Athlone Press, London, p 151.
19 Seebohm, F *Report of the Committee on the Local Authority and Allied Personal Social Services*, Cm 3703 (1968) HMSO, London; Welshman, J 'Rhetoric and reality: community care in England and Wales, 1948 – 74' in Bartlett, P & Wright, D (eds) *Outside the Walls of the Asylum: The History of Care in the Community 1750 – 2000* (1999) Athlone Press, London, p 213.
20 Goffman, E *Asylums* (1961) Anchor Books, London; Szasz, T *The Myth of Mental Illness: Foundations of a Theory of Personal Conduct* (1961) Harper & Row, New York; Szasz, T *Law, Liberty and Psychiatry* (1963) Macmillan, New York.

'[t]he recruit comes into the establishment with a conception of himself made possible by certain stable social arrangements in his home world. Upon entrance, he is immediately stripped of the support provided by these arrangements .... [H]e begins a series of abasements, degradations, humiliations, and profanations of self. His self is systematically ... mortified'.[21]

Absolute reliance on the institution vanished as negative images of the institution continued to surface.

However, despite the increasing professional dissociation from the institution and the reduction in hospital facilities, the modern impetus for community care would not have been possible without the pharmacological developments of the 1950s. These advances provided psychiatrists with sufficient support to embrace a less restrictive care environment. The discovery of anti-psychotic drugs and anti-depressants represented a significant breakthrough, as they stimulated developments in psychiatric practice.[22] Professions outside the inner circle of mental health provision such as social workers and community psychiatric nurses had, prior to these developments, barely any status. The freedom that these drugs afforded encouraged a growing professionalism of these groups.[23] It cannot be said that these advancements provided all the necessary elements for the creation of a modern community care system, but this gradual restructuring allowed for the initial framework required for community care to begin to be built in earnest.

4 Guardianship

(a) The history of guardianship

The notion of guardianship has existed since the Mental Treatment Act 1930 and was intended as the 'community care equivalent of compulsory admission for treatment or an ordinary hospital order'.[24] The Mental Deficiencies Act 1913 enabled guardians of mental defectives to control those in their care. The guardian was provided with all the powers a father of a child under the age of 14 would have. Since the introduction of

21 Goffman, E *Asylums* (1961) Anchor Books, London, p 24.
22 Jones, K *Asylums and After* (1993) Athlone Press, London, p 150.
23 The Younghusband Report of 1959 proposed an extensive training programme to be undertaken specifically for social workers attached to local authority Health and Welfare Departments: The Younghusband Report *Report of Working Party on Social Workers in the Local Authority Health and Welfare Services* (1959) HMSO, London.
24 Hoggett, B *Mental Health Law* (4th edn 1996) Sweet & Maxwell, London, p 218.

guardianship in this legislation the importance of a less restrictive care environment has continued. The Mental Treatment Act 1930 further recognised the importance of techniques, which aimed at improving the patient's reaction to normal everyday settings. These techniques were known as 'normalising techniques'. The 'open door' system endorsed the unlocking of doors in some wards so that patients were free to come and go independently. Likewise, the granting of 'parole' was also found to be particularly beneficial to patients. Patients began with 'hospital parole' where they were allowed out of the ward and progressed to 'weekend parole' where they could go home on trial prior to their final discharge. The objective of the parole system was to acclimatise the patient gradually to greater levels of freedom and independence so that the patient would not become too dependent on the regimented routine of hospital and would be able to cope upon discharge. Each system developed from the Mental Treatment Act 1930 and validated the importance of maintaining social norms and community contact. While attitudes gradually shifted away from the institution emphasis was placed on community care. In 1957 the 'Percy Commission'[25] accepted that there were 'limits to persuasion in relation to those with chronic disorder; and a proper reluctance to use detention in hospital for those with mild disorders'.[26] Guardianship offered an alternative to institutional care and it was anticipated that the provision of care in a more flexible community environment would lead to fewer institutionally dependent patients needing care in the future. This re-orientation of attitude towards psychiatric care was mirrored in the Mental Health Act 1959.

(b) The guardian's powers

The guardian was provided with wide powers under the Mental Health Act 1959. Despite these, it was anticipated that guardianship would only be used where the patient was reluctant to cooperate and accept the authority of those looking after him. The guardian could prevent the patient from leaving home or giving up a job. He could restrict or prohibit social interaction with certain people and he could prevent the individual adopting behaviour, which was perceived to be anti-social. As the individual was living in the community under the control of the guardian the patient had to conform to accepted social behaviour. However, despite the encouragement of guardianship and less restrictive care in the Mental

---

25 The 'Percy' Commission: *Royal Commission on the Law Relating To Mental Illness and Mental Deficiency 1954-1957* Cm 169 (1957) HMSO, London.
26 See paras 387, 399, 400 and 411. Also see, Fisher, M 'Guardianship under the Mental Health Legislation: a review' *Journal of Social Welfare Law* 1988, p 316.

Health Act 1959, reliance on confinement in hospital remained. For many working within the psychiatric field during the 1960s and 1970s, segregation still typified the optimal approach for achieving the right balance between third-party protection, patient liberty and welfare. Control of the mentally ill remained a priority. While guardianship fostered community care, the 1959 Act still reflected the need to control the mentally disordered individual. The guardian's powers were broad and open to a variety of interpretations, thereby providing the guardian with highly paternalistic powers to control the vulnerable individual.

By the 1970s, guardianship was considered a dismal failure principally because the guardian had too much control over the vulnerable individual.[27] The Department of Health viewed the 'paternalistic approach' adopted in the Mental Health Act 1959 as 'out of keeping with modern attitudes to the care of the mentally disordered'.[28] The 1959 Act was viewed as being paternalistic despite the reduction of strict legal rules governing the application of psychiatric care, because the medical profession continued to wield significant power over their patients. It was further noted that the extensive powers of the guardian were rarely necessary and only required for a small number of mentally disordered patients. It was assumed that those who needed more restrictive care would be detained and cared for in hospital. Those who might benefit from a more flexible care environment, however, would still need to be supervised in the community in order to protect third parties and to promote patient welfare. The guardianship powers within the Mental Health Act 1959 were viewed as hostile, extensively paternalistic and led to the patient's position being infantilised rather than encouraging the development of skills required for independent living. Despite these problems, the policy of embracing a less restrictive environment of care remained popular. The benefits of care in the community, such as enhancing patient skills and encouraging independent living, were sufficient for attempts to be made to overcome the problems that continued to persist.

The Mental Health Act 1959 created a highly paternalistic community environment, thereby preventing the patient from experiencing effective care which would enable him to re-establish self-sufficiency. Yet by the mid-1970s the foundation of guardianship had shifted from 'in the interests of the patient', which reflected an adherence to paternalistic control to 'for the welfare of the patient', which indicated a recognition that patients had to learn basic skills in order to eventually care for themselves. The 1981 White Paper embraced the idea of promoting patient welfare by

27 Department of Health *A Review of the Mental Health Act 1959* (1976) HMSO, London.
28 Department of Health and Home Office *Reform of Mental Health Legislation* Cm 8405 (1981) HMSO, London.

conferring on the guardian only those powers which were 'essential to promote the well-being of the patient'.[29] The 'welfare principle' has traditionally been the cornerstone of child law[30] and was viewed by Lord MacDermott in *J v C*[31] as amounting to the weighing up of:

'all relevant facts, relationship claims and wishes of parents, risks, choices and other circumstances .... [T]he course to be followed will be that which is most in the interests of the child's welfare as that term is now understood .... [It is] the paramount consideration because it rules upon or determines the course to be followed'.[32]

The White Paper acknowledged that the paternalistic approach of guardianship adopted in the Mental Health Act 1959 was not flexible enough to enable guardianship to benefit the patient. The adoption of essential guardianship powers would 'clarify the purpose of guardianship and ensure that the power is not so wide', thereby allowing the patient to develop appropriate social skills.[33]

The guardianship provision is laid down in the MHA 1983, s 7. A guardianship application may be made either by the patient's nearest relative or by an approved social worker.[34] The patient must be at least 16 years of age and must be suffering from mental illness, psychopathic disorder, severe mental impairment or mental impairment of a nature which warrants his reception into guardianship under the MHA 1983. If the patient is severely mentally impaired or mentally impaired, guardianship may only be available if it can be demonstrated that the individual is abnormally aggressive or seriously irresponsible. The objective of guardianship is to provide a safe and secure environment for the individual in the community rather than to ensure medical treatment is administered. Therefore, the patient's condition does not have to be treatable.[35] If an application for guardianship is made but the patient's nearest relative

29 Department of Health and Home Office *Reform of Mental Health Legislation* Cm 8405 (1981) HMSO, London.
30 See Bromley, P M & Lowe, N V *Family Law* (1998) Butterworths, London, pp 336-38 and also, Cretney, S M & Masson, J M *Principles of Family Law* (1996) Sweet & Maxwell, London, pp 517-24.
31 [1970] AC 668.
32 [1970] AC 668 at 710H-711A.
33 Department of Health and Home Office *Reform of Mental Health Legislation* Cm 8405 (1981) HMSO, London, para 43.
34 The MHA 1983, s 11(1). However, for such an application to be considered, the applicant must have seen the patient within 14 days of making the application: the MHA 1983, s 11(5)
35 *R v Canons Park Mental Health Review Tribunal, ex p A* [1995] QB 60. See Glover, N 'Treatability: its scope and application' *Journal of Forensic Psychiatry* 1996, Vol 7, No 2, p 353.

objects, the application can go no further.[36] In *Re S-C (Mental Patient: Habeas Corpus)*,[37] the nearest relative's objection was disregarded by the approved social worker. The Court of Appeal found the application could not be duly completed under the MHA 1983, s 6 and the detention was unlawful. The power of the nearest relative to veto a guardianship application can cause difficulty, as:

> 'often social workers are concerned not that the patient may act irresponsibly, but that the relatives may act irresponsibly towards the patient. Where there is a caring relative, guardianship may not be needed. It is where ... [the] ... nearest relative ... is neglectful, exploitative or unable to care, that guardianship may well be required'.[38]

Fortunately where the nearest relative's veto is considered unreasonable or inappropriate the MHA 1983, s 29 provides the approved social worker with the facility to apply to the county court for the nearest relative's replacement.[39] For a guardianship order to be granted, there must be evidence that the patient is suffering from one of the specific forms of mental disorder found within the MHA 1983.[40] The application requires two registered medical practitioners certifying that the patient does indeed fulfil the statutory requirements and that it is necessary for his welfare or for the protection of other persons that the patient should be received into guardianship.

The MHA 1983, s 8 confers specific 'essential powers' on the local social services authority or on the person named as guardian. These powers replace the very wide position laid down in the Mental Health Act 1959, and restrict the liberty of the patient subject to guardianship only to the extent of ensuring the necessary treatment and care is undertaken. The power to ensure the patient 'reside[s] at a ... [certain] ... place' does not include the power to require the patient to live with a particular person, although use of persuasion may discourage the patient from sleeping rough or living with people who may take advantage of his psychiatric state. If the patient absconds from his abode without the guardian's permission, the guardian has the power to take the patient into custody and return

---

36   The MHA 1983, s 11(4).
37   [1996] QB 599.
38   Fennell, P 'The Beverly Lewis case: was the law to blame?' *New Law Journal* 1988, vol 139, 17 November p 1557.
39   The MHA 1983, s 9(3)(c). See also *R v Central London County Court; R v Managers of Gordon Hospital, ex p AX London* (12 March 1997, unreported), QBD.
40   The MHA 1983, s 1.

him to the stated place of residence within 28 days of his departure.[41] Requiring the patient to reside at a particular place does not extend to requiring the patient to reside in hospital. The guardian can require the patient to attend places for the purpose of medical treatment but this does not authorise the administration of non-consensual treatment. The patient under guardianship is not subject to the consent to treatment provisions contained in the MHA 1983, Pt IV. Treatment may only be undertaken if the patient freely consents. In $T \ v \ T$[42] Wood J noted that:

> '[t]he wording of section 8 ... [is much more] ... restricted than the wider powers of the guardian under section 34 of ... [the Mental Health Act 1959]. One important effect is to remove the guardian's implicit power to consent to treatment on behalf of the patient. In my judgement there is no power to consent to ... [treatment] ... in section 8 ... and indeed on a construction of the statute as a whole I am satisfied that medical treatment means psychiatric treatment.'[43]

The final power available to the guardian is the power to require access to the patient's residence although this does not allow for forced entry. However, proceedings can be brought against any person denying access under the MHA 1983, s 129, which specifies when a person commits an obstruction under the MHA 1983.

(c) Difficulties associated with guardianship

It has been stated that the guardianship provisions within the Mental Health Act 1983 allow a 'committed interest by professionals to provide good care in the community'.[44] However, as a community-based power, guardianship has faced a number of difficulties, the most problematic of which is the lack of sanctions available to the guardian when attempting to execute his powers. For unlike the provision of care within hospital where sanctions can be invoked upon the unco-operative patient, such sanctions cannot be used within the community environment. The level of compulsion remains low and '[i]n essence, the effective use of compulsory powers is inherently linked to the institutional context: the

---

41 The MHA 1983, s 18(3) and (4). Such a power has to be clearly expressed in the legislative provisions. In *R v Hallstrom, ex p W* [1986] 2 All ER 306 at 314g, McCullough J said 'there is a canon of construction that Parliament is presumed not to enact legislation which interferes with the liberty of the subject without making it clear that this was the intention'.
42 [1988] 1 All ER 613.
43 Per Wood J at 617g.
44 DHSS Draft Code of Practice 1985, para 3.5.2.

awkward reference to the person living in the community as the 'patient' is revealing of the contradictions of the power'.[45] The use of sanctions within the community introduces a real conflict with the underlying principle of guardianship. The introduction of coercion within the community does not reflect the concept of a 'least restrictive' care environment and therefore, the effectiveness of guardianship is limited.

Guardianship relies upon patient compliance. Those who are willing to accept the guardian's directions are already likely to be co-operative and, therefore, the guardianship order is 'almost redundant'.[46] The lack of sanctions has led to the abandonment of guardianship, yet for those situations where guardianship might be useful, such as where the relative is irresponsible or neglectful, frequently the patient does not fulfil the criteria. In order for a guardianship order to be made the patient must be suffering from mental illness, psychopathic disorder, severe mental impairment or mental impairment, of a nature that warrants his reception into guardianship under the MHA 1983. If the patient is severely mentally impaired or mentally impaired, guardianship may only be available if it can be demonstrated that the individual is abnormally aggressive or seriously irresponsible. This narrows the field of application considerably and persons who are considered to be learning disabled, who may have benefited from a guardianship order, may not be considered. Beverly Lewis, a learning-disabled woman who died of neglect was one such example. Her mother's mental illness was attributed to Beverly's death but the social services authority did not consider guardianship because Beverly was not abnormally aggressive or seriously irresponsible in behaviour. At the time it was argued that if a form of community treatment order had existed, which would have enabled the forced treatment of her mother, Beverly's death may have been averted. However, Fennell argues that mechanisms within the MHA 1983 could have been used to prevent such neglect irrespective of whether community treatment orders had been available.[47]

The MHA 1983 made coercive measures illegal under guardianship, and this has led to professional frustration. The guardian's lack of powers has created despondency and led to the growing debate about community treatment orders and the future of community care. The practical failure of guardianship can largely be attributed to the inadequate sanctions available to the guardian and the narrow application criteria. In practice,

45 Fisher, M 'Guardianship under the Mental Health Legislation: a review' *Journal of Social Welfare Law* 1988, p 316, at p 322.
46 Gunn, M 'Mental Health Act guardianship: where now?' *Journal of Social Welfare Law* 1986, p 144, at p 149.
47 Fennell, P 'The Beverly Lewis case: was the law to blame?' *New Law Journal* 1988, vol 139, 17 November p 1557.

guardianship has failed to live up to expectations and has not provided a workable community care measure. As the benefits of community care were gradually recognised practitioners working within the field soon realised that guardianship did not fulfil the needs of the patient or the psychiatrist and alternative courses of action were considered.

5 Leave of Absence

(a) Application of leave of absence

The low application of guardianship has been greatly influenced by the shortcomings of the provision.[48] From the early 1980s extended leave proved increasingly popular with practitioners as it was thought to provide a 'medically controlled power to impose treatment in the community which ... [did] ... not involve the cumbersome decision-making procedures of guardianship'.[49] Extended leave, otherwise known as leave of absence, is an order which allows a patient who has been detained in hospital to be granted leave in the community.[50] Application of extended leave is restricted to patients who fulfil the MHA 1983, s 3 'admission for treatment' criteria, but who may positively gain from a less restrictive method of care. Leave of absence is not the same as discharge, for while the patient is on leave he remains 'liable to be detained' and continues to be subject to the mental health legislation. Owing to this, the patient also remains subject to the consent to treatment provisions under the MHA 1983, Pt IV, the purpose of which is to clarify the extent to which treatment for mental disorder can be imposed on detained patients in hospitals and mental nursing homes.

The responsible medical officer has the authority to grant leave. In the *Fourth Biennial Report*[51] the Mental Health Act Commission issued advice about the procedure to be followed when granting leave:

48 In 1998, there were 11,550 admissions to hospital, 89% of which were under the MHA 1983, s 2. By 31 March 1999, there were only 600 new guardianship cases nationwide. See Department of Health *Guardianship Under the Mental Health Act 1983* (2000) TSO, London.
49 Fennell, P 'Community care, community compulsion and the law' in Ritter, S et al (eds) *Collaborative Community Health Services: Together We Stand* (1996) Edward Arnold, London, p 104.
50 Leave of absence is governed by the MHA 1983, s 17. Application of extended leave is restricted to patients who fulfil the MHA 1983, s 3 admission for treatment criteria, but who may positively gain from a less restrictive method of care. Those patients, who cannot satisfy these criteria, cannot be subject to leave of absence.
51 Mental Health Act Commission 1991, HMSO, London.

'[t]he recommendation of the Commission is that all absences from hospital should be regarded as constituting leave with a need for responsible medical officer authorisation but that such leave should be agreed periodically, the weekly multi-disciplinary conference being an ideal occasion, with a written statement of the maximum licence that is granted for a defined period and with any relevant conditions.'[52]

Leave of absence can be used for temporary purposes, such as to enable a patient to receive treatment for a physical disorder in a general hospital or to move a patient, who is proving difficult to manage, to a regional secure unit. Leave of absence may also be granted for longer periods as long as they are within the legitimate detention period. As the patient remains 'liable to be detained' and continues to be subject to the consent to treatment provisions under the MHA 1983, Pt IV, professionals are provided with greater flexibility: the patient can live in the community but can still be regarded as if detained. If treatment is necessary and the patient does not co-operate, the leave can be revoked and the patient will be re-admitted to hospital. These provisions give the responsible medical officer more force and support when attempting to ensure the patient complies with the leave of absence order. Leave can be granted with or without conditions attached. Such conditions may include the need to receive medication, to live at specified residences, or to undergo therapies such as occupational therapies. In *L v Sweden*,[53] the European Commission on Human Rights held that a decision to grant provisional leave from detention in a psychiatric hospital with a condition of treatment constituted an interference with the right to respect for private life under Article 8 of the European Convention, unless the measure was justified in the interests of the person's health under Article 8(2).[54] It is therefore necessary to ensure the conditions are reasonable and can be complied with, yet do not lead to an unreasonable restriction of liberty.

Extended leave allows for a less restrictive method of care to be implemented, yet the responsible medical officer maintains overall control over the patient's behaviour and actions within the community. The responsible medical officer continues to hold significant power over the patient. Leave of absence may be revoked and the patient recalled to hospital when it is necessary in the interests of the patient's health and safety or for the protection of others. With the threat of revocation, the

52 Para 9.7.
53 (1988) 61 DR 62.
54 House of Commons Health Committee *Report on Community Supervision Orders*, Vol 11, p 8. Memorandum submitted by the Law Society Mental Health and Disability Committee, para 8.

patient's behaviour is restricted, as he must comply with what is expected of him. The consent to treatment provisions are still applicable: therefore removal of the patient from the community can be swiftly achieved provided there is evidence that without the medication the patient could represent a risk to third parties. Furthermore, the patient's detention may be renewed while on leave as long as there are inpatient elements to the patient's treatment programme. In *B v Barking, Havering and Brentwood Community Healthcare NHS Trust*,[55] the patient challenged the legality of a decision to renew her detention period while she was subject to a leave of absence order. The patient claimed that it contravened McCullough J's ruling in *R v Hallstrom, ex p W (No 2), R v Gardner, ex p L*, that a patient's detention could not be renewed whilst she was 'liable to be detained' during a period of leave.[56] However, the Court of Appeal held that as long as the patient's treatment contained an element of inpatient treatment the detention period could be renewed. Extended leave provides a method of care, within the MHA 1983, which allows greater flexibility in the provision of patient care.

(b) The objective of extended leave

A principal aim behind the use of extended leave has been to enable hospital and social services authorities to work together towards the patient's rehabilitation in the community.[57] Extended leave has thereby been used as a preliminary measure to establish the extent of a patient's needs in order to achieve successful integration into society.[58] The increasing use of extended leave since the early 1980s illustrates the gradual acceptance of community care as a viable method within mental health provision. With the 1980s came the closure of many psychiatric

55 [1999] 1 FLR 106.
56 [1986] 2 All ER 306.
57 The concept of 'partnership' has been fully accepted in contemporary community care. Efficient interdependence between health and social care authorities has been encouraged for successful implementation of community care in the future. See Department of Health *Developing Partnerships in Mental Health* Cm 3555, (1997) HMSO, London.
58 See generally, Morris, F & Mullins, M 'Assessing mental patients in less secure environments' *New Law Journal* 1996 Vol 146, p 855. Fears have been raised about the over-use of the MHA 1983, s 17. NHS Executive guidelines have been issued on the use of trial leave. There may be no renewal of a patient's detention while he is on trial leave although the use of the MHA 1983, s 17 is not barred altogether (may be used for short periods of time). The recommendation is for an increased usage of the MHA 1983, s 19 so that the managers and clinicians involved in the latter stages of patient care (whether in a less secure hospital or in the community) may assume all the statutory authority for the patient.

hospitals and the decommissioning of beds, and although attitudes clearly warmed to the idea of community care, extended leave provided practitioners with a practical way of maintaining control over patients when hospital beds were not available.

This apparent preference for extended leave led psychiatrists to develop other ways of creating their own community care order. The adopted practice was based upon the use of extended leave where leave was granted to patients with the condition that medication was continued. If the patient refused the medication or became otherwise unco-operative, leave was revoked and the patient recalled to hospital. However, if the patient complied with the conditions, leave of absence could last for up to six months. When this period had nearly elapsed, psychiatrists could recall the patient to hospital for a nominal time so that a further application could be made to renew detention. The granting of leave would then follow.[59] This arrangement became known as the 'long leash' technique.[60] The 'long leash' technique was popular as it could be continued indefinitely and throughout the period of leave the patient would remain subject to legislative control. The 'long leash' was regarded as the best treatment method for patients who did not require the highly-controlled environment of a psychiatric institution. It enabled the patient's right to liberty to be satisfied, yet also promoted a strong control framework, thereby allowing the protection of third parties. The medical profession appreciated the scope within this measure for it allowed patient liberty and third party protection to be achieved simultaneously. The 'long leash' was widely practised until the decision of *R v Hallstrom, ex p W (No 2) and R v Gardner, ex p L*.[61]

(c) The Hallstrom decision

Miss W and Mr L had a long history of mental illness[62] and although both had spent long periods within the confines of psychiatric institutions, at the time their cases were heard both lived in the community. On the day of Miss W's admission, her responsible medical officer granted her leave of absence with the condition that she live at a specified hostel and continue to take her medication. Mr L had been on leave for nearly six months, at which point his responsible medical officer recalled him back to hospital for the leave to be renewed. The provision to renew the order

---

59 The MHA 1983, s 20(2).
60 See the Mental Health Act Commission *First Biennial Report 1983-1985* (1985) HMSO, London.
61 [1986] 2 All ER 306.
62 Which fell within the ambits of the MHA 1983.

could only be invoked where it was believed the patient's mental condition required detention for treatment in a hospital.[63] In both cases, the patients were living in the community and coping well when they were recalled. The recall was directed in order for the leave to be granted for a further six-month period. 'Inpatient treatment' since the *Hallstrom* decision has been interpreted narrowly. McCullough J said, 'Parliament did not intend that the provisions for renewal should embrace those liable to be detained but not in fact detained'.[64] Use of the renewal provision for anything other than to administer inpatient treatment is contrary to the purpose of the MHA 1983. McCullough J observed:

> '[E]ven a night's detention is an infringement of personal liberty. Had Parliament intended to grant the power to overbear the refusal to consent of patients such as Miss W, who could be monitored in the community provided they were given appropriate treatment, it would have so provided by a clear provision which involved no unnecessary detention. The differences between the 1959 Act and the 1983 Act in relation to consent to treatment, ... underline the unlikelihood that Parliament intended in the later Act to provide for cases like Miss W's in the indirect way contended for by counsel for the doctors'.[65]

In the *Hallstrom* decision, the actions of the psychiatrists were found to be unlawful and to lead to an interference of the subject's liberty thereby ending the flexibility upon which psychiatrists had come to rely. The remaining treatment options were limited. The *Hallstrom* decision was the catalyst, which led the Royal College of Psychiatrists and the Mental Health Act Commission to issue discussion documents about the future of community care and possible replacements of the 'long leash' technique.[66] The 'long leash' had been so greatly relied upon that *Hallstrom* created a problem for psychiatrists: how to monitor effectively patients who did not require treatment within a restrictive institutional environment. It must be noted that although the *Hallstrom* decision played a key role in the re-assessment of contemporary community care methods from the mid-1980s, the finding of McCullough J that a decision to renew the authority to detain a patient cannot be made at a time when the patient is on leave of absence was overruled by the Court of Appeal in

---

63   [1986] 2 All ER 306 per McCullough J at 310a.
64   [1986] 2 All ER 306 per McCullough J at 317.
65   [1986] 2 All ER 306 per McCullough J at 316e.
66   See Royal College of Psychiatrists *Community Treatment Orders - A Discussion Document* (1987) Royal College of Psychiatrists, London. See also MHAC *Fourth Biennial Report* 1989–1991 and MHAC *Fifth Biennial Report* 1991–1993.

B v Barking, Havering and Brentwood Community Healthcare NHS Trust.[67] A renewal can now be made while the patient is on leave if the patient's treatment, taken as a whole, involves an inpatient element.

The *Hallstrom* decision added to the arguments made in favour of a formalised community care order.[68] The significant impact of the decision gave the campaign's armamentarium an added boost in the struggle to achieve an official community care order. The stance taken by the *Hallstrom* decision launched an increasingly intense discussion about the future of community care. In practice, it led to further unofficial developments in treatment techniques to counterbalance the effect of the decision.

6 Greater Reliance on Pharmacology

The *Hallstrom* decision had devastating consequences for psychiatric practice. Since Enoch Powell's Hospital Plan in 1962 a clear correlation was made between the furtherance of the community care policy and a reduction in the number of hospital beds for the mentally ill. By the mid-1980s continued closures of psychiatric hospital facilities had placed a significant strain on the mental health service. Inpatient amenities were no longer easily available and the community as a care environment was being relied on through necessity. Owing to crisis levels in community psychiatric nursing, the adoption of alternative care measures emerged. Reliance was gradually being placed on long-term neuroleptic drug depots that usually last for a period of a week. Drug depots are drugs that can be stored in the body for a period of time so that they can be administered less frequently. Patients detained in hospital under the MHA 1983, s 3 are then treated with depots and granted leave of absence under the MHA 1983, s 17. Invariably the leave of absence is qualified by the condition that the patient return to the depot clinic every week for further injections. The use of neuroleptic drug depots is effectively a contemporary variation of the typical leave of absence provision.[69] If the patient does not comply, he is followed up and either persuaded to return to the depot clinic or recalled to hospital. If the patient does not co-operate, the patient's leave will be revoked in the interests of his health or safety or for the protection of other persons.[70] This is rarely needed, for the depots usually ensure a

67 [1999] 1 FLR 106.
68 See Royal College of Psychiatrists *Community Treatment Orders - A Discussion Document* (1987) Royal College of Psychiatrists, London. See also MHAC *Fourth Biennial Report* 1989–1991 and MHAC *Fifth Biennial Report* 1991–1993.
69 Glover, N 'Community care – same problems, different epithet? *Journal of Medical Ethics* 1998, Vol 24, p 336.
70 The MHA 1983, s 17(4).

high level of patient compliance, unlike the oral neuroleptics, which, as they are administered more frequently, provide more opportunities for patient non-cooperation. However, the technique raises questions concerning its legality, for it closely resembles the 'long leash' procedure, which was held to be unlawful in *Hallstrom*.[71] As the depot treatment is administered under the guise of extended leave, it means that the MHA 1983, Pt IV can be invoked if the patient does not co-operate. The provision of drug depots would fall under the MHA 1983, s 58, which requires either the consent of the patient or a second medical opinion in favour of the treatment. The patient can be treated in hospital without his consent and then granted leave of absence into the community. The patient may find himself living in the community, yet still subject to the mental health legislation and he will continue to be under the lingering influence of pharmacological treatment. There is little literature upon the use of drug depots, and that which does acknowledge its use[72] does not question the legality of the technique, simply accepting its presence within contemporary psychiatric practice. The drug depot technique reflects yet another attempt to create an unofficial community care order from the existing mental health provisions in order to meet the new challenges of community care.

7 The Provision of After-Care Services

Since the early 1980s, a definite shift in attitude within psychiatric practice has become apparent. Reliance on the hospital setting has gradually diminished and been replaced by the provision of care within a less restrictive environment. In this period hospital admission figures escalated, but the increase reflected the growing phenomenon of the 'revolving door' patient where short-term inpatient stays were used to handle acute phases of illness while chronic conditions were managed in the community. This changing focus in service provision and care management has required an injection of community support. Without the provision of additional community facilities, services and staff assistance, care within the community cannot operate effectively. It was accepted prior to the enactment of the Mental Health (Amendment) Act 1982 that a positive duty to provide after-care services should be included. The MHA 1983, s 117 was incorporated into the Act to satisfy this acknowledged need.

71 However, note *Barking Havering and Brentwood Community Healthcare NHS Trust* [1999] 1 FLR 106 and see the Mental Health Act Commission *First Biennial Report 1983-1985* (1985) HMSO, London.
72 Pastor, T 'Community treatment orders' *Psychiatric Bulletin* 1989, Vol 13, p 201.

The MHA 1983, s 117 imposes a duty upon health authorities and local social services authorities to provide after-care services, such as social support, for certain categories of mentally disordered patient who are no longer detained within a psychiatric hospital. Therefore, those patients that have been detained under the MHA 1983, Pt II, ss 2, 3 or 4 should be provided with appropriate after-care services. Furthermore, because the MHA 1983, s 117 relates to those patients who have ceased to be detained in hospital, it is considered that patients who are not physically detained in hospital but who are 'liable to be detained' or 'liable to be recalled to hospital', such as those who have been granted leave of absence, may also receive after-care services under the MHA 1983, s 117. Provision for after-care services was not considered necessary in the Mental Health Act 1959 and, even after the MHA 1983, s 117 had been included in the Act, the Government at the time viewed such a step as superfluous owing to such services already being provided under the National Health Service Act 1977.[73] The statutory duty placed upon local authorities is contained in the National Health Service Act 1977, Sch 8, para 2(1) and states:

> '[a] ... local social services authority may ... make arrangements for the purpose of the prevention of illness and for the care of persons suffering from illness and for the after-care of persons who have been so suffering'.[74]

However, the argument that the MHA 1983, s 117 merely duplicates the existing duty under the National Health Service Act 1977 is incorrect because under that Act health authorities and local social services authorities are under a *general* duty of care to provide services to fulfil the after-care needs of the mentally disordered. The MHA 1983, s 117 places a duty of care to provide services for the patient concerned, thereby placing an *individual* duty of care on the relevant authorities.[75] The purpose behind after-care provision is to ensure that a mentally disordered patient can return quickly to the community with the intention that he will retain the skills needed for independent living. This duty requires authorities to co-operate with voluntary organisations to set up a system of appropriate after-care. In *Clunis v Camden and Islington Health*

73 National Health Service Act 1977, Sch 8, para 2(1).
74 This after-care duty was approved by the Secretary of State in a Department of Health circular (No LAC (93) 10, Appendix 3, and in paragraph 3(2)(a) of Appendix 3) where it is required that local authorities provide 'centres (including training centres and day centres) and other facilities (including domiciliary facilities), whether in premises managed ... [by the said local authority] ... or otherwise, for training and occupation of persons suffering from or who were suffering from mental disorder'.
75 Jones, R *Mental Health Act Manual* (6th edn, 1999) Sweet & Maxwell, London, p 353.

Authority[76] it was observed that the after-care provision was designed to promote the social welfare of a class of individuals and ensure that the services required were made available.

The provision of after-care extends to those patients who have ceased to be physically detained within the institution but remain 'liable to be detained'. This status can be achieved if the patient is a restricted patient who has been granted a conditional discharge or if the patient has been granted leave of absence under the MHA 1983, s 117.[77] The Mental Health Act Commission[78] and the Code of Practice[79] regard the use of the MHA 1983, s 117 as amounting to a patient being away from institutional care, but remaining subject to hospital powers. However, difficulty arises with the conflicting dicta found in *R v Hallstrom (No 2)*[80] and *R v Ealing District Health Authority, ex p Fox*.[81] *Ex p Fox* involved a patient who had been detained in Broadmoor. The tribunal decided the patient should be conditionally discharged once specified conditions had been fulfilled. During a period of deferment after-care facilities and supervision were to be arranged. However, the local authority did not consider the patient suitable for community living and, consequently, would not provide the necessary supervision. Otton J accepted that the duty under the MHA 1983, s 117 to provide after-care facilities was a constant duty, but would only be triggered upon discharge from hospital.[82] The duty remained suspended until the necessary conditions were fulfilled. However, McCullough J in *Hallstrom* was unconvinced that 'detained' in the MHA 1983, s 117 meant 'liable to be detained'.[83] In practice, after-care assists a patient to integrate within the community. Whether the discharge from hospital is temporary under extended leave or more permanent under a conditional discharge, after-care continues to play a significant role. The MHA 1983, s 117 is the first statutory acknowledgment of the need to provide after-care for those that are no longer confined in psychiatric institutions. This provision has allowed those working within the psychiatric field to embrace a more flexible approach to mental health care because it has established a more structured environment of care and support within the community.

In *Johnson v United Kingdom* the European Court of Human Rights held that the absence of safeguards to ensure that a patient's release from

76 [1998] 3 All ER 180.
77 The MHA 1983, s 73(2).
78 *Second Biennial Report* 1985-87, para 11.4.
79 *Second Biennial Report* 1985-87, para 20.3.
80 [1986] 2 All ER 306.
81 [1993] 1 WLR 373.
82 [1993] 1 WLR 373 per Otton J at 385H.
83 [1986] 2 All ER 306 at p 317.

detention in a psychiatric hospital would not be unreasonably delayed, after it was established that he was no longer mentally ill, could potentially be the cause of a breach of Article 5(1) of the European Convention on Human Rights.[84] In 1989, the patient's responsible medical officer had written a report, which stated that the applicant was free of any symptoms of the mental illness that had led to his confinement and should be conditionally discharged into a suitable hostel environment. However, the hostels in the area were unwilling to take him because of his history of alcohol abuse and attacks on women. Accordingly, the applicant's discharge was deferred. In 1993, the tribunal ordered an absolute discharge, having seen the most recent report, which stated that the applicant had not suffered from mental illness since 1987 and did not need to be detained in hospital. The Court noted that the imposition of the hostel requirement between 1989 and 1992 had led to the indefinite deferral of the applicant's release, because the tribunal in practice ordered his continued detention because the condition had not been implemented. The applicant argued that as he was no longer suffering from the form of mental illness that led to the initial confinement, he should be unconditionally discharged into the community. However, the Court rejected this argument. It was considered that, having regard to the need to balance the interests of the individual against those of the community into which he would be released, the Mental Health Review Tribunal could retain discretion to assess the most appropriate course of action. In *R v Tower Hamlets NHS Trust, ex p Appleby*, McCullough J granted leave to an applicant who had been discharged from hospital, where he had been cared for under the MHA 1983.[85] The discharge had been in breach of guidance issued by the Department of Health on the 'Care Programme Approach', which requires community care services to be in place before such a person is discharged. A situation has arisen where failure to discharge because community care facilities are not in place breaches Article 5(1) of the Convention but if discharge of a patient is granted without appropriate facilities this breaches government guidance. This situation presents a problem when it is accepted that community facilities are always likely to be short of patient need.

In *Ex p Fox*, Otton J concluded that, subject to *R v Oxford Regional Mental Health Review Tribunal, ex p Secretary of State for the Home Department*,[86] which makes it impossible for a tribunal to re-open the issues, the tribunal can defer 'direction ... to allow time for the District Health Authority concerned to give effect to the conditions that the Mental

---

84 (1997) 40 BMLR 1 (case no 119/1996/738/937).
85 (1997) CO/1289/97.
86 [1988] AC 120.

Health Review Tribunal has ... determined'.[87] The duty extends to ensure that, where a disagreement about how such conditions should be fulfilled arises, the health authority must endeavour to enable the patient to comply with the specified conditions. To prevent an impasse the matter can be referred back to the tribunal.[88] *Ex p Fox* illustrates the nature of the obligation because while the MHA 1983, s 117 is applicable an unequivocal duty is placed upon the relevant health authority and local social services authority to provide the appropriate services. If the pertinent authorities are not willing to provide these services themselves, they are required to seek them from elsewhere. The obligation to provide facilities is accepted and is one that is dependent on patient need. The assessment of need is an issue for medical discretion. In *R v Gloucestershire County Council, ex p Mahfood*,[89] and *R v Islington London Borough Council, ex p McMillan*,[90] it was argued that the duty to provide after-care is 'absolute and specific ... [and] ... aimed at the satisfaction of individual need' and, therefore, was not a target duty, as explained by Woolf LJ in *R v Inner London Education Authority*[91] as a 'very broad and general type of duty which is a common feature of legislation which is designed to benefit the community'.[92] The House of Lords decision of *R v Gloucestershire County Council, ex p Barry*[93] found that a local social services authority may take account of resource constraints when it assesses and identifies patient need. Once those needs have been fully recognised, resource limitations can no longer be factored into the decision to provide.

Invariably, the supply of after-care services raises the issue of how such services are to be funded. In January 1994, advice by the Social Services Inspectorate was issued which stated that:

'services provided under section 117 of the Mental Health Act 1983 are not subject to charging under section 17 of the Health and Social Services and Social Security Adjudications Act 1983'.[94]

In 1998, the Government confirmed this by stating that '[c]harges cannot be levied for services, residential or non-residential, which are provided

87 [1993] 1 WLR 373 at 386E-F.
88 MHA 1983, s 71(1)
89 On appeal, *R v Gloucestershire County Council, ex p Barry* [1996] 4 All ER 421. This decision has since been heard in the House of Lords [1997] AC 584, which affirmed the position taken by the Court of Appeal.
90 (1995) 30 BMLR 20.
91 (1990) 2 Admin LR 822.
92 (1990) 2 Admin LR 822 per Woolf LJ at 828B.
93 [1997]AC 584.
94 Advice Note for use by Social Security Inspectorate – Discretionary Charges for Adult Social Services, January 1994.

under section 117 of the Mental Health Act 1983'.[95] In *R v London Borough of Richmond, ex p Watson*,[96] Sullivan J stated that the wording of the MHA 1983, s 117 imposed a 'freestanding duty' on the local social services authority to provide after-care directly under the MHA 1983 as opposed to a 'gateway' duty requiring the local social services authority to secure provision of after-care under other powers and legislation. Sullivan J reasoned that as no other powers and no other statutes were mentioned in the MHA 1983, s 117(2) it meant that the power to provide after-care was restricted to the MHA 1983, s 117 alone thereby making it a freestanding duty. The intention behind section 117 is clear. The Care Programme Approach is to be maintained and encouraged.[97] Patients are to be cared for in the least restrictive environment and, if they are suitable candidates for community care, they should be provided with appropriate after-care under the MHA 1983, s 117 free of charge.

In 1990, a Care Programme Approach for the mentally ill was formally adopted.[98] This approach followed the Department of Health's recognition in 1989 that 'community care ... [meant the provision of] ... the right level of intervention and support to enable people to achieve maximum independence and control over their ... lives'.[99] The provision of adequate and flexible community services was an essential element of this. However, only a year before, the Griffiths Report[100] had clearly documented countless examples of services failing to meet current patient demand. Gostin postulates that:

'access to health and social services should not be based upon charitable or professional discretion but upon enforceable right ... [and that if] ... there is an unreasonable denial of a service, the remedy is or should be provided by ... law'.[101]

---

95 HC Deb vol 317 col 172wa, 28 July 1998 (Mr Paul Boetang MP).
96 *R v London Borough of Richmond, ex p Watson*; *R v Redcar & Cleveland Borough Council, ex p Armstrong*; *R v Manchester City Council, ex p Stennett*; *R v London Borough of Harrow, ex p Cobham* (28 July 1999, unreported), QBD.
97 See Department of Health, Health Circular (90) 23/Local Authority Social Services Letter (90) 11 and Department of Health *Social Services Departments and the Care Programme Approach: An Inspection* (1995) HMSO, London.
98 Department of Health *Social Services Departments and the Care Programme Approach: An Inspection* (1995) HMSO, London.
99 Department of Health, *Caring for People: Community Care in the Next Decade and Beyond*, Cm 89, 1989, HMSO, London.
100 Griffiths, Sir Roy *Community Care: An Agenda for Action: A Report to the Secretary of State for Social Services* (1988) HMSO, London.
101 Gostin, L O 'The ideology of entitlement: the application of contemporary legal approaches to psychiatry' in Bean, P *Mental Illness: Changes and Trends* (1986) Wiley, Chichester, p 27.

This view incorporates a responsibility on the part of the health authority and the local social services authority to provide the required after-care services. This responsibility can be seen to originate from statutory provision. The National Health Service and Community Care Act 1990, Pt III implemented many of the recommendations laid down in the Griffiths Report. The objective of the National Health Service and Community Care Act 1990 was to move the provision of 'community care' services from health authorities to local social services authorities and to implement the 'Care Programme Approach'. Local social services authorities were given the task of ensuring that patient need was assessed, packages of care devised and services co-ordinated between the different responsible agencies. The National Health Service and Community Care Act 1990, s 47(1) provides that where an individual may need community after-care services, the authority must:
(a) carry out an assessment of the individual's needs; and
(b) having regard to the results of the assessment, the authority must then decide whether his needs call for the provision of such services.

'Community care services' are defined as services which a local authority may provide or arrange to be provided under:
(a) the National Assistance Act 1948, Pt III;
(b) the Health Services and Public Health Act 1968, s 45;
(c) the National Health Service Act 1977, s 21 and Sch 8; and
(d) the MHA 1983, s 117.[102]

Under the National Health Service and Community Care Act 1990 provision must be made for those who appear to be in need of community care services. The National Health Service and Community Care Act 1990 requires local authorities to prepare, publish and keep under review a care plan, which must take account of the views of other multi-disciplinary teams and the views of the carers and the patients alike. It requires the local authority to assess the person involved and upon completion of the assessment decide whether community assistance is necessary. Although the National Health Service and Community Care Act 1990 provides a general duty to consider people for assessment and service provision, patients who are subject to the MHA 1983, s 117 are also entitled to assessment under the 1990 Act. The National Health Service and Community Care Act 1990, s 47 plays a similar role to the MHA 1983, s 117. However, if a detained patient becomes subject to the MHA 1983, s 117, the patient is 'expressly entitled' to the assessment and subsequent after-care facilities if required,[103] while under the National Health Service

---

102 National Health Service and Community Care Act 1990, ss 46(3)-47(8).
103 Fennell, P 'Community care, community compulsion and the law' in Ritter, S et al (eds) *Collaborative Community Health Services: Together We Stand* (1996) Edward Arnold, London, p 104.

and Community Care Act 1990, s 47 an absolute right to assessment does not exist.[104] The National Health Service and Community Care Act 1990, s 50 further provides a system to review failures in the discharge of social services duties. If a failure to provide occurs, the Secretary of State may order a declaration that the local authority has defaulted in its duties. The provision of community care services is usually brought about by a combination of services supplied by the local social services authority under the National Health Service and Community Care Act 1990 and health services provided under the National Health Service Act 1977.

The Mental Health Act Commission[105] has found a lower rate of usage of the MHA 1983, s 117 in places with a high density of discharged psychiatric patients, thereby indicating that the availability of resources has influenced after-care provision. In *R v Islington London Borough Council, ex p McMillan* McCowan LJ held that a local authority has a right to take account of resources and other practical considerations both when assessing needs and when deciding whether it is necessary to meet those needs.[106] The courts have held that consideration of resources can be given expressly or impliedly within the statutory provision itself.[107] Applying this in the mental health context the patient is provided with an express entitlement to assessment and after-care but it allows for an implied consideration of resources when making a decision as to the after-care to be provided.

The provision of adequate after-care services is essential in the implementation of the community care policy and, as the emphasis has shifted towards community care, the role of after-care services and the strength of the patient's claim to such facilities has become increasingly an issue of contention. 'The objective of the ideology of entitlement is to establish the right to a service which can be enforced at the behest of a client group or individual.'[108] Despite attempts to promote the Care

104 However, even where an assessed need has been accepted a local authority remains entitled to take certain issues into consideration (eg resources) when deciding the appropriate level of care to be provided: *R v Hertfordshire County Council, ex p Three Rivers District Council* (1992) 90 LGR 526 and see also, *R v Gloucestershire County Council, ex p Mahfood* and *R v Islington London Borough Council ex p McMillan* (1995) 30 BMLR 20. For Court of Appeal judgment see [1996] 4 All ER 421 and for the House of Lords judgment see [1997] AC 584.
105 See Mental Health Act Commission *Crisis in Inner City Mental Health Services* (1993) HMSO, London.
106 *R v Islington London Borough Council, ex p McMillan* (1995) Times, 21 June and LEXIS transcript. This was in relation to the National Health Service and Community Care Act 1990, s 47.
107 *R v Cambridge Health Authority, ex p B* [1995] 2 All ER 129.
108 Gostin, L.O 'The ideology of entitlement: the application of contemporary legal approaches to psychiatry' in Bean, P *Mental Illness: Changes and Trends* (1986) Wiley, Chichester, p 30.

Programme Approach and to ensure the provision of appropriate aftercare services, some overt failures in care provision have been visible.[109] There are increasing levels of complaint regarding the inadequacy of community care provision and judicial review proceedings are instigated to review decisions concerning after-care assessment.[110] In response to the difficulties arising from the provision of community services, the Department of Health issued *After Care Form for the Discharge of Psychiatric Patients* in 1995.[111] The failures in community care reflect the real conflict between policy-oriented medicalism and the legalist rights-based approach. Policy is a flexible and dynamic concept, as it can develop swiftly in accordance with changing patterns of care practice. The law is much more static in its response. The issue of resources and after-care provision demonstrate the conflict between the need to respond effectively to patient need while also ensuring such facilities can be funded. The MHA 1983, s 117 places a legal duty on local social services authorities to provide after-care, but owing to considerable changes in psychiatric practice since 1983 when the MHA 1983, was enacted, a gap has emerged between what *should* be provided to patients in the community and what *can* be provided to patients.

8 Conclusion

Strong images of incarcerated lunatics continue to pervade the social historic view of mental health care, yet this is a false representation of past psychiatric provision. The notion of community care has a long history. Indeed, it was the primary basis upon which care was supplied prior to the erection of the large, domineering Victorian asylums that have come to be associated with psychiatric provision. The vulnerable were cared for in familiar 'home' environments while the carers claimed parochial relief to finance the care. Yet, despite this long history, community care did not receive statutory recognition, albeit limited to mental defectives, until the Mental Deficiency Act 1913. For the mentally ill, the benefits of community care as a care method did not fully emerge for some time due to fears that third parties might be at risk from their behaviour.

109 For example, in December 1992, Christopher Clunis, a recently released psychiatric patient, killed Jonathon Zito in a London tube station.
110 Gordon, R *Community Care Assessments: A Practical Legal Framework* (1993) Longman, London.
111 Department of Health *'After Care Form for the Discharge of Psychiatric Patients'* (1995) HMSO, London. However, since the publication of this circular care failures have continued to arise. In August 1995, Anthony Smith killed his mother and brother a month after having discharged himself from hospital.

However, by 1930, when the Mental Treatment Act 1930 was enacted, voluntary admission to hospital was embraced and by the time of the Mental Health Act 1959 had been fully approved. The acceptance of voluntary admission played a vital role in the changing social perception of mental illness. It was accepted that many of those with mental health problems were able to recognise their difficulties and seek help for themselves without having to wait for their condition to deteriorate to such an extent that the civil commitment provisions needed to be invoked. The Mental Health Act 1959 further confirmed the use of guardianship as a means of endorsing the community as a care environment. However, the guardian's extensive powers prevented the acknowledged benefits of a less restrictive environment from materialising, owing to the measure's highly paternalistic nature.

Despite these hesitant steps the modern impetus to re-orientate psychiatric care provision towards community care did not emanate directly from these early legislative provisions. Instead, it can be drawn from three factors, which set in motion the move towards acquiring a formally recognised community care order. Enoch Powell's Hospital Plan in 1962 launched the initial stages of reducing inpatient hospital beds for the mentally ill and mentally impaired. From this time, the closure of psychiatric hospital facilities gathered pace. At the same time, the work of Goffman, Szasz and Foucault managed to sway both professional and public opinion against reliance on the institution for the provision of psychiatric care and treatment.[112] The negative impact of hospital care on the patient and the threat of institutionalisation encouraged the support of a less restrictive environment. These combined factors led to the patronage of other professions involved in the care of the mentally ill. Community-based professions such as social work and community psychiatric nursing had been given little support prior to the 1960s, yet after the closure of many hospitals and the attitudinal shift away from institutional care these professions were relied on to support patients in the community. The creation of a modern community care framework had begun.

However, in spite of many being in favour of a less restrictive care environment, the re-orientation of psychiatric services towards community care was partially a measure to address need rather than an autonomous decision to extend the liberty of the patient. Psychiatric inpatient facilities were run down and beds decommissioned, yet the mentally ill continued to need care. Practitioners had to consider alternative measures. Guardianship under the MHA 1983 proved to be inadequate, for the guardian was provided with no sanctions if the patient

---

112 Jones, K *Asylums and After* (1993) Athlone Press, London, p 165.

was unco-operative and, furthermore, narrow application criteria prevented its use being more widespread. Leave of absence offered greater flexibility for practitioners and soon its use was extended to meet the current challenges of the psychiatric care system.

Despite clear indications that practitioners embraced the modern notion of community care (whether through choice or through necessity) the provision of such care under any measure requires adequate community services and support in order to make it effective. The MHA 1983, s 117 placed local social services authorities and health authorities under a duty to provide appropriate after-care services to those who had been detained under the MHA 1983. Recognition of this need to provide was a fundamental step forward, yet problems with community provision have continued to surface. Attempts to provide community care throughout the 1980s and early 1990s have suffered from inadequate financial support and inter-agency disputes over provision responsibility. Local social services authorities and health authorities are required under the National Health Service and Community Care Act 1990 to work together to achieve an effective partnership, yet, owing to different institutional cultures, miscommunication and opposing objectives, community care has been blighted. By the early 1990s, it became clear that community care attempts had proved a dismal failure. On 31 December 1992 Ben Silcock, a young man with schizophrenia, brought the inadequacies and confusions of community care clearly into focus. A gentle person who wished to 'talk to the animals' was savagely mauled as he climbed into the lion enclosure at London Zoo. The timing of the incident resulted in widespread reportage. The Government was forced to act. No longer was community care to be a makeshift and improvised method of mental health care provision. Ben Silcock's activities had managed to instigate change in official Government policy: something that many practitioners, campaigners and academics had so far failed to do.

Chapter 4
Decision-making on behalf of the mentally incapacitated

1 Introduction

The move towards community care has highlighted a number of problems, one of which is the issue of how important decisions relating to treatment and other care options are to be made when an individual is incapable of making his own decisions. As support for the provision of psychiatric care in a less restrictive environment gained momentum throughout the 1970s and 1980s, increasing numbers of mentally disordered and mentally incapacitated individuals were cared for in the community. At the same time, the MHA 1983 encouraged the use of voluntary hospitalisation and treatment with the result that the consent to treatment provisions in the MHA 1983, Pt IV could not be invoked. The situation that emerged from these changes in psychiatric practice was one that proved problematic for those involved in caring for such individuals. The mental health legislation could not be applied to these people because they either lived in the community or because they were voluntary patients. The question that emerged was how could necessary care and treatment be given to those who could not cooperate with prescribed treatment regimes and who could not make their own decisions?

This chapter will consider the impact of re-orienting psychiatric support to the community on decision-making on behalf of others. In addition, the means by which treatment and other serious decisions are given and made, and who, other than the individual concerned, has the right to make them, will be explored. Individual autonomy and the right to be self-determining are universally-promoted concepts enabling adults to decide what happens to their bodies. Owing to this right, individuals can consent to or refuse medical treatment regardless of any possible consequences. However, this freedom to choose can be revoked in a number of situations:

(a) where an individual is detained under the MHA 1983[1];
(b) where an individual is admitted to hospital informally, but is able neither to consent nor dissent;[2] or
(c) where an individual lacks mental capacity at common law.

The position of a patient detained under the MHA 1983 has been fully examined in Ch 2; this chapter, therefore, will focus on those who fall outside the legislation's ambit.

As was illustrated in Ch 2, the MHA 1983 endorses a welfarist approach in that it emphasises prompt therapeutic intervention and the need to evidence 'treatability' when initiating the detention process. Andrew Ashworth and Larry Gostin have suggested that the proposed treatment must 'effect some change in the ... [patient's] ... mental condition – in the sense either that the condition can be cured or remedied or that it can be prevented from getting worse'.[3] However, if a patient is classified as mentally ill or severely mentally impaired the 'treatability test' does not apply. The MHA 1983 requires some justification for the removal of individual liberty, and demonstrating that detention in hospital is necessary to treat or prevent harm coming to an individual or third parties provides this. Yet, for those who are hospitalised on an informal basis and are not subject to the statutory provisions, their rights are less likely to be upheld. As Lord Steyn observed in *R v Bournewood Community NHS Trust, ex p L*, the position of such patients is legally inadequate because, despite the fact that their mental conditions are frequently viewed in a similar manner to that of detained patients, they benefit from none of the safeguards which have been built into the MHA 1983.[4] Where individuals lack the necessary mental capacity to make their own treatment choices, treatment may only be administered to them without their consent when it is in their best interests.[5] The *Bournewood* case concerned those lacking mental capacity to consent to their admission to hospital, and it did not overtly introduce any new mechanisms for the treatment of such patients. However, it would seem that this decision has eliminated a large

---

1   See Ch 2.
2   *R v Bournewood Community NHS Trust, ex p L* [1999] 1 AC 458.
3   Ashworth, A & Gostin, L 'Mentally disordered offenders and the sentencing process', in Gostin, L (ed) *Secure Provision: A Review of Special Services for the Mentally Ill and Mentally Handicapped in England and Wales* (1985) Tavistock, London, p 215.
4   *R v Bournewood Community NHS Trust, ex p L* [1999] 1 AC 458. See also, Eastman, N & Peay, J 'Law Without Enforcement. Theory and Practice' in Eastman, N & Peay, J (eds) *Law Without Enforcement. Integrating Mental Health and Justice* (1999) Hart Publishing, Oxford, pp 11–12.
5   *F v West Berkshire Health Authority* [1990] 2 AC 1.

degree of scrutiny in relation to such vulnerable people and possibilities for non-consensual treatment (under the guise of *Re F* and the 'best interests' test) have opened up.

The role of the common law in ascertaining capacity will be explored in relation to the provision of treatment for both mental and physical conditions. Consideration will then be given to the position of the informal hospitalised patient. Finally, we look at the Law Commission proposals on mental incapacity,[6] the more recent Government reform proposals and the suggestion of a generic Mental Incapacity Bill.[7]

2 Establishing Incapacity

Mental competence plays a crucial role in decision-making. Where such competence is deemed to be lacking, then substituted decision-makers are often justified. Yet establishing the meaning of competence is more complicated than merely suggesting that an individual lacks the wherewithal to understand. Complete mental incompetence is rarely obvious to all. Only the individual in a persistent vegetative state, for example, can be said to be completely lacking in mental capacity for he will rarely ever improve and will rarely (if at all) have moments of lucidity.[8] For the vast majority of individuals with varying health and psychiatric problems, capacity to make a decision will be affected by their current state of health, the environment in which they find themselves, the degree of information given to them and the assistance offered to help explain the issues. Competence is therefore, 'decision-relative'.[9] In relation to mentally disordered individuals and those who are mentally impaired, this is often recognised in daily activities. For example, a mentally impaired person will be allowed to make certain decisions such as what clothes to wear and what to eat for lunch. However, serious choices such as whether to accept or reject medical treatment, are more commonly taken out of the hands of the person concerned.

The general presumption of competence in adults is supported by the values of promoting individual well-being and self-determination. Butler-Sloss LJ noted in *Re MB (an adult: medical treatment)* that '[e]very person is presumed to have the capacity to consent to or refuse medical treatment

---

6 Law Commission Report No 231 *Mental Incapacity* (1995), HMSO, London.
7 See Lord Chancellor's Department *Making Decisions: The Government's Proposals for Making Decisions on Behalf of Mentally Incapacitated Adults* Cm 4465 (1999) TSO, London.
8 *Airedale National Health Service Trust v Bland* [1993] AC 789.
9 Buchanan, A & Brock, D *Deciding For Others: The Ethics of Surrogate Decision-Making* (1998) Cambridge University Press, Cambridge, p 18.

unless and until that presumption is rebutted'.[10] These values have a long tradition within medical ethics and are reflected in the law of consent.[11] However, frequently the ability to be self-determinative or to promote personal well-being is questioned when the individual involved has certain health or psychiatric problems. Certain capacities are deemed necessary in order for a person to make competent decisions about health care. The first is the ability to understand and communicate with others; the second is the capacity for reasoning and the ability to deliberate; and finally, the ability to evaluate particular outcomes of a decision as benefits or potential harms.

At a general level, the ability to understand and communicate means that an individual can comprehend the nature of and reasons for a proposed treatment. This ability can only be evidenced if certain information is given to the patient. Such information will include the patient's diagnosis, a prognosis, which will depend on the alternative treatment methods available, the risks and benefits of each treatment option and the doctor's recommendation regarding treatment. 'Understanding requires the capacities to receive, process, and make available for use the information relevant to particular decisions'.[12] Efforts must also be made by professionals to provide this information in a patient-friendly way. Medical jargon should be avoided where possible, willingness to spend time with the patient in discussing treatment options must exist and, where patients have difficulty communicating their views, every effort should be made to facilitate communication.

Competence also requires the ability of the patient to rationalise and deliberate. Making certain decisions requires time. Inherent within treatment decisions is the need to consider possible outcomes and alternatives. Therefore, decisions of this nature are not made instantly and as such, patients need to be able to take in and retain the information they are given by the doctor. The patient must have the ability to draw inferences about the consequences of making a particular decision. As part of the need to deliberate and reason is the need for the decision-maker to have a sense of what is good and what is harmful. In other words, without being able to classify an outcome as good or bad, the patient will not be

10   [1997] 2 FLR 426 at 436. Gunn criticises the emphasis placed on the protection of competent individual's rights to be self-determining while neglecting the difficulty of how to make decisions on behalf of those who lack capacity. Gunn, M 'Treatment and mental handicap' *Anglo-American Law Review* 1987, Vol 16, p 242.
11   For detailed discussion on the law of consent in England and Wales, see McHale, J, Fox, M & Murphy, J *Health Care Law: Text, Cases and Materials* (1997) Sweet & Maxwell, London, ch 6.
12   Buchanan, A & Brock, D *Deciding For Others: The Ethics of Surrogate Decision-Making* (1998) Cambridge University Press, Cambridge, p 24.

able to rationalise the information he is given and come to a conclusion. Therefore, the patient must be able to weigh up information, decide what would be best for him and then arrive at a decision.

The capacities, which are necessary for a person to arrive at a competent decision about healthcare, mean that mental competence acts as a threshold. If the patient possesses the necessary capacities to make a decision, intervention by a third party cannot be justified regardless of how irrational or bizarre the decision seems to others. However, if such abilities are not evident, the substituted decision-maker will make the decision irrespective of the patient's views and wishes. Under the MHA 1983, the provision of treatment without patient consent applies only to treatment for mental disorder and does not extend to the treatment of physical conditions. If a detained patient needs treatment for a physical condition, then he has the right to refuse such treatment providing it is established that the patient has capacity at common law to make such treatment choices. Despite the psychiatric patient's status, a presumption of capacity is maintained and has to be rebutted by those questioning the patient's capacity. Likewise, for those who are not subject to the mental health legislation, capacity acts as the threshold to intervention by others. It is not until mental incapacity is established that proxy decision-making is ethically acceptable. A comprehensive definition of legal capacity was proposed by the High Court in *Re C (adult: refusal of treatment)*.[13] Mr C was a 67-year-old schizophrenic patient and was detained in hospital under the MHA 1983. He developed a gangrenous foot and his doctors wanted to amputate it, but he refused to give his consent despite the possibly life-threatening consequences of his decision. To determine whether a person is incapable at common law of making a decision, the test of capacity, which was laid down by Thorpe J in *Re C*, must be satisfied. A person must be able to:
(a) take in and retain treatment information;
(b) believe the information; and,
(c) be able to balance the information up to arrive at a choice.

This test reflects each of the capacities, which were discussed above. An individual must be able to understand information and communicate with others; he must be able to reason and deliberate; and finally, he must be able to evaluate the possible outcomes of a decision and arrive at a choice. If the individual meets the requirements laid down in *Re C*, mental capacity

---

13   [1994] 1 All ER 819. For a detailed discussion on how to evaluate competence, see Buchanan, A & Brock, D *Deciding For Others: The Ethics of Surrogate Decision Making* (1990) Cambridge University Press, Cambridge, pp 317–21. For a recent consideration of the law of capacity, see *B v A NHS Hospital Trust* [2002] EWHC 429 (Fam).

will be established and the individual's decision cannot then be substituted by another.

The determination of incompetence in patients who have refused all treatment or a type of treatment for a physical condition could be criticised on the basis that doctors rarely challenge competence if the patient accepts the proposed treatment and agrees with the doctor. However, Appelbaum and Roth have shown that where a patient refuses treatment and competency is questioned, most treatment refusals are withdrawn once greater efforts are made to inform the patient of the reasons behind the treatment recommendation.[14] In the case of psychiatric patients who refuse treatment for mental conditions, the case is slightly different for two reasons. The first is that a psychiatric condition is often, although not always, viewed as impairing the person's ability to make a competent decision about his need to receive treatment. The onus of proving competence seems to shift to the patient to prove he has the mental capacity to decide. The second reason is that in England and Wales the MHA 1983, Pt IV removes the problem of patient consent except in the case of very extreme treatments, most notably, psycho-surgery which requires both patient consent and a second medical opinion in favour of the treatment.[15]

3 Providing Non-Consensual Treatment for Physical Conditions

Despite attempts to limit the administration of treatment for physical conditions without consent, there has been a gradual expansion of such incidents over recent years. These cases fall into two groups: first, where the definition of certain treatments is 'stretched' so that it is interpreted as treatment for mental disorder under the MHA 1983; and secondly where treatment (some of which with seemingly dubious therapeutic credentials) for individuals who lack capacity at common law is justified as being in the patient's best interest. The MHA 1983, s 63 provides that the consent of the patient is not required for treatment for mental disorder that does not fall within the MHA 1983, s 57(which applies to the most serious forms of treatment such as psychosurgery) and the MHA 1983, s 58 (which governs less serious (and reversible) treatments such as electro-convulsive

14 Appelbaum, P S & Roth, L H 'Treatment Refusal in Medical Hospital' in President's Commission for the Study of Ethical Problems in Medicine and Biomedical and Behavioural Research *Making Health Care Decisions: The Ethical and Legal Implications of Informed Consent in the Patient-Practitioner Relationship* (1982) US Government Printing Office, Washington DC, Vol 2, Appendices.
15 The MHA 1983, s 57.

therapy and drug therapy). The MHA 1983 only applies to 'treatment for mental disorder', which has been given a broad interpretation.[16] It can cover any form of 'nursing care, habilitation or rehabilitation' as long as it can be connected with the mental disorder. Therefore, taken with the breadth of the MHA 1983, s 63, a vast spectrum of treatment measures could be justified if the objective is to provide 'treatment for mental disorder'. Where the condition is physical but is closely connected to the psychiatric condition, it is often difficult to determine whether the treatment can lawfully be given without the patient's consent because the distinction between 'physical' and 'mental' has blurred. In *R v Mental Health Act Commission, ex p X*,[17] Stuart-Smith LJ observed that where the mentally disordered man was sexually deviant, the treatment for the sexual deviancy was inextricably linked with the treatment of the mental disorder. When establishing the scope of the MHA 1983, s 63, the question as to what amounts to treatment for physical and psychiatric conditions remains open to interpretation. The plight of anorexia-sufferers and force-feeding is a prominent example in this discussion. In *Re KB (adult) (mental patient: medical treatment)*, it was held that force-feeding a detained patient with anorexia nervosa could be regarded as 'treatment for mental disorder' and therefore covered by the MHA 1983, s 63.[18] Anorexia nervosa is a mental illness and force-feeding through a naso-gastric tube is regarded as treatment for the underlying mental disorder as well as for the physical manifestations of the condition.[19] In *B v Croydon Health Authority*, the patient suffered from a personality disorder, which was coupled with post-traumatic stress disorder leading to self-harm.[20] This manifested itself in the patient starving herself. The decision to stop eating stemmed from the personality disorder rather than the mental illness; nevertheless the MHA 1983, s 63 was applied despite the ongoing debate about how treatable personality disorders actually are. Hoffman LJ recognised that the MHA 1983, s 145(1) provides a wide definition of medical treatment:

'it would seem ... strange if a hospital could, without the patient's consent, give him treatment directed to alleviating a psychiatric disorder showing itself in suicidal tendencies, but not without such consent be able to treat the consequences of a suicide attempt ...

16 The MHA 1983, s 145. See also *R v Canons Park Mental Health Review Tribunal, ex p A* [1995] QB 60 and Glover, N 'Treatability: its scope and application' *Journal of Forensic Psychiatry* 1996, Vol 7, No 2, p 353.
17 (1988) 9 BMLR 77.
18 (1994) 19 BMLR 144.
19 For a detailed examination of the treatment for anorexia nervosa, see, Dresser, E 'Feeding the hunger artists: Legal issues in treating anorexia nervosa' *Wisconsin Law Review* 1984, p 297.
20 [1995] Fam 133.

the term "medical treatment" ... for the mental disorder in section 63 includes such ancillary acts'.

The controversy surrounding Ian Brady's decision to starve himself to death emphasises the continued difficulty in separating out mental illness, personality disorder and mental incapacity.[21] Brady's treatment was authorised under the MHA 1983, s 63, as his refusal to eat was a 'symptom, manifestation [and] consequence of his mental disorder'. However, it was also found that Brady could have been treated under common law principles of necessity as he lacked the capacity to make 'treatment choices'.[22]

Force-feeding is a highly invasive procedure, which does little to improve the trust between the vulnerable patient and his doctor.[23] 'Force-feeding crushes the patient's will, destroying who the patient is'.[24] Despite the anti-therapeutic nature of such procedures, extension to the scope of the MHA 1983, s 63 has not stopped here. In 1996, 'treatment for mental disorder' was extended to authorise a caesarean section operation on a detained woman in order to deliver her baby safely.[25] The patient was a paranoid schizophrenic and although she consented initially to the operation, her psychiatrist was worried she might change her mind later on. The court considered it in the patient's interests to have the baby delivered as soon as possible. Wall J accepted that the patient failed the test in *Re C* and was deemed to lack the capacity to consent to or to refuse medical treatment in relation to her pregnancy. 'It is only by stretching [the] logic and the language of section 63 almost to breaking point that caesareans can be viewed as treatment for mental disorder'.[26] The decision to include treatment for a successful pregnancy and childbirth, as part of an overall treatment plan, for the patient's mental disorder was accepted. However, this dictum must now be read in light of Judge LJ's observations in *St George's Healthcare NHS Trust v S* that 'a woman detained under the Act for mental disorder cannot be forced into medical procedures unconnected with her mental condition unless her capacity to consent to

21 *R v Dr James Donald Collins and Ashworth Hospital Authority, ex p Ian Stewart Brady* CO/68/2000, (10 March 2000, unreported).
22 Dyer, C 'Force-Feeding of Ian Brady Declared Lawful' [2000] *British Medical Journal* 731.
23 MacLeod, S *The Art of Starvation* (1989) Little, Brown and Company (UK), Virago Press, London.
24 Lewis, P 'Feeding Anorexic Patients Who Refuse Food' [1999] *Medical Law Review* 21 at p 37.
25 *Tameside and Glossop Acute Services Trust v CH* [1996] 1 FLR 762.
26 Fagan, E & Fennell, P 'Feminist Perspectives on Mental Health Law' in Sheldon, S & Thomson, M (eds) *Feminist Perspectives On Health Care Law* (1998) Cavendish Publishing Limited, London, p 93.

such treatment is diminished'.[27] The attempt to confine such actions to those who were already detained under the mental health legislation failed and before long the common law principles of necessity and best interests were used to justify non-consensual medical intervention. In *Rochdale Healthcare (NHS) Trust v C*[28] a caesarean section was authorised at common law as it was considered necessary in the interests of the patient's health to operate immediately to save the foetus' life. The patient was thought unable to rationally weigh up the treatment information and come to a final decision as she was in the 'throes of labour'. These cases indicate that the right of an adult of sound mind to make 'treatment choices' irrespective of possibly grave consequences has been eroded significantly. In *Re MB*[29] the patient needed a caesarean section operation but she had a needle phobia that prevented her from consenting to the anaesthetic. Butler-Sloss LJ noted that 'if … a compulsive disorder or phobia from which the patient suffers stifles belief in the information presented to her, then the decision may not be a true one'. Treatment choices (which include refusal of treatment) that are made on the basis of apparently bizarre reasons or which may lead to death, are increasingly being set aside. With the absence of any clear principles governing how patients lacking mental capacity should lawfully be treated for physical illness, the House of Lords have effectively allowed doctors the freedom to provide proxy consent.[30] Moving away from the use of formal powers, which are enshrined in the mental health legislation, has ultimately allowed doctors to invoke the vague concept of best interests to detain a patient without the patient enjoying any of the safeguards that are built into the MHA 1983.[31]

Caesarean section operations without patient consent have been justified on the basis of mental incapacity and best interests.[32] Despite the foetus having no legal status in the UK, its presence has inevitably been felt in each of these cases. The courts have taken the view that it is in the best interests of any woman to give birth to a healthy child. Such arguments may have some force, as the existence of a foetus will inevitably sway the views of the court despite its lack of legal status in England and Wales. However, similar arguments have been used in relation to the sterilisation of mentally incompetent women, a procedure that has less obvious

27 [1999] Fam 26.
28 [1997] 1 FCR 274.
29 (1997) 38 BMLR 175.
30 *Re F* [1990] 2 AC 1.
31 *R v Bournewood Mental Health and Community NHS Trust, ex p L* [1999] 1 AC 458.
32 Brazier, M & Glover, N 'Does Medical Law Have a Future?' in Hayton, D (ed) *Law's Future(s)* (2000) Hart Publishing, Oxford. See also, Glover-Thomas, N 'The Impact of Law Reform on Treating the Psychiatric Patient' *Contemporary Issues in Law* 2001, p 89.

therapeutic benefits for the woman concerned. In *Re F (Mental Patient: Sterilisation)*[33] F was a 36-year-old woman with serious learning difficulties who had formed a sexual relationship with a male patient. Professionals involved in her care believed sterilisation was the best option as pregnancy was inadvisable. However, she was unable to consent to the operation. The House of Lords found that at common law where the need for an operation on a mentally impaired or mentally disordered person is urgent, it can be carried out without their consent if the operation is in their best interests. The common law provides a solution when treatment is deemed necessary but the individual concerned appears to be incapable of providing consent. A doctor can lawfully operate on, or give other treatment to, adult patients who are incapable of consenting to his doing so, as long as the operation, or other treatment concerned, can be shown to be in the best interests of the patient if it is carried out in order either to save the patient's life or to ensure improvement or prevent deterioration in his physical or mental health.[34] Therefore, the 'best interests' test would be satisfied if the operation would save that person's life or improve or prevent deterioration of the patient's mental or physical condition. A doctor, if he operates on the patient, will be immune from liability in trespass to the person, if he can establish that the operation is carried out with regard to the best interests of the patient, and the action taken conforms to 'the practice that a responsible body of medical opinion would take'.[35] It was further recognised in *Re F* that good medical practice would be adhered to if court declarations were obtained before such procedures were undertaken. The procedures to be followed when applying for a court declaration that a proposed sterilisation operation is lawful were developed by the Official Solicitor.[36] The procedure to adopt is as follows:

(a) any application for a declaration that a proposed operation for sterilisation of a patient can lawfully be carried out despite the inability of such a patient to consent thereto should be by way of originating summons issuing out of the Family Division of the High Court;

(b) the applicant should normally be the person responsible for the care of the patient or intending to carry out the proposed operation or other treatment, if it is declared to be lawful;

(c) the patient must always be a party and should normally be a respondent. In cases in which the patient is a respondent, the patient's guardian ad litem should normally be the Official Solicitor. In any

33 *Re F* [1990] 2 AC 1.
34 *Re F* [1990] 2 AC 1.
35 *Bolam v Friern Barnet Hospital Management Committee* [1957] 1 WLR 582.
36 *Practice Note (Official Solicitor: sterilisation)* [1996] 2 FLR 111. See also Department of Health *The Handbook of Contraceptive Practice* (1990) HMSO, London.

cases in which the Official Solicitor is not either the 'next friend' or the guardian ad litem of the patient or an applicant he shall be respondent; and
(d) with a view to protecting the patient's privacy, but subject always to the judge's direction, the hearing will be in chambers, but the decision and the reasons for that decision will be given in court.

There have been several cases concerning the reproductive capabilities of mentally incompetent people since 1987, which indicates a growing trend towards the justification of proxy decision-making on the basis of best interests. In *Re B (a minor) (wardship: sterilisation)*, the House of Lords unanimously endorsed the sterilisation of B, a mentally impaired girl of 17 with a mental age of 6.[37] She was thought to be incapable of understanding the relationship between sexual intercourse and pregnancy but as she exhibited a normal sexual drive and inclinations for someone of her chronological age, sterilisation seemed the best option.[38] It was found that to allow B to become pregnant was inappropriate as she 'displayed no maternal feelings and indeed had an antipathy to small children'.[39] Despite the clear human rights implications raised by sterilising individuals without consent, by 1991 court declarations were no longer considered necessary when the procedure was for 'therapeutic purposes'.[40] Of further interest is the case of *A (Mental Patient: Sterilisation)*,[41] which was heard by the Court of Appeal in 1999. An application was made to carry out a vasectomy on a 28-year-old Down's syndrome man. However, the judge found that, although the patient was sexually active, he did not understand the link between intercourse and pregnancy and the effect of the operation on the patient would, therefore, be minimal. An appeal was refused because male sterilisation on non-therapeutic grounds could only be carried out if in the best interests of the patient, taking into account not just medical but emotional issues as well. The court noted that a fresh application could be made if the patient moved to a local authority home and his freedom was restricted because of fears that he would have a sexual relationship with another resident. However, in such circumstances, it was considered that it was more likely that the female concerned would be subject to *extra supervision*, as opposed to the male patient. It would appear that this extra supervision might well amount to sterilisation of the woman. The legal and ethical inconsistencies of this approach can clearly be seen! The decision-makers continue to be the medical professionals and the

37 [1987] 2 All ER 206. See also Freeman, M 'Sterilising the Mentally Handicapped' in *Medicine, Ethics and the Law* (1988) Current Legal Problems.
38 [1987] 2 All ER 206.
39 [1987] 2 All ER 206 at 216h per Lord Oliver of Aylmerton.
40 *Re E (a minor) (medical treatment)* [1991] 2 FLR 585; *Re GF* [1992] 1 FLR 293.
41 [2000] 1 FLR 549.

individual's carers and the potential for conflicting interests plainly exists. Exactly whose best interests are served by such procedures – the mentally incapacitated individual or those caring for them – is open to question.

4 *Bournewood* and the Informal Patient[42]

The case of *R v Bournewood Community NHS Trust, ex p L* could have had far-reaching consequences for psychiatric practice had the House of Lords affirmed the position adopted by the Court of Appeal. The House of Lords rejected the Court of Appeal's decision that patients like L, who were unable to consent to admission to hospital but who did not show any positive dissent, could not be admitted and effectively detained, unless the admission provisions within the MHA 1983 were used. The Court of Appeal's decision would have overturned accepted practice within the psychiatric field, creating huge practical difficulties across the country because every patient with similar problems to L would have had to be formally detained in hospital under the mental health legislation. However, the House of Lords considered the Court of Appeal's reasoning to be flawed and informal admission for such individuals was reinstated.

The patient, L, was a 48-year-old autistic man with profound mental impairment. His ability to comprehend things around him was restricted, and he was thereby considered incapable of consenting to hospitalisation or medical treatment. In July 1997, while attending a day centre, L became agitated and hurt himself; his carers could not be contacted. L was taken to hospital and it was decided that he should be admitted and treated. However, as L seemed compliant and did not resist admission, no steps were taken to detain him formally under the MHA 1983. The Court of Appeal found that the statutory framework of the MHA 1983 ousted any common law jurisdiction but the hospital trust appealed to the House of Lords. The House of Lords considered the Court of Appeal's reasoning to be flawed and it was confirmed that informal admission for those who are unable to consent, but who do not object, is acceptable practice. The House of Lords considered that the incident, which led to the patient's hospitalisation, was an emergency and, therefore, intervention was necessary for L's best interests to be served. The House of Lords confirmed the common law doctrine of necessity and it concluded that the common law principle justified any interference with L's human rights.[43]

---

42   *R v Bournewood Mental Health and Community NHS Trust, ex p L* [1999] 1 AC 458.
43   See Glover, N 'L v Bournewood Community and Mental Health NHS Trust' *Journal of Social Welfare and Family Law* 1999, Vol 21, No 2, p 151.

The House of Lords has confirmed that when hospitals are faced with informal patients who can neither consent not dissent to treatment because they 'lack the wherewithal to express their objection by leaving',[44] it will not be necessary to apply the MHA 1983. However, Lord Steyn recognised many benefits, which could be associated with the Court of Appeal's approach. Informal patients would only be admitted for assessment and detained for up to 28 days under the MHA 1983, s 2, or admitted for treatment and detained for up to six months under the MHA 1983, s 3 on the written recommendation of at least two doctors; patients would gain the protection of the consent to treatment provisions within the MHA 1983; patients would have the right to apply to or be automatically referred to Mental Health Review Tribunals; after-care services provided by health authorities and local authorities would be made available; and the Mental Health Act Commission would supervise the provision of care. Therefore, the formal detention of patients like L would invoke an extensive scheme of statutory safeguards. Despite this, the majority of the House of Lords found favour in established clinical practice. The lack of statutory safeguards for the informal incapacitated patient raised many concerns and demands for reform were inevitable.[45]

It can be argued that the House of Lords' decision was swayed by pragmatism. Lord Goff acknowledged that had the Court of Appeal's decision been upheld large numbers of incapacitated patients would now have to be detained. In production of a written submission to the Appellate Committee, the Mental Health Act Commission found evidence to suggest that an additional 22,000 detained patients resident on any one day would be the consequence of the Court of Appeal's judgment. Despite the House of Lords re-affirming psychiatric practices, recent figures suggest that the *Bournewood* decision has, nevertheless, led to an increase in the MHA 1983, ss 2 and 3 applications to convert informal patients into formally detained patients. In 1993-94, 3,000 informal patients were subsequently admitted under the MHA 1983, s 3; in 1998-99, this figure rose to 5,000.[46] The majority of patients to whom this judgment would apply would be

44 Eastman, N & Peay, J 'Law Without Enforcement. Theory and Practice' in Eastman, N & Peay, J (eds) *Law Without Enforcement. Integrating Mental Health and Justice* (1999) Hart Publishing, Oxford, p 11.
45 See *Law Commission Consultation Papers No 119, No 128, No 129, No 130* (1991-93) HMSO, London; Glover, N & Brazier, M 'Ethical aspects of the Law Commission Report on Mental Incapacity' *Reviews of Clinical Gerontology* 1996, Vol 6, pp 365-70; Lord Chancellor's Department *Who Decides? Making Decisions on Behalf of Mentally Incapacitated Adults* Cm 3803 (1997) HMSO, London; Keown, J & Gormally, L 'Human dignity, autonomy and mentally incapacitated patients: A critique of *Who Decides?*' *Web Journal of Current Legal Issues* 1999, Issue 4; and Glover-Thomas, N 'Making decisions on behalf of mentally incapacitated adults' *Reviews in Clinical Gerontology* 2001, Vol 10, p 375.
46 Department of Health *Statistical Bulletin* (1999) Vol 25, p 7.

those in need of long-term care. Had the Court of Appeal's decision been upheld, the administration of treatment to an incapacitated individual would have been subject to intense scrutiny. However, as such patients are not subject to the compulsory powers of the MHA 1983, any decision to treat would have to be justified on the basis of mental incapacity and would be dealt with in the same way as the provision of treatment for physical conditions. As a result, it is difficult to say whether *Bournewood* has influenced the levels of patients being found mentally incompetent to make their own treatment choices. The *Bournewood* decision did not overtly introduce any new mechanisms for providing treatment to those who are unable to decide for themselves, but it is contended that when an individual is in hospital on an informal basis, and little scrutiny as to their daily care is in place, it seems possible that the finding of mental incapacity could arise and non-consensual treatment could follow.

5 Law Reform and the Mentally Incapacitated

(a) Reform

Before *Re C*, which was decided in 1994, there was no comprehensive definition of capacity in English law, despite the existence of a substantial number of people who were not legally competent. Individuals who have not yet reached the age of majority, those suffering from dementia and other degenerative organic conditions and those who are mentally incompetent owing to mental impairment or injury frequently are not in a position to make their own choices. In addition, because of advances in medical technology and knowledge, the lives of individuals who are, or are likely to become, mentally incompetent in the future, are being prolonged. As the population ages and the number of elderly people with dementia or some other mental impairment affecting their capacity rises, it has become increasingly important to consider possible reform.[47] The process by which decisions can be made on behalf of those who are incapable of making their own decisions needs to be clarified. The challenge of developing services which meet the needs of such individuals and protects their interests, is intensifying. The concern surrounding this issue has grown since the National Health Service and Community Care Act 1990 shifted the emphasis of care towards the community and community-based services. Placing incapable and vulnerable people in the community environment without sufficient

---

47   Jacques, A *Understanding Dementia* (1992) Churchill Livingstone, Edinburgh.

protective measures raises the possibility of abuse and exploitation.[48] Therefore, efforts to reform the law in this area are vital.

The Law Commission published its report on *Mental Incapacity* in February 1995.[49] The report was the outcome of a lengthy and wide-ranging process of consultation. This process resulted in four consultation papers over a period of four years.[50] However, the Government did not support the Law Commission's draft bill on mental incapacity and a further consultation period was initiated.[51] This process culminated in October 1999 when the Department of Health issued the Green Paper *Making Decisions*.[52] This policy statement sets out the Government's proposals to improve the decision-making process for those who are incapable of making decisions for themselves or who cannot communicate their decisions. The importance of clarifying the law governing care and treatment decisions on behalf of people without capacity must not be underestimated. The number of people who will fall into this category will undoubtedly increase as the population ages and medical technology improves to such a degree that more people survive after life-threatening illness and injury.

The Government has put forward plans to change both procedural and substantive aspects of the law governing this area. The policy statement supports many of the Law Commission's recommendations to create an efficient and effective system for managing the affairs of the mentally incapacitated adult. It will cover decision-making in the medical, financial and personal arena. The proposed reforms include a new test for assessing incapacity and recommend that ways be sought to enable a person without capacity to communicate their decisions if possible. The policy statement also addresses the need for legal safeguards for carers, a new continuing power of attorney and the end of the Court of Protection in its current form.

48 McCreadie, C *Elder Abuse: Update on Research* (1996) Age Concern/Institute of Gerontology, London.
49 Law Commission Report No 231 *Mental Incapacity* (1995) HMSO, London.
50 *Law Commission Consultation Papers No 119, No 128, No 129, No 130* (1991-93) HMSO, London. See also Glover, N & Brazier, M 'Ethical aspects of the Law Commission Report on Mental Incapacity' *Reviews of Clinical Gerontology* 1996, Vol 6, p 365.
51 Lord Chancellor's Department *Who Decides? Making Decisions on Behalf of Mentally Incapacitated Adults* Cm 3803 (1997) HMSO, London. See also, Keown, J & Gormally, L 'Human dignity, autonomy and mentally incapacitated patients: A critique of *Who Decides?*' *Web Journal of Current Legal Issues* 1999, Issue 4 and Glover-Thomas, N 'Making decisions on behalf of mentally incapacitated adults' *Reviews in Clinical Gerontology* 2001, Vol 10, p 375.
52 Lord Chancellor's Department *Making Decisions: The Government's Proposals for Making Decisions on Behalf of Mentally Incapacitated Adults* Cm 4465 (1999) TSO, London.

(b) Mental capacity

The central issue is what constitutes legal capacity. After all, it is only when lack of capacity has been established that the decision-making process can be removed from the individual. Where an individual is clearly competent to make a choice, proxy decision-making would be wholly unethical. Even where others consider a decision irrational it must nevertheless be accepted if the decision-maker has the mental capacity to make that decision. This position is strengthened by the Government's decision to confirm the presumption of legal capacity in all individuals. The test recommended by the Law Commission to establish mental capacity has been confirmed. A person will be viewed to be without capacity where *by reason of mental disability* a person is either:

(a) unable to understand the information relevant to the decision;
(b) incapable of retaining that information; or
(c) cannot communicate the decision to another.

Some important points need to be made about this test. The proposed capacity test is functional in nature and is based on the status of the individual concerned. Incapacity can be proven once a diagnostic threshold of mental incompetence is met. It focuses on whether the individual is able, at the time when a particular decision has to be made, to understand the nature and effect of the decision. The functional test is only applied to those who are unable to make a given decision because they are suffering from a *mental disability*. Mental disability has been defined by the Law Commission (and confirmed in the Green Paper *Making Decisions*) as 'any disability or disorder of the mind or brain, whether permanent or temporary, which results in an impairment or disturbance of mental functioning'. 'Mental disability' is to be broadly interpreted and could include recognised psychiatric conditions and confused or impaired states following physical illness. A person's capacity cannot be compromised because they hold peculiar, and perhaps irrational, views on life. '[T]he patient's right of choice exists whether the reasons for making that choice are rational, irrational or even non-existent'.[53] Likewise old age, infirmity or learning disabilities cannot be regarded as a justification for intervention in an individual's personal affairs. However, it has been argued that the adoption of a broad test of incapacity will inevitably result in the lowering of diagnostic thresholds. David Carson notes that the approach is likely to be: '[t]his person ... is severely mentally ... [impaired]. Therefore, it is reasonable to conclude that he is incapable'.[54]

53 *Re T* [1992] 4 All ER 649 at 662.
54 Carson, D 'Disabling Processes: the Law Commission's Proposals on Mentally Incapacitated Adults' Decision-Making' *Journal of Social Welfare and Family Law* 1993, p 304.

Once it has been established that a person is suffering from a mental disability, any person seeking the right to make decisions or treatment choices on the person's behalf must prove that the individual is *unable to make* a decision for himself. An individual may be able to understand and retain treatment information but if they are then unable to act on it, they may be viewed as incompetent. For example, a person suffering from body dysmorphia who has a firmly fixed belief that he is meant to be an amputee may be unable to make a treatment decision concerning the deep ulcers on his leg. A person with this condition is subject to a powerful obsession. He may be able to understand and retain the treatment information but his obsession prevents him from making the necessary decision.

Finally, it is confirmed in *Making Decisions* that emphasis should be placed on establishing good lines of communication between the health care professional and the mentally incapacitated adult. A patient who appears unable to communicate his decision should not automatically be labelled as mentally incapacitated. All efforts must be made to facilitate communication. People should be 'enabled' to make their own decisions where possible. Information must be offered in broad terms and in simple language. Where there is difficulty in communicating, for example owing to aphasia consequent upon a stroke, all practical steps should be taken to aid communication.

(c) Best interests

The Law Commission recommended that statutory provision should be made to the effect that decisions made by others on behalf of people without capacity must be made in the incompetent person's best interests. The Government shares this view. However, the common law test of 'best interests' that was established in *F v West Berkshire Health Authority*, has been criticised because it is vague and difficult to apply in practice.[55] The 'best interests' test would be satisfied if the proposed treatment would save that person's life or improve or prevent deterioration of the patient's mental or physical condition. No further detail was provided in the case as to how this test could and should be applied in practice. In *Airedale NHS Trust v Bland*, 'best interests' was thought to include 'having respect paid to what seems most likely to have been [the patient's] views on the subject'.[56] This approach entails an element of the 'substituted judgment' test. When applying the 'substituted judgment' test the decision-maker should seek to arrive at the judgment that the incapable person would

55 [1990] 2 AC 1.
56 [1993] AC 789.

have made, could they have done so. The Law Commission rejected this test for two, largely practical, reasons. First, the legal principles to be implemented are designed to apply to *all* mentally incapacitated persons. 'Substituted judgment', in the case of a person who has never had capacity, is a fiction. Secondly, the best interests test needs to be applied easily, not just by medical practitioners and judges, but also by the people who care for the individual on a daily basis. Therefore the criteria must be straightforward and simple to grasp. Moreover, the Law Commission saw no conflict between the concepts of substituted judgment and best interests. Where someone's preferences are known, their 'best interests' require that such preferences be taken into account even if these preferences cannot be said to qualify as a rational judgment. In seeking to clarify the definition of best interests, the Government embraces the notion of incorporating statutory guidance on how the best interests of a person without capacity should be determined. The decision-maker should have regard to four factors:

(a) the ascertainable past and present wishes and feelings of the person concerned, and the factors that person would consider if able to do so;
(b) the need to permit and encourage the person to participate or improve his ability to participate as fully as possible in anything done for and any decisions affecting him;
(c) the views of other people whom it is appropriate and practicable to consult about the person's wishes and feelings and what would be in his best interests; and
(d) whether the purpose for which any action or decision is required can be as effectively achieved in a manner less restrictive of the person's freedom of action.

Despite the initial appearance that 'best interests' will continue to be classified on common law criteria, the test is transformed because the statutory guidance will be prescribed. These criteria will seek to balance the welfare needs of patients with whatever residual ability they might retain to express their own preferences. However, the Government confirms that the prescribed criteria will only have to be referred to and taken account of when making a decision on behalf of an incapacitated adult, as the promotion of flexibility must continue.

(d) General authority to act reasonably

The Law Commission recognised that lay carers and relatives rather than medical professionals usually carry out the care of mentally incapacitated adults. It was envisaged that a general empowerment of those caring for incapacitated persons on a daily basis was needed. The authority for day-to-day decision-making often develops informally and in a piecemeal fashion that affords protection to neither the incapacitated adult nor the decision-maker. The Law Commission recommended that the informality in the decision-making should remain but that a legal context should be provided to give clarity to carers and adequate protection for those without capacity. In recommending the 'general authority to act reasonably', the Law Commission sought to put in a statutory format the common law principle of necessity that provides for actions on behalf of a person without capacity when action is necessary and is in their best interests. The definition of 'to act reasonably' is to do anything for the personal welfare or healthcare of a person who is, or is reasonably believed to be, without capacity in relation to the matter in question, if it is in all the circumstances reasonable for it to be done by the person who does it. However, certain decisions may not be made under the general authority to act: eg consent to marriage and to sexual relations. Certain financial decisions may be made under the authority to act, such as payment for goods and services incurred on behalf of a person without capacity. Details of this authority to act will either be included in the legislation or in a Code of Practice.

(e) Continuing powers of attorney

The Government recommends the establishment of a capacity threshold. Although this threshold is quite low, there will always be people who fall below it. The concept of best interests and a general authority to act reasonably suggests that the incapacitated person may have appointed an individual, when capable, to make decisions for them when they can no longer do so themselves. The notion that people can appoint proxies in the event that they will not be able to make decisions for themselves in the future has an established history. The Power of Attorney Act 1971 provided for the appointment of a proxy decision-maker by the donor. However, this Act provided that any such power given by the donor would last only as long as his own powers, and accordingly could not survive if he lost his decision-making capacity. The Enduring Power of Attorney Act 1985 extended this earlier power so that certain decision-making powers vested in the 'attorney' could endure beyond the donor's loss of capacity. The Act limited these powers to financial matters. However, there has been a widespread failure by attorneys to register powers with the Public Trust Office when they believe the individual concerned is becoming mentally incapacitated and this has provided opportunities for fraud and abuse. For example, it has been estimated that up to 15% of cases involving registered powers have been tainted by fraud or abuse.[57]

57 Robins, J 'Increased capacity' *Gazette* 1999, Vol 96 No 47, p 20.

The Government also intends to replace the enduring power of attorney with Continuing Powers of Attorney. The continuing power of attorney will allow individuals to delegate decision-making powers on finance, healthcare, and personal welfare to a person of their choice. Although the powers of the continuing power of attorney are significantly broader than those under the enduring power of attorney, it will not be possible to authorise consent or refusal of consent to any treatment unless the individual is reasonably believed to be without capacity or is subject to the compulsory powers of the MHA 1983. An attorney will not be able to make decisions on behalf of the individual about withdrawal of artificial nutrition or hydration unless that power has specifically been included within the continuing power of attorney. Owing to the problems experienced by the current system of enduring power of attorney, the Government proposes to include some additional safeguards in the continuing power of attorney. The document must be signed, witnessed and dated. There will be a compulsory registration system and a registering authority. Without registration, the attorney will not be able to use the continuing power of attorney. Furthermore, to prevent abuse, the attorney will have to notify others of the intention to apply to register the continuing power of attorney before registration takes place so that any disputes and challenges can be settled by the modernised Court of Protection before the continuing power of attorney becomes effective. Although steps have been taken to ensure the continuing power of attorney provides greater safety for both the incapacitated person and the attorney, many of the problems experienced with the enduring power of attorney may continue. The proxy under the continuing power of attorney does not have to be a relative but many elderly people are cared for by members of their family and it is likely that the proxy will be a relative. Will a daughter who has carried the burden of caring for her elderly mother be able to make decisions in her mother's best interests? There seems to be the same potential for 'selfish' decisions under the continuing power of attorney as the enduring power of attorney. The continuing power of attorney should not be regarded as a panacea to abuse and exploitation but the proposals put forward by the Government will certainly be a vast improvement on the current system.

(f) A new Court of Protection

Decisions made on behalf of incapacitated adults must be in their interests alone. Actions must not be governed by the desires of other individuals. In order to protect the interests of the vulnerable a new jurisdiction, which would be operated by the court system, was recommended by the Law Commission. This single court jurisdiction will be able to make decisions concerning financial, personal welfare and healthcare issues. However, it is hoped that the court will be seen as an option of last resort where disputes have failed to be resolved by other means. Where no solution has been found, then application may be made to this new enhanced court, which is essentially based on the old Court of Protection. In the consultation process, concerns were raised about the lack of regional presence of the Court. This question of accessibility has, to some extent, been answered by the recommendation that, where possible, cases will be dealt with at a local level rather than in London. A central administration will provide support and carry out administrative functions, while a body of High Court judges, circuit judges and district judges will be assigned to the Court of Protection and will hear cases around the country. However, where medical professionals seek clarity on the lawfulness of certain medical interventions, the High Court will maintain its inherent jurisdiction to decide such matters.

All decisions made by the Court should be made with the key principles (outlined above) in mind. Consideration must be given to the capacity of the individual concerned, whether they are able to play a role in the decision-making process and what would be in the individual's best interests. The Court will have the power to make decisions on behalf of these individuals or appoint a manager to make the decisions. Furthermore, the Court will be able to make declarations about an individual's capacity.

The Court's powers are to be extended from the current powers of the Court of Protection. The Law Commission recommended that the Court should be able to approve or refuse approval of particular types and forms of healthcare, depending on the individual concerned, his level of mental capacity and whether it would be in his best interests. The decision to consent to certain forms of treatment may also be delegated to a manager when appropriate. The Court may also require the substitution of a person responsible for the healthcare of a patient with another person. Finally, the Court may direct that the patient's healthcare records be accessed for the purposes of making a decision regarding the individual. Certain decisions raise some concern: most notably, the controversial issues of discontinuing artificial nutrition and hydration to a patient in a persistent vegetative state (PVS) who may be said to have no interests, let alone best interests,[58] and the validity of advance treatment statements made by patients when mentally capable. These healthcare decisions must be a matter for the Court and should not be made by a manager. The Law Commission Report endorsed the possibility of withdrawing treatment from such patients where it can be shown that 'no activity in the cerebral cortex [is evident] and [there is] no prospect of recovery'. The need for

---

58 *Airedale National Health Service Trust v Bland* [1993] AC 789.

judicial involvement in such decisions is obvious. There must be no opportunity for abuse or exploitation and the growing elderly, demented population must be free from the threat of involuntary euthanasia. Healthcare decisions are just one aspect of the Court's newly-extended powers. It will also have powers to make welfare decisions: eg where the incapable individual is to live; who may and may not have contact with the individual (in the interests of protecting the vulnerable person); and obtaining social security benefits and community services which the individual is entitled to and in need of.

The Government also supports the idea of the Court appointing a manager, on some occasions, to make decisions on behalf of mentally incapacitated adults. However, it will be an exceptional case when the manager has responsibility for making *all* decisions concerning the person's welfare. The Government proposes to allow the Court to appoint suitable managers and to set the scope of their responsibilities. It is thought likely that the Court may appoint a number of managers with responsibility for the different aspects of the mentally incapacitated adult's life. This will ensure the manager has the suitable skills, which are required for making the decisions, and it will minimise any conflict of interests.

However, as with the general authority to act reasonably, the manager will be unable to make certain decisions on behalf of the incapacitated adult, for example providing consent to marriage and sexual relations. The Government also takes the view that most healthcare decisions could be made by the Court without the need to appoint a manager. The power to refuse consent to certain forms of treatment will not be given to the manager but will remain an issue for the Court. For property and finance decisions, the Court may appoint a manager. The manager will be able to deal with a number of issues pertaining to the incapacitated adult's finances:
(a) the control and management of any property, its disposal and acquisition;
(b) carrying on a business;
(c) dissolution of a partnership;
(d) carrying out a contract; and
(e) discharging a debt or obligation.

Other financial decisions, such as the setting up of a trust for the person concerned and the making of a will, must be made by the Court instead of the manager. Apart from the specific issues, which are laid down in the report, the Government considers it necessary to promote flexibility in the decision-making process. Each case will raise different issues and considerations. The Court must therefore be given the freedom to make the appropriate decision in the interests of each particular vulnerable adult. The decision to appoint a manager will be subject to regular review and the Government intends to provide the Court with the power to fix a time limit or order a periodic review for cases where a manager has been appointed to make decisions on financial and welfare issues. In cases where managers have been appointed to make healthcare decisions, the Court should always place a time limit (of no more than five years) on these appointments. For those vulnerable adults who are unable to make their own decisions, the system of proxy decision-making by a manager must be watertight in order to prevent their rights and interests being disregarded. It is hoped that the inclusion of an exhaustive list of issues where managers may not intervene and the use of a system of periodic review will achieve this.

6 Conclusion

Making decisions on behalf of those who are incapable of making their own is becoming an increasingly prominent issue as more vulnerable people find themselves being cared for in the community environment. As voluntary hospitalisation and community care continue to provide the means of care for the majority of mentally disordered and impaired individuals, a clarification of the way in which important decisions are made on their behalf is needed. Where patients are not subject to the mental health legislation because they are being cared for in the community, because they are voluntary patients in a psychiatric hospital or because the individual is informally cared for in hospital but is unable to consent or dissent to care, substituted decision-making may be necessary. Proxy decision-making can only be ethically justifiable when a person has been classified as legally incompetent. Such a label is awarded when an individual is unable to take in and retain information pertaining to a planned care regime; where they cannot believe the information and deliberate over it to arrive at a choice; and where they have difficulties in communicating their choice. In such circumstances, the person's carer must act in their best interests.

The Government has published its recommendations on how the law is to be reformed in this area. Where an individual is considered to have the necessary mental capacity to make his own choices, then those choices will be respected. Incapacity can be proven once a diagnostic threshold of mental incompetence is met. The question to be asked is whether the individual concerned is able, at the time when a particular decision has to be made, to understand the nature and effect of the decision. Where such capacity is lacking, it seems likely that treatment choices and other important decisions will continue to be made at the behest of carers, doctors and judges, who will apply the 'best interests' test in accordance with prescribed statutory criteria. Although the test is transformed because guidelines are to be incorporated into the legislation, its application will remain flexible. Therefore, whether the mentally incapacitated adult will benefit from these proposed changes remains to be seen.

The question of how decisions can be made on behalf of mentally incapacitated adults has been subject to some scrutiny over recent years. This chapter has examined these questions and has considered the recent Government proposals on this issue. It was feared that the Law Commission's Report on *Mental Incapacity* would be disregarded and left to gather dust. It now seems that the final consultation period, which culminated in the report, *Making Decisions*, has gained some momentum and active steps may well be taken in the near future. However, it cannot be denied that these proposals are cautious ones and no time-scale for their implementation has been proposed. Certainly, there are many aspects which are to be welcomed as they do address some of the problems experienced in the past by those caring for vulnerable individuals, but the Government has decided to avoid the contentious issues of advanced statements in healthcare, public law protection of people at risk and non-therapeutic research. These areas will not be subject to statutory control and will continue to be governed by the common law. The Green Paper *Making Decisions*, is a watered-down version of the Law Commission Report on Mental Incapacity and although exclusion of these important issues is disappointing, the proposed measures indicate some progress, which can only be of benefit to vulnerable individuals. However, the issues raised in the consultation process which are not to be advanced by the Government seem likely to return, and debate seems set to continue. As the population ages and the incidence of dementia and other mentally debilitating conditions increase, these thorny issues will inevitably need to be faced once again.

Chapter 5
Community care: law and policy

1 Introduction

Once professionals and patients alike had accepted community care, the next challenge was to formalise the care approach so that it could be applied consistently around the country. During the 1980s official community care attempts failed, owing to the paucity of community service provision and the *Hallstrom* decision, which led to the 'long leash' technique being declared unlawful. Attempts to overcome the adverse affects of this decision and practical inadequacies were undertaken with varying success. This chapter will consider the manner in which community care failures of the 1980s were dealt with, how effective the suggestions for alternative care methods were and, finally, how successful the Mental Health (Patients in the Community) Act 1995 has been in responding to the needs of increasing numbers of psychiatric patients living in the community.

MIND continued to play a leading role in the libertarian movement, although as the years went by it adopted a less confrontational approach.[1] The National Schizophrenia Fellowship continued to highlight the plight of sufferers of chronic mental health difficulties and those who cared for them. However, the work of *The Times* journalist, Marjorie Wallace, achieved the most positive results at the time. In 1985, she ran a campaign on schizophrenia, which highlighted some of the very difficult problems faced by people with mental health difficulties living in the community. The campaign instigated great media interest in mental health and a variety of programmes were aired on television. As a result of Wallace's work, a new organisation was set up called SANE (Schizophrenia – A

1 Jones, K *Asylums and After* (1993) The Athlone Press, London, p 236.

National Emergency). The publicity which Wallace's work engendered ensured SANE's success in raising funds for research purposes. The work of SANE reflected the intense ambition of Marjorie Wallace to place mental health at the forefront of public debate and to promote it from the Cinderella status to which it had become accustomed. The work of all three organisations played a vital role in providing a support structure to those directly affected by psychiatric difficulties. All three continued to highlight the confusion within the system and the huge gaps in provision. However, despite the very real impact each organisation had on the development and adoption of policy, they were each independent of Government and could do nothing more than sway public and Governmental feeling.

The provision of community support to people who had been discharged from psychiatric facilities continued on an ad hoc and informal basis. This provision continued to be supplemented by the work of the above organisations and a variety of charities. However, by the end of 1992 it became clear that makeshift psychiatric provisions could no longer continue. In December 1992, Ben Silcock, a young man with schizophrenia, climbed into the lions' enclosure at London Zoo.[2] Ben believed he could 'talk to the animals' and in his attempt to do so, he was savagely mauled. The timing of the incident resulted in widespread news reporting. New Year's Day 1993 brought little other news and, with London Zoo providing the backdrop to this dramatic event, it ensured an intense period of media coverage. Community care could not be sustained as an improvised method of dealing with the needs of such vulnerable individuals. Ben Silcock's activities had managed to instigate the first murmurs of change in official Government policy: something that many people had failed to do. In the years leading up to the Silcock case, various recommendations for change had been published, most notably by the Royal College of Psychiatrists. Yet, each attempt to deal with the inadequacies of the system was politely ignored. The Silcock incident ensured that the community care debate was brought back into focus and serious consideration had to be given to how alternative psychiatric facilities were to be provided and financed.

The purpose of this chapter is to examine and assess the official response to the needs of increasing numbers of psychiatric patients who were, and continue to be, discharged into the community. We will consider the alternative measures (such as community treatment orders) which were contemplated towards the end of the 1980s. The chapter will further

2   This story attracted comments from all the major broadsheet newspapers in January 1993. See *The Times*, *Guardian* and *Independent*, 5 January 1993. See also an article by Ben Silcock's father, Bryan: Silcock, B 'Which way for community care?' *Sunday Times* News Review, 10 January 1993, p 5.

explore the international influences on England and Wales in the quest to respond appropriately and adequately to the needs of these vulnerable people, and finally the provisions of the Mental Health (Patients in the Community) Act 1995 and the introduction of supervised discharge will be critically assessed.

2 Community Treatment Orders

Psychiatrists, hospital managers and Government officials have embraced the notion of community care for a variety of reasons. A mentally disordered individual who was living in the community among family and friends was thought to maintain a degree of independence, an independence that is all too frequently lost after long spells in hospital. Likewise, by promoting community care, already under-resourced psychiatric facilities would not continue to be over-stretched, and the humanitarian objective of protecting individual liberty, where possible, would be achieved. Yet for all the positive attributes that could be associated with community care, by the mid-1980s it was clear that the reality was somewhat different. The idea of removing patients from 'bleak old Victorian institutions'[3] was an accepted goal but the difficulty of providing adequate levels of community facilities and ensuring patient cooperation made this objective much harder to achieve in practice. Once away from the intense scrutiny of a hospital ward, some mentally disordered people were failing to take their medication and comply with conditions. The non-compliance of patients was focused on an aspect of community care that it was thought possible to improve, while the inadequate financial support of the policy was carefully overlooked. Therefore, the policy of subjecting patients to some means of compulsory medication in the community environment was much debated throughout the 1980s, and was most commonly referred to as the community treatment order.

In 1987 the Royal College of Psychiatrists published a discussion document on community treatment orders.[4] At this time the psychiatric

3   Jones, K *Asylums and After* (1993) The Athlone Press, London, p 239.
4   MIND *Contemporary Treatment in the Community* (1987) MIND Policy Paper, London; Bingley, W 'Compulsory practices' *Openmind* 1987, No 26; Fennell, P 'Inscribing paternalism in the law: consent to treatment and mental disorder' *Journal of Law and Society* 1990, Vol 17 p 29; Cavadino, M *Mental Health Law in Context: Doctors' Orders?* (1989) Dartmouth Publishing, Aldershot; Cavadino, M 'Coercion is not the best method' *Community Care* 1990, 22 March; Cavadino, M 'Community control?' *Journal of Social Welfare and Family Law* 1991, p 482. See also Scott-Moncrieff, L 'Comments on the discussion document of the Royal College of Psychiatrists regarding community treatment orders' *Bulletin of the Royal College of Psychiatrists* 1988, Vol 12, p 220.

profession was still suffering the effects of the *Hallstrom* decision, which prevented practitioners from using provisions within the MHA 1983 to create informal community care measures. This decision had severely restricted options for caring and controlling individuals with mental health difficulties. The benefits of a less restrictive care environment could not be embraced for a large proportion of mentally disordered people because there was now no effective means of ensuring they complied with their medication. The community treatment order envisaged by the Royal College would apply to people like Ben Silcock, who had refused to take his medication while in the community, and lacked the responsibility and capacity to make his own decisions.

By the end of the 1980s, there was a continuing trend to avoid hospitalising mentally disordered patients for long periods. The tradition of admitting severely disturbed people to hospital had eroded and much greater reliance was placed on the patient's home, friends and family to offer the support he needed. The Royal College recognised that this trend was far better than that adopted up to the late 1960s and 'community care' offered greater therapeutic benefits. Yet the College also recognised that the same problem surfaced when patients, having been successfully treated in hospital, were released. They frequently discontinued their medication after leaving hospital and their mental state deteriorated. In such situations psychiatrists would not be able to act unless the patient consented to being re-admitted to hospital or the patient's condition deteriorated to such an extent as to justify compulsory admission. The proposed community treatment order sought:

> 'to remedy this inability to provide necessary treatment, and also to avoid not only admission to hospital but the gradual erosion of the patient's social supportive network which inevitably follows repeated distressing relapses'.[5]

The community treatment order would permit 'medical treatment for mental disorder' outside hospital. It was expected, however, that the use of force would only be applied to a small number of patients suffering from schizophrenia and closely related disorders, and that every effort should be made to encourage voluntary hospitalisation and treatment where possible.

It was envisaged by the Royal College that the order would only apply to patients who require compulsory treatment where this treatment could be satisfactorily provided in the community. Furthermore, only patients

---

5   The Royal College of Psychiatrists *Community treatment orders: A discussion document* (1987) RCP London.

whose conditions fell within the category of mental illness could be subject to the order. Of course, the value of this limitation is questionable when it is accepted that the 'mental illness' category has come to be regarded as the 'dustbin category' of the mental health legislation. The absence of a definition of 'mental illness' has ensured that any behaviour or disorder of mind can potentially be viewed as a mental illness for the purposes of the MHA 1983. For a patient to be subject to the order he should have had a previous period of severe mental illness which responded to treatment and it should be likely that the patient will relapse unless treatment is administered. The Royal College recommended that patients subject to the order should have immediate access to a second medical opinion in order to assess the medical value of the order. As with admission to hospital, it was envisaged that the order would last for six months and could be renewed. Likewise, patients would have an immediate right of appeal to a Mental Health Review Tribunal and if they did not seek review, the Mental Health Review Tribunal would automatically review the patient's position.

The point of the order was to ensure patients continued their medication when released from hospital. It was anticipated that most patients, once subject to the order, would willingly comply with medication. Yet, it was also recognised that some patients would still refuse treatment. Forceful treatment of an individual in the community was not proposed by the Royal College; instead where such a situation arose, the patient would be compulsorily re-admitted to hospital.

The community treatment order tried to combine the use of a less restrictive care environment with the need to ensure the continuance of medication. The advantages of such a proposal were that the patient would be free to live in the community with family and friends, maintain skills for independent living and not be labelled a 'psychiatric inpatient'; while at the same time, it was thought that the cost of providing treatment in this way would be significantly lower than that of hospital care. Proponents, like the Royal College of Psychiatrists, argued that the order enabled the humanitarian ideal of protecting individual liberty to be endorsed, but it can be argued that this was far from the truth. Although patients would technically be free to live in the community, they would still be subject to intervention by the authorities. Moreover, patient compliance could remain limited under the order. The only aspect of psychiatric care and treatment that can be forced on an unwilling person is medication. Other aspects of the community care approach, such as occupational therapy, day centres and so on, cannot be forced on anyone. To benefit from these aspects of community care, the individual must actively wish to cooperate. Community care was embraced because it was heralded as a new and inspiring way of dealing with the mentally disordered. It was envisaged that greater freedoms would be made available to patients and that such patients would not suffer from some of the more negative aspects of institutional care, most notably increased dependence on others. However, the community treatment order, as proposed by the Royal College of Psychiatrists in 1987, seemed to run counter to these intentions. The only benefit of the order would be to ensure patients continued to receive medication, but where they refused to comply they would merely end up back in hospital. At this time, the community treatment order was viewed as a 'very obvious form of social control, forcing medication which has marked side-effects on people who do not want it, and who are not in hospital'.[6]

The community treatment debate subsided for a few years owing to the lack of support for the Royal College of Psychiatrists' proposals. Yet, the debate had not disappeared altogether. After Ben Silcock's activities, community treatment became a live issue once again. The Government asked for views from mental health organisations as to an appropriate response to the inadequacies of the mental health system that Ben Silcock has so clearly highlighted. MIND considered such orders would lead to an unacceptable breach of civil liberties, while the National Schizophrenia Fellowship viewed continued closure of psychiatric inpatient facilities and the chronic lack of resources as being the main culprits for continued failures in the system. The Royal College of Psychiatrists noted that its proposals for community treatment orders in 1987 had not been fully supported by its members and stated that another working party had been set up to consider new options.

The working party focused on a modified version of its previous proposals. Rather than introducing a community treatment order, it proposed a scheme of community supervision. The Royal College published its discussion document on community supervision orders in January 1993. The Reed Committee Report had been published the year before and therefore any new arrangements had to be consistent with the principles laid down in the Report.[7] The Royal College recognised that patients should be cared for:
(a) with regard to the quality of care, and with proper attention to their individual needs;
(b) as far as possible outside hospital and other institutions;
(c) in conditions of no greater security than is justified by the degree of danger they present to themselves and others;

6   Jones, K *Asylums and After* (1993) The Athlone Press, London, p 239.
7   Department of Health, *Home Office Review of Health and Social Services for Mentally Disordered Offenders and Others Requiring Similar Services, Final Summary Report* Cm 2088 (1992) HMSO, London.

(d) in such a way as to maximise rehabilitation and their chances of sustaining an independent life; and
(e) as near as possible to their own homes or families, if they have them.

The Royal College considered six principles would apply when implementing a community supervision order:
1   It is undesirable to give compulsory *treatment* to a patient in the community in the absence of consent.
2   Compulsory *supervision* (ie a requirement to be seen and supported by a community psychiatric nurse) in the community is in the interest of a limited and defined group of patients.
3   Compulsory arrangements in the community must have safeguards and should not be used as an alternative to circumventing community care.
4   Arrangements should not be open-ended.
5   The grounds for compulsory arrangements should be clear.
6   There should be opportunities to apply for a discharge from such an order.

Once again, it was anticipated by the Royal College of Psychiatrists that this order would be limited to a particular group of psychiatric patients who had previously spent time in hospital. Unlike the community treatment order, where compliance with medication was the primary objective, the community supervision order was designed to allow practitioners to intervene before a patient's mental state deteriorated to the extent where compulsory detention was necessary. The purpose of the supervision order was to require patients to maintain contact with the healthcare services to enable practitioners to detect when the patient's condition was beginning to decline. When this occurred, the patient would be recalled to hospital at a relatively early stage in order to prevent a worsening of the condition. It was envisaged that such an order would be particularly useful for those 'revolving door' patients who frequently found themselves in and out of hospital.

Despite the toned-down nature of the Royal College's modified proposals, some difficulties continued. The order would have enabled practitioners to intervene early on when the patient refused medication or became uncooperative. Such intervention would come in the form of re-admission to hospital. However, this right to intervene counteracts the inherent aims of community care and acts as a threat to patients who, for whatever reason, do not want to accept treatment. The supervision order would work in potentially the same way as the proposed community treatment order: the patient refuses treatment then finds himself re-admitted to hospital. The six-year interval between the Royal College of Psychiatrists' first and second attempt to bridge the gap between hospitalisation and release into the community had failed to achieve results or win support.

3 International Influences

(a) Introduction

Despite the internal struggle experienced in England and Wales over the rights and wrongs of adopting a community treatment/supervision order, many countries around the world have revised legislation in order to enable involuntary treatment of the mentally disordered in the community.[8] Some countries adopted outpatient commitment models before the debate emerged in England and Wales while others have only recently changed their laws, most notably Canada, with the introduction of Brian's Law in Ontario.[9] Various states in the US and Australia have some form of community treatment provision while development of such approaches in Europe has been more limited.[10]

(b) Community treatment models

There are two principle models for community treatment. The first is community treatment as a condition of leave or discharge from hospital, and the second is community treatment, which is used as an alternative to hospitalisation. The need to show that the patient concerned has undergone a period of inpatient hospital care is a far more common model of community treatment, although more recent law reform proposals have been more willing to embrace the spirit of the community care approach and the less restrictive care environment. Community treatment that is dependent on the patient having spent time in a psychiatric facility as an inpatient is thought to have a different objective to the other model. Where such inpatient stays must be evidenced, community treatment seems focused on preventing relapse. Høyer and Ferris suggest this will 'tend to add further coercion to the existing inpatient coercion', whereas

---

8   These changes have been wrought as a result of increasing attention being placed on non-compliance of patients living in the community. See for example, Dennis, L & Monahan, J (eds) *Coercion and Aggressive Community Treatment – A New Frontier in Mental Health Law* (1996) Plenum Press, New York.
9   See Dedman, P 'Community treatment orders in Victoria, Australia' *Psychiatric Bulletin* 1990, Vol 14, p 462. Stein, L & Test, M 'Alternative to mental hospital treatment: 1. Conceptual model treatment program and clinical evaluation' *Archives of General Psychiatry* 1980, Vol 37, p 392; Wilk, R J 'Implications of involuntary outpatient commitment for community health services' *American Journal of Orthopsychiatry* 1988, Vol 58, p 580; Geller, J L 'The quandaries of enforced community treatment and unenforceable outpatient statutes' *Journal of Psychiatry and Law* 1986, p 149.
10 Høyer, G & Ferris, R 'Outpatient commitment. Some reflections on ideology, practice and implications for research' *Journal of Mental Health Law* 2001 Vol 1, p 56 at p 57.

community treatment 'as an alternative to hospitalisation may have the potential to reduce the total amount of coercion in psychiatric care'.[11]

Alaska, New Hampshire and Tennessee have systems of conditional release, that require a person to meet inpatient standards and be detained on an inpatient basis before the court can order involuntary outpatient commitment. Since the late 1990s, there has been renewed interest in involuntary outpatient commitment schemes in the US. Involuntary outpatient commitment has recently been considered in California, Massachusetts and Connecticut and enacted in New York (Kendra's Law), whereas in Maryland, Pennsylvania and Iowa, attempts to expand the use of involuntary outpatient commitment were defeated. In Australia and New Zealand most jurisdictions have outpatient commitment measures in place, which include the power to treat patients forcibly in the community.[12]

In 2000 Brian's Law was enacted in Ontario, Canada. Brian's Law is a form of community treatment order and arose as a result of increasing political pressure to control persons with mental health problems in the community. Brian's Law is only applicable to patients who have been inpatients in a psychiatric facility on two or more occasions or for a cumulative period of thirty days or more in the previous three years. It therefore follows the community treatment model, which aims at preventing further relapses, rather than as a means of embracing the notion of the least restrictive care environment. Although this law provides a means of enforcing a treatment programme on an unwilling patient, the idea behind the law is to ensure discharged patients have a support structure within the community upon which they can rely. In England and Wales, the MHA 1983, s 117 introduced a duty to provide after-care services to the mentally ill, Ontario has had no such statutory duty upon which patients could rely until now. Therefore Brian's Law is rather the means by which community treatment (and support) plans are devised and implemented. The community treatment order places a duty upon the treatment providers to ensure adequate care is provided. Therefore the 'Ontario community treatment order can be seen as enforcing standards

---

11 Høyer, G & Ferris, R 'Outpatient commitment. Some reflections on ideology, practice and implications for research' *Journal of Mental Health Law* 2001 Vol 1, p 56 at p 58.
12 Høyer, G & Ferris, R 'Outpatient commitment. Some reflections on ideology, practice and implications for research' *Journal of Mental Health Law* 2001 Vol 1, p 56 at p 62. See also Power, P 'Community treatment orders: The Australian experience' *The Journal of Forensic Psychiatry* 1999, Vol 10, p 9; McIvor, R 'The community treatment order: Clinical and ethical issues' *Australian and New Zealand Journal of Psychiatry* 1998, Vol 32, p 223.

of care from treatment providers as much as enforcing compliance in the patient population'.[13]

(c) Criticisms surrounding community treatment orders

Different forms of community treatment and outpatient commitment have existed around the world for some years, although not all measures have been favourably received. When attempting to evaluate the effectiveness of these measures difficulties arise owing to the fact that research remains very thin on the ground and the literature available is limited.[14] The Bazelon Center has been highly critical of the involuntary outpatient commitment schemes in operation around the US.[15] It suggests that involuntary outpatient commitment is being offered as a solution to the problem of mentally disordered offenders in prison, the homeless on the streets and those who are disruptive or violent in society, but some fundamental flaws exist within the approach. Recent research carried out in Bellevue Hospital in New York also indicates that some of the positive attributes associated with outpatient commitment might also be exaggerated.[16] The assumption that outpatient commitment reduces the likelihood of re-hospitalisation and shortens hospital stays appears to have no statistical substance. Likewise, outpatient commitment has not been shown to improve compliance with medication and continuation of treatment, or reduce the number of arrests or violent acts committed. The study provides strong evidence that outpatient commitment may be of little intrinsic value apart from forcing the mental health system to commit

13   Bartlett, P 'English Mental Health Reform: Lessons from Ontario?' *Journal of Mental Health Law* 2001, Vol 1, p 27 at p 39.
14   However, see, Swartz, M S et al 'Can involuntary commitment reduce hospital recidivism? Findings from a randomized trial with severely mentally ill individuals' *American Journal of Psychiatry* 1999, Vol 12, p 1968; Fernandez, G A & Nygard, S 'Impact of involuntary outpatient commitment on revolving-door syndrome in North Carolina' *Hospital and Community Psychiatry* 1990, Vol 41, p 1001; Zanni, G & deVeau, L 'Inpatient stays before and after outpatient commitment (in Washington DC)' *Hospital and Community Psychiatry* 1986, Vol 37, p 941; Munetz, M R, Grande, T, Kleist J & Peterson, G A 'The effectiveness of outpatient civil commitment' *Psychiatric Services* 1996, Vol 47, pp 1251-53; Rohland, B *'The Role of outpatient commitment in the management of persons with schizophrenia'* (May 1998) Iowa Consortium for Mental Health Services, Training and Research; Hiday, V A & Scheid-Cook, TL 'The North Carolina experience with outpatient commitment: A critical appraisal' *International Journal of Law and Psychiatry* 1987, Vol 10, p 215.
15   See http://www.bazelon.org.
16   Final Report: Research Study of the New York City Involuntary Outpatient Commitment Pilot Program, (at Bellevue Hospital) 4 December 1998) Policy Research Associates at www.prainc.com/IOPT/opt_toc.htm.

itself to helping patients find acceptable and effective treatment for their illnesses.

Similar concerns about the use of community treatment exist in England and Wales. MIND and other mental health organisations fear that if compulsion within the psychiatric system is taken up those in need of support will be driven away from services.[17] Trust within the therapeutic relationship between the patient and psychiatrist will diminish if the patient fears reprisals within the community if he does not actively co-operate. Compulsion may also be used disproportionately against particular minorities within the patient population.[18] Moreover, such orders are likely to focus on medication to the detriment of other services, such as talking treatments, housing, employment and benefits, and may be employed as an easier option than engaging service users in discussion concerning their own wishes. Proposals for such orders ignore the realities of neuroleptic medication. In particular, they assume medication is always effective and necessary.[19] Psychiatric medication still has some serious and irreversible side-effects, including weight gain, impotence, tardive dyskinesia and neuroleptic malignant syndrome. Drug reactions are a significant and continuing feature of taking psychiatric drugs. Therefore, a patient's decision to forego medication can often be a rational decision and lead to an improved quality of life.[20] The community treatment route also assumes that diagnosis of mental illness is a foolproof predictor of violence. Community treatment and/or supervision provisions are frequently justified on the basis that the risk mentally disordered individuals present to third parties will be reduced. However, Wallace has found clear evidence to suggest that alcoholics and drug addicts are twice as likely to commit crime as someone who suffers from schizophrenia. Where mentally disordered individuals do offend, the incident is more likely to be associated with drugs and alcohol abuse than with their condition.[21]

17 Pedlar, M 'Arguments against community treatment orders' (A Note for Local MIND Associations) (1999) MIND, London at http://www.good.co.uk/gustav.mahler/Pedler1.html.
18 See Department of Health, Home Office 'Services for people for black and ethnic minority groups: Issues of race and culture' *Review of Health and Social Services for Mentally Disordered Offenders and Others Requiring Similar Services* (1992) HMSO, London.
19 Davis, D et al 'Important issues in the drug treatment of schizophrenia' *Schizophrenia Bulletin* 1980, Vol 6, p 70.
20 *Psychiatric Drugs: Users' Experiences and Current Policy and Practice* (1988) MIND, London. See also, Cobb, A *Safe and Effective? MIND's View on Psychiatric Drugs, ECT and Psychosurgery* (1993) MIND, London.
21 Wallace, C et al 'Serious criminal offending and mental disorder' *British Journal of Psychiatry* 1988, Vol 172, p 477.

Overall, it would seem that proposals for community treatment and supervision are impracticable. Experiences in other countries suggest that where patients continue to refuse treatment, there is little alternative but to re-admit the patient to a psychiatric facility. Persuasive and cajoling community psychiatric nurses can only do so much with a patient who refuses to co-operate. Community treatment in whatever guise does not condone forcible treatment of a patient in the community environment. There therefore appears to be no effective sanction to ensure community treatment orders succeed.

4 The Position in England and Wales

(a) Introduction

Despite the existence of outpatient commitment and community treatment orders in parts of the US, Australia, New Zealand, Canada and elsewhere, such measures have been rejected in England and Wales. Those against the adoption of community treatment orders raised the practical difficulties associated with such orders as justification for their position. However, it was the possibility of abuse and the limited nature of the order that engendered the greatest concern.

(b) The Ten-Point Plan and supervision registers

After Ben Silcock's activities, the need for policy redevelopment in psychiatric provision was obvious and could no longer be sidelined. This one example of care failure was subject to a brief period of intense media exposure and from that time on recommendations for review and reform of the mental health system has never been far from the surface. In 1992 the Government instigated an internal review to develop a community care order.[22] The culmination of this review process was the ten-point plan, which was intended to reinforce current methods of caring for the mentally disordered in the community. The ten-point plan incorporated short-term expedients, which would allow much greater use of the existing legislative provisions within the MHA 1983. In addition, supervision registers were introduced to act as a central record of all mentally disordered people in the community who were at risk of causing harm to others or suffering

---

22 See Department of Health *The Ten Point Plan* (1993) Press Release, H93/908 and NHS Executive *Introduction of Supervision Registers for Mentally Ill People* (1994) HSG (94) 5.

harm themselves.[23] The introduction of these provisions was viewed as the foundation upon which a new supervised discharge order would be based; an order that would be the official response to community care in the future.

The NHS Management Executive introduced the supervision register in 1994[24] and all psychiatric units record patients who are discharged into the community. The aim of the register is to reduce the likelihood of harm being caused to the discharged patient, while at the same time minimising the potential risk of harm to third parties. However, not every patient is automatically placed on the register at the point of discharge from hospital. A risk assessment of the patient is carried out and its findings will direct the decision. The risk assessment criteria are:
(a) significant risk of suicide;
(b) significant risk of serious violence to others; or
(c) significant risk of severe self-neglect.[25]

Once the decision to include a patient on the register is made, evidence as to particular instigators of risk must be provided. Such factors might be the patient's failure to continue taking his medication or the likely impact of familial/societal attitude towards the patient. The decision must be supported by the evidence and recorded in writing, thereby enabling the decision-making process to be accessed by other professionals. The patient must be informed of the decision to include him on the register, both orally and in writing.[26]

The supervision register was introduced in order to rationalise records of mentally disordered individuals living in the community environment. The nature of the register requires the accumulation of information about designated people and such information can be made available to any person who is clinically involved with the patient, whether in the community or in hospital. Inclusion of the individual's name on the register may hinder effective integration in to the community. There is

23 NHS Management Executive 1994.
24 See Baker, E 'The introduction of supervision registers in England and Wales: a risk communications analysis' *Journal of Forensic Psychiatry* (1997) Vol 8, No 1, p 15; Prins, H 'I've got a little list (Koko: Mikado) But is it any use?: comments on the forensic aspects of supervision registers for the mentally ill' *Medicine, Science and Law* 1995, Vol 35, p 218.
25 NHS Executive *Introduction of Supervision Registers for Mentally Ill People* (1994) HSG (94), para 9.
26 All medical professionals and social workers involved and the patient's GP will have access to the information placed on the register, but the case of *R v Cardiff Crown Court, ex p Kellam* (1993) 16 BMLR 76 held that records of patient's movements which could be found within medical records were 'excluded material' within the meaning of the Police and Criminal Evidence Act 1984, s 11 and, as such, could not be disclosed to the police.

no time limitation for inclusion on the register and, therefore, a patient's name could remain on the register indefinitely. Inevitably, when a patient is included on the register they will be regarded as a risk to themselves or others and as such, this will influence the way in which those who have access to the register treat them. Clearly, there is an increased opportunity for discrimination against an individual on the register. The Disability Discrimination Act 1995 acknowledges the necessity for fair and equal treatment of people with disability within society, yet how the supervision register can be reconciled with the objective of the 1995 Act is unclear. The supervision register requires the segregation of psychiatric patients in the community who could represent a significant risk to themselves or others from those with mental health problems who are not considered to present a risk. By including an individual's name on the register, they are distinguished from others, and it is this distinction which could lead to discrimination. The function of supervision registers was promoted as a means of monitoring and supporting those deemed most at risk. MIND raised concerns about confidentiality and the possibility of people in need not seeking help for fear of inclusion on the register. There is no means to appeal against being placed on the register and it therefore presents clear possibilities for social control.[27]

(c) The Mental Health (Patients in the Community) Act 1995

The ten-point plan and the introduction of supervision registers were preliminary exercises in the lead-up to enacting new legislation. Since 1992 it had been recognised that new powers to subject an individual, on leaving hospital, to continued care in the community was needed. The Mental Health (Patients in the Community) Act 1995 came into force on the 1 April 1996 and introduced after-care under supervision.[28] The Mental Health (Patients in the Community) Act 1995 inserted new sections into the MHA 1983 (the MHA 1983, ss 25A – 25J). The Mental Health (Patients in the Community) Act 1995 was designed to provide greater control over mentally disordered individuals in the community. Baroness Cumberledge observed that 'the central principle of the ... [1995 Act] ... is that supervision cannot be separated from the after-care services ... [provided under the MHA 1983, s 117] ... which it exists to support'.[29]

27 Lowe-Ponsford, F, Wolfson, P & Lindesay, J 'Consultant psychiatrists' views on the supervision register' *Psychiatric Bulletin* 1998, Vol 22, p 409.
28 See generally, Hewitt, D 'The supervised discharge of former mental patients: part one and part two' *Litigation* 1997, Vols 16 and 17, nos 4 and 5, pp 149 and 197. See also, Bynoe, I 'Supervised discharge: what does it mean?' *Openmind* 1993, Vol 65, p 6.
29 HL Deb vol 564, cols 184-189, 11 May 1995 (Baroness Cumberledge).

Up until this time, control over discharged patients was limited, with the result that many were often caught in the 'revolving door'. Although the mental health system was at breaking point in the early 1990s, many argued against the introduction of greater coercion in the community, fearing that the European Convention on Human Rights (that endorsed removal of liberty where 'lawful detention' was required) would be contravened.[30] Provisions within the Mental Health (Patients in the Community) Act 1995 have consequently been limited and instead offer little more than a compromise between community treatment orders, as advocated by the Royal College of Psychiatrists in the 1980s, and guardianship.[31]

The supervised discharge order provides for a patient to be discharged from hospital, yet remain subject to a framework of support within the community. A level of compulsion in the use of after-care services is added by the Mental Health (Patients in the Community) Act 1995. The supervised discharge order is intended to provide a mutual obligation between the patient and the social services authority: the patient is required to fulfil the conditions attached to the order while the social services authority is obliged to provide the after-care services needed by the patient. The new sections within the MHA 1983 (namely the MHA 1983, ss 25A-25J) govern after-care under supervision. An application for supervision cannot be freestanding. In other words, an application cannot be made regardless of the patient's statutory status, ie whether the patient is detained and is closely connected to a patient's prior detention.[32]

Upon discharge, each patient is assigned a supervisor, who will ensure the necessary after-care facilities are provided, and a community responsible medical officer who ensures the medical treatment required by the discharged patient is administered. One professional may undertake both roles.[33] The supervisor's objective is to ensure contact between the patient and caring framework is maintained after discharge. This contact

30 Harrison, K 'Growing opposition to 'unconventional' bill' *Openmind* 1995, April/May, p 5. See also Crichton, J 'Supervised discharge' *Medicine, Science and Law* 1994, Vol 34, No 4, p 319.
31 Fennell, P 'Community care, community compulsion and the law' in Ritter, S et al (eds) *Collaborative Community Health Services: Together We Stand* (1996) Edward Arnold, London.
32 An application for supervision may only be made if the patient is liable to be detained in hospital for treatment and is over the age of 16 years (the MHA 1983, s 25A(1)).
33 However, the person fulfilling these roles has to be approved under the MHA 1983, s 12. This approval is carried out by the Regional Health Authorities whose power to approve has been delegated by the National Health Service Functions (Directions to Authorities and Administration Arrangements) Regulations 1991 (SI 1991/554, regs 3, 5, Sch 1). Guidance on the procedures for approval is

will enable the supervisor to remain aware of any changes in the patient's mental condition; any problems experienced by the patient in the community setting and satisfy any additional needs the patient might have. The patient may only be subject to after-care under supervision if over the age of 16 and previously formally detained in hospital under the MHA 1983.[34] The patient must have been diagnosed as suffering one of the following conditions: mental illness, severe mental impairment, psychopathic disorder or mental impairment. It must also be evidenced that if the patient was not to receive after-care services or supervision after discharge from hospital 'there would be a *substantial* risk of serious harm to the health or safety of the patient or the safety of other persons, or of the patient being seriously exploited'.[35] As the risk of harm must be substantial, this indicates that the after-care under supervision criteria is narrower than that for admission to hospital for treatment under the MHA 1983, s 3, thereby making it more difficult to satisfy. It must also be shown that if the patient were subject to supervision he would have a greater chance of securing after-care services, thereby ensuring a more successful transition from hospital to community.

Once the patient has been placed under supervision, the 'responsible after-care bodies' (which are the health authority and the local social services authority) have the power to impose, on the recommendation of the responsible medical officer, requirements for securing after-care facilities. These conditions are:

(a) that the patient reside as a specified place;
(b) that the patient attend at specified places and times for the purpose of medical treatment, occupation, education or training; and
(c) that access to the patient be given, at any place where the patient is residing, to the supervisor, any registered medical practitioner or any approved social worker or to any other person authorised by the supervisor.

These powers are clearly moulded on the essential powers of guardianship found in the MHA 1983. The powers allow the supervisor to reach the patient and, by specifying where the patient is to live and how he is to maintain contact with the caring framework, the chance of the patient becoming lost to the caring infrastructure may be lessened. However, the power to enforce these requirements is not found within the supervisor's

---

contained in Department of Health Circular No HC (90) 21. The medical practitioners should have special experience in the diagnosis or treatment of mental disorder, have three years or more post-registration clinical experience and should be members of the Royal College of Psychiatrists.
34   The MHA 1983, s 25A(4).
35   The MHA 1983, s 25A(4)(b).

role but is given to the 'responsible after-care bodies'. This attempts to create a centralised system rather than rely upon the individual professionals involved in each case, thereby creating a more fluid and consistent approach to the care of the mentally disordered in the community.

What makes the after-care under supervision power different from guardianship is the additional power, under the MHA 1983, s 25D(4), for the supervisor to 'take and convey' the individual subject to supervision to the place in question.[36] Clearly, this section provides the supervisor and the 'responsible after-care bodies' with more power to ensure the patient fulfils the requirements attached to the order. It was expected that the power to take and convey could be delegated to other bodies, such as the police or psychiatric facility staff. This provision is controversial and has been condemned as a socially acceptable form of civil arrest. In the initial stages of debate as to the future of community care in the late 1980s and the early 1990s, the main concern was that medical professionals, nurses and social workers would be required to force treatment upon unwilling patients within the community environment. The take and convey provision attempts to circumvent this as it allows the professional to take the patient out of the community and back into the institutional environment, which is considered a traditionally acceptable place for treatment to be carried out. Although the MHA 1983, s 25D(4) does not explicitly provide a power to treat without consent, if the individual is unco-operative he will be removed from the community and dealt with in hospital.

The European Court of Human Rights case of *Winterwerp v The Netherlands*[37] provides the criteria which amount to lawful arrest and detention in the case of a psychiatric patient with regard to the European Convention on Human Rights, Art 5. Article 5 provides that everyone has the right to liberty and security of the person except where detention is lawful for the prevention of the 'spreading of infectious diseases, of persons of unsound mind, alcoholics or drug addicts or vagrants...'.[38] It was observed that:

'Article 5(1) obviously cannot be taken as permitting the detention of a person simply because his views or behaviour deviate from the norms prevailing in a particular society.[39] To hold otherwise would

---

36 The MHA 1983, s 137 defines 'convey' as 'any other expression denoting removal from one place to another'.
37 (1979) 2 EHRR 387.
38 Article 5(1)(e).
39 (1979) 2 EHRR 387 at para 37 of the judgment.

not be reconcilable with the text of Article 5(1), which sets out an exhaustive list of exceptions calling for a narrow interpretation'.[40]

In *X v United Kingdom*,[41] the criteria were confirmed. It was observed that:

> 'except in emergency cases, the individual concerned must be reliably shown to be of unsound mind, that is to say, a true mental disorder must be established before a competent authority on the basis of objective medical expertise; the mental disorder must be of a kind or degree warranting compulsory confinement; and the validity of continued confinement depends upon the persistence of such a disorder'.[42]

If a person is to be lawfully apprehended on the grounds of mental disorder or impairment, there must be expert evidence to support the contention that the person is suffering from some mental instability which necessitates detention within hospital.[43] However, in the case of an emergency, *X v United Kingdom*[44] did not regard the *Winterwerp* decision as necessarily binding. In an emergency, the expert opinion can be obtained after the patient has been admitted to hospital. The court held that '[a] wide discretion must in the nature of things be enjoyed by the national authority empowered to order such emergency confinements'.[45] The evidential requirement is high and it must support the view that detention in hospital is vital. If the refusal of an individual to attend a place for treatment is not regarded as an 'emergency', then it seems unlikely that the individual's refusal to attend a day-centre, training or occupational therapy class will be considered an emergency. In which case, how a professional would be able to justify use of the take and convey provision in light of the position adopted by the European Court of Human Rights is unclear. Despite this difficulty, in 1995 Baroness Cumberledge obviously regarded the 'take and convey' provision as something that could be steered according to the circumstances.

> 'If a patient is on supervised discharge, the health authority would have accepted a supervision application at the outset, and ... the authorisation of a power to convey is implicit in that original

---

40   (1979) 2 EHRR 387 at 401-2.
41   (1981) 4 EHRR 188.
42   (1981) 4 EHRR 188 at para 40 of the judgment at 202.
43   This must be accepted by a panel of like professionals: see *Lubert v Italy* (1984) Series A, No 75, judgment of 23 February.
44   (1981) 4 EHRR 188.
45   (1981) 4 EHRR 188 at para 41.

acceptance. [The] ... power would be used only under limited circumstances ... it may be particularly valuable in emergencies.'[46]

Once the patient has been taken to hospital, the consent to treatment provisions within the MHA 1983, Pt IV can only be used if, once the patient has been conveyed to the hospital, he is then formally admitted to hospital under the MHA 1983, s 3. Once this has taken place, Part IV can be used and the patient can then be subject to medication and treatment without his consent if all the other requirements are satisfied.

The Mental Health (Patients in the Community) Act 1995 represents a clear contradiction of one of the aims of the MHA 1983: that of the 'clean legal break'. With the enactment of the 1983 Act, it was envisaged that once a patient was discharged from hospital, he would be in exactly the same position as any other member of society. The only route to enable the enforced treatment of a former patient was to apply for admission for treatment under the MHA 1983, s 3, which would only be successful if the former patient fulfilled the requirements laid down by the provision. The supervised discharge order in conjunction with the take and convey provision erodes this 'clean legal break' as it prevents former patients being treated like everyone else.[47]

After-care under supervision can last for a period of six months in the first instance, is renewable for a further six months[48] and thereafter annually.[49] The procedure for renewal requires the community responsible medical officer to furnish a report[50] within the last two months of the current supervision period. This report has to examine whether the patient continues to satisfy the conditions for supervision:

(a) the patient is suffering from mental disorder, being mental illness, severe mental impairment, psychopathic disorder or mental impairment;

---

46 HL Deb vol 563, col 1254, 4 April 1995 (Baroness Cumberledge).
47 Modern psychiatry relies upon pharmacological treatment and therefore 'how [can] it be demonstrated that the treatment was no longer necessary if it was genuinely believed that it was only the treatment which was preventing the deterioration?': Parkin, A 'Mental Health (Patients in the Community) Act 1995' (1996) *Modern Law Review* Vol 59, No 3, p 414.
48 The MHA 1983, s 25G(2)(a).
49 The MHA 1983, s 25G(2)(b).
50 The report should be kept with the patient's admission documents so that future consideration as to whether the patient should cease to be subject to supervision can be made having regard to the report. See Mental Health (Hospital, Guardianship and Consent to Treatment) Regulations 1983, SI 1983/893, reg 10, and form 30.

(b) there would be a substantial risk of serious harm to the health or safety of the patient or the safety of other persons, or of the patient being seriously exploited, if he were not to receive the after-care services provided for him under the MHA 1983, s 117 below; or
(c) his being subject to after-care under supervision is likely to secure that he receives the after-care services so provided.[51]

In addition, the community responsible medical officer must examine the patient to ensure that living within the community is still benefiting the patient and that inpatient care is unnecessary.[52] The report cannot be made unless the MHA 1983, s 5 is fulfilled. This requires the community responsible medical officer to consult with:
(a) the patient;
(b) the supervisor;
(c) one or more persons who are professionally concerned with the medical treatment of the patient;
(d) one or more persons who are professionally concerned with the after-care services; and
(e) any other person that the community responsible medical officer believes to have a substantial role in the care of the patient, but who is not professionally concerned with the provision of care.

A statutory duty to review the position of a patient subject to after-care under supervision is enshrined in the MHA 1983, s 25E. It provides two categories in which review of the after-care provisions is necessary. The first is where the patient refuses to or neglects to satisfy the requirements attached to the supervised discharge order.[53] Upon review of the patient's position within the community, if he fails to cooperate, modification of the order may be required. However, where the patient fails to continue taking his medication, then the 'responsible after-care bodies' are under a duty to consider whether the patient needs to be admitted to hospital for treatment. The second category is where the patient's condition has improved to the extent where it is thought unnecessary to continue after-care under supervision.[54] Before any modifications are made to the order, the 'responsible after-care bodies' are required to consult with the patient, the carers of the patient and (unless the patient objects) the nearest relative. Once the modifications have been made, the 'responsible after-care bodies' are required to:

---

51 The MHA 1983, s 25G(3)(b).
52 The MHA 1983, s 25G(3)(a).
53 The MHA 1983, s 25E(2).
54 The MHA 1983, s 25E(4)(a).

'(a) inform the patient both orally and in writing;
(b) inform any person who has been consulted under paragraph (b);
(c) inform in writing any person who has been consulted under paragraph (c)'

that the modifications have been made and are in operation.

Perhaps the most innovative aspect of the Mental Health (Patients in the Community) Act 1995 is the statutory recognition of consultation in the decision-making process. The importance of this is clear because, in addition to the express duty being placed upon the decision-maker to consult parties involved in the patient's care, it also recognises the need to discuss care options with the patient. Consultation embodies an obligation to provide information to all persons concerned with the care of the patient. During this process views and objections to the proposed course of action may be given. However, the obligation to consult does not include the requirement to take up the opinions and suggestions expressed, but merely to consider these when making the final decision. A decision-making body may fail to comply with a duty to consult not only by total inaction, but also by inadequate consultation. Consultation must be made at a time when the proposals are at an early stage and hence can be easily changed.[55] Those proposing possible treatment or care must have adequate reasons for these proposals and they must give the recipient sufficient time to consider and respond. Consultation with the individual concerned must be clearly and conscientiously taken into account during the process of finalising any care or treatment plans.[56] In *R v Secretary of State for Social Services, ex p Association of Metropolitan Authorities*[57] Webster J observed that the:

'essence of consultation is the communication of a genuine invitation to give advice and a genuine receipt of that advice. To achieve an effective consultation, the consultor must supply sufficient information so that helpful advice can be tendered'.

Simon Brown LJ observed that:

'Prominent amongst the considerations relevant to determining the precise demands of consultation in a given case will be:

---

55 *R v Brent London Borough Council, ex p Gunning* (1985) 84 LGR 168.
56 *R v Brent London Borough Council, ex p Gunning* (1985) 84 LGR 168 per Hodgeson J at 189.
57 [1986] 1 WLR 1.

(a) whether the obligation is statutory and absolute or implied in common fairness;
(b) the urgency with which it is necessary to reach a decision. This may impose constraints lest the very process of consultation itself causes delay such as to pre-empt a particular proposal or other possibly appropriate decisions; ... [and] ...
(c) the extent to which during earlier discussions or consultative processes opportunities have been afforded for views to be expressed by interested, and in particular opposing, parties and the likelihood, therefore, of material and informed additional views or information emerging upon further consultation'.[58]

Although the need to consult interested parties (including the patient) has been explicitly recognised, at each stage of the application process where consultation is required the responsible decision-making bodies may overrule the patient's objection for the nearest relative to be consulted. If:
(a) the decision-maker considers the patient has a propensity to violent or dangerous behaviour towards others; and
(b) the community responsible medical officer considers it appropriate for steps to be taken,

the patient's view may be overruled.

A patient who is subject to after-care under supervision is entitled to make an application to a Mental Health Review Tribunal under the MHA 1983, s 66.[59] However, this power does not include a right for the medical member of the Tribunal to examine the patient without the patient's consent.[60] Therefore, in addition to the Mental Health Review Tribunal carrying out its established role regarding detained patients, it will also hear appeals against supervision and make recommendations to the community responsible medical officer that supervision ought to be considered. However, the Tribunal has no power to ensure these suggestions are followed. The Mental Health (Patients in the Community) Act 1995 will allow the Mental Health Review Tribunal to reconsider the case if the community responsible medical officer decides not to apply its recommendations.[61] However, applications to the Mental Health

---

58 *R v Secretary of State for Education, ex p Morris* [1996] ELR 162, (1995) LEXIS transcript, 21 December.
59 Department of Health *Caring for People: Training for the Future* (1993) HMSO, London, para 7.16.
60 Where the patient refuses to be examined the Mental Health Review Tribunal Rules 1983, SI 1983/942, r 19(2) provides that in such instances the application will be deemed as having been withdrawn.
61 Mental Health (Patients in the Community) Act 1995, Sch 1, para 10(2).

Review Tribunal from patients who are subject to supervision have been low, owing to the minimal usage of after-care under supervision.[62] After-care under supervision has not been actively embraced by the psychiatric profession for a variety of reasons, not least the restrictive nature of the order in practice and the complexity of applying the order. The responsibility of applying the order falls largely on the shoulders of the relevant health authority and the individual responsible medical officer, yet to ensure the patient's needs are satisfied in the community the relevant social services authority has to be actively involved in the planning and implementation of after-care. This detailed preparation might seem rather disproportionate to the actual benefits to the patient concerned or the authorities. As the order has no sanctions to ensure it is adhered to by the patient in the community, the fall-back position of re-admission to hospital must be relied on. The Mental Health (Patients in the Community) Act 1995 has been little more than a compromise between advocates of extensive community treatment provisions and the human rights lobbyists who have argued against any form of community coercion. The result is a toothless legislative provision, which offers little to anyone, a criticism that sounds all too familiar.

5 Conclusion

After the tragic circumstances surrounding Ben Silcock's injuries in 1992, the mental health system was exposed to intense media interest. This coverage highlighted the failings of community care and galvanised the then Conservative Government into action. Ben Silcock managed to achieve something which professionals within the psychiatric profession, service users, academics and mental health charities had failed to do: bring the question of reform to the top of the political agenda. After a number of false starts in the 1980s with the suggested adoption of community treatment orders, the Mental Health (Patients in the Community) Act 1995 was enacted, and introduced after-care under supervision. At the time, the supervised discharge order was heralded as a new way forward for the provision of mental health care in the community environment, but in reality it was a compromise between two camps. Advocates of community treatment orders believed community care would only be successful if professionals had access to sufficient control over patients, while social control theorists were concerned that the community environment should remain free from coercion at all costs. The result of this has proved

62 Knight, A, Mumford, D & Nichol, B 'Supervised discharge order: the first years in the south and west region' *Psychiatric Bulletin* 1998, Vol 22, p 418; Mohan, D, Thompson, C & Mullee, M 'Preliminary evaluation of supervised discharge in the south and west region' *Psychiatric Bulletin* 1998, Vol 22, p 421.

disappointing. After-care under supervision adds little to the existing provisions within the MHA 1983 and the threat of re-admission to hospital remains the only sanction to unco-operative patients. Both community treatment orders and after-care under supervision are principally concerned with the enforcement of medication. The other advantages to community care, such as the maintenance of the familial support network and patient independence, have been overshadowed by this apparent emphasis on medication. Owing to this, the need for adequate support structures within the community has been seriously underestimated and it is this that has so far proved to be the undoing of community care.

Chapter 6
Community care: the road to disillusionment

1 Introduction

In the early years of the community care policy, its implementation was thought to involve little more than removing the patient from the confines of the psychiatric hospital and ensuring the continuation of medication in the community environment. This approach was flawed, as it failed to recognise the important role that community services played. For many discharged patients their support needs remain high and ongoing supervision and treatment are essential. By the mid-1990s, people were increasingly disillusioned by community care and what the policy could offer. Service users who invariably sought a less restrictive care environment were frequently left to fend for themselves upon discharge from hospital. Service providers also favoured a non-hospital approach where possible, as not only was it regarded as more cost-effective but it was also recognised as having numerous advantages for the patient.[1] Yet despite the support of community care in theory, the policy was far from perfect in practice. Numerous reports throughout the 1990s have indicated serious failings in the policy's practical implementation[2] and the enactment of the Mental Health (Patients in the Community) Act 1995 did little to allay the increasing levels of criticism. The introduction of

1 Department of Health *Better Services for the Mentally Ill* Cm 6233 (1975) HMSO, London.
2 See for example, Ritchie, J et al *Report of the Inquiry into the Care and Treatment of Christopher Clunis* (1994) HMSO, London; Woodley Team Report (The) *Report of the Independent Review Panel to East London and The City Health Authority and Newham Council* (1995), London: East London and The City Health Authority and Newham Council; *Steering Committee Report of the Confidentiality into Homicides and Suicides by Mentally Ill People* (1996) Royal College of Psychiatrists, London.

after-care under supervision by the 1995 Act had been heralded as the way forward for the provision of mental health care in the community environment, but it failed because too little control was injected into the order. Professionals had inadequate control over patients under community supervision and the order added little to the existing provisions within the MHA 1983. The threat of re-admission to hospital remains the only sanction to unco-operative patients.

The purpose of this chapter is to consider two of the key factors that contributed to the failure of community care. One of the most startling oversights has been the disregard of housing provision and its role in the integration of patients into the community. Housing provision was overlooked and was not actively considered until the final stages of the policy's implementation, yet housing represents a critical link connecting psychiatric patients in the community with the mental health system. It has been acknowledged that 'adequate housing has a major role to play in community care and is often the key to independent living'.[3] It is essential that released psychiatric patients be provided with an adequate base in the community. Indeed, its importance should not be underestimated. In *The Report into the Care and Treatment of Christopher Clunis* it was observed that Christopher Clunis had been 'treated as ... single, homeless, and itinerant with no family ties, and the more they treated him as such the more he began to fulfil that role'.[4] The improvement of his condition was hampered by spasmodic homelessness resulting in loss of contact with the mental health structure. Similar housing inadequacies were found to exist in the care of Stephen Laudat, leading him to experience difficulties with the re-integration process.[5] Although the reports observed a connection between failures in housing provision and subsequent deterioration in the patient's mental condition, it was noted in the *Report of the Confidential Inquiry into Homicides and Suicides by Mentally Ill People* that these failures continued to occur, and it seemed that little was being done to rectify the problem. This report went on to say that, '[t]his leads us to the alarming conclusion that these individual reports make little lasting impact on services for mentally ill people'.[6] What the reports do illustrate is the necessity of ensuring that

---

3   See generally, Cunningham, R & Spenser, S 'The role of housing managers in the implementation of community care' *Social Policy and Administration* 1996, Vol 30, No 3, p 227.
4   Ritchie, J et al *Report of the Inquiry into the Care and Treatment of Christopher Clunis* (1994) HMSO, London.
5   Woodley Team Report (The) *Report of the Independent Review Panel to East London and The City Health Authority and Newham Council* (1995), London, East London and The City Health Authority and Newham Council.
6   Ritchie, J et al *Report of the Inquiry into the Care and Treatment of Christopher Clunis* (1994) HMSO, London, p 64.

patients discharged from hospital are provided with adequate housing to enable them to establish roots in, what might be, unfamiliar territory.

A second factor which has prevented the effective integration of psychiatric patients into the community is the lack of occupational/ employment prospects and the social activity associated with these opportunities. Patients in psychiatric facilities are offered a ready-made social setting, which enables them to improve essential skills for independent living in the community. Opportunities to maintain these skills need to be made available once the patient has been discharged. Regular social activity is an inherent part of the community care policy, for such integration helps to obliterate the social 'outcast' which has commonly been associated with released patients in the past. Such integration allows the patient to become more secure in the community environment, thereby allowing him to benefit more fully from the policy. However, the clear benefits associated with these occupational opportunities have been threatened, because of the high levels of disability discrimination and ongoing problems with stigma. The Disability Discrimination Act 1995 provides a legislative framework which attempts to limit discrimination in employment, education, the provision of goods and services and public transport. The 1995 Act therefore attempts to ensure that fundamental aspects of societal living are not restricted to the able-bodied or those who are free from mental illness.

2 Inter-Agency Co-operation

Many of the practical difficulties that have been associated with community care provision, such as ensuring adequate housing, maintaining regular contact between the patient and the mental health services and the assumption of responsibility for providing these services, also relate to ongoing difficulties in achieving successful inter-agency co-operation. Staite and Martin recognise that '[w]orking together is not easy. Old rivalries, old misconceptions – even old personal animosities – can act as a barrier to creative multi-agency working'.[7] For the community care policy to be successful, it is essential that adequate provision be made for its practical implementation. Legal responsibility for supplying such services can be found with a variety of agencies: local social services authorities, health authorities and housing departments. Each agency has its own approach to supplying services and the difficulty has, therefore, been the creation of a uniform co-operative of agencies working together

---

7   Staite, C & Martin, N 'What else can we do? New Initiatives in diversion from custody' (1993) 157 Justice of the Peace, p 280.

for the patient's benefit. Lack of inter-agency co-operation was found to be one of the main shortcomings in the preparations for Christopher Clunis' discharge.[8] Minimising the extent to which communication failures occur could ultimately improve the clinical and social outcomes for many discharged psychiatric patients. However, despite the recognition of communication failures in the Clunis Report, subsequent inquiries have continued to highlight similar problems and it is questionable whether effective inter-agency co-operation can ever be achieved in practice owing to the constant pressures on agencies.[9]

3 The National Health Service and Community Care Act 1990

Since the enactment of the National Health Service and Community Care Act 1990 the system of health and social service provision has become more complicated and the difficulties outlined above have been magnified and compounded. Before the enactment of the National Health Service and Community Care Act 1990, regional health authorities managed the health service. The 1990 Act introduced the internal market for provision of services and created a tier system whereby the NHS Management Executive became the governing body of the healthcare system and is accountable to the Department of Health. Health service providers and those purchasing services were separated. Providers of health services are NHS trusts and the purchasers consist of district health authorities and fund-holding GPs. The purchasers of services buy the necessary services they need, whether for the district or for patients, from the service providers. The increased level of complexity has inevitably influenced the ability to co-ordinate service provision, making careful planning and constant communication between agencies essential. Difficulties which have existed since the creation of the internal market may be dispelled somewhat as the Labour Government has shifted its policy and intends to abolish the internal market. In 1998, proposals were introduced to create a *new NHS*, which would provide greater opportunity to combine both social care and health care budgets.[10] It is hoped that these changes will

---

8   Prins, H 'All tragedy is the failure of communication: The sad saga of Christopher Clunis' *Medicine, Science and Law* 1994, Vol 34, p 277. See also, Ritchie, J et al *Report of the Inquiry into the Care and Treatment of Christopher Clunis* (1994) HMSO, London.
9   *Report of the Confidential Inquiry into Homicides and Suicides by Mentally Ill People* (1996). See also Blom-Cooper, L et al *The Falling Shadow: One Patient's Mental Health Care 1978 – 1993* (1995) Duckworth, London.
10 Department of Health *Modernising Mental Health Services: Safe, Sound and Supportive* (1998) HMSO, London.

provide the possibility for improving links between different agencies in the future. Improvements to inter-agency co-operation will depend largely on the willingness of agency workers to collaborate with other agencies in an effort to achieve a worthwhile outcome for the individual patient concerned.[11]

Since the enactment of the National Health Service and Community Care Act 1990, local authorities have been provided with greater power to provide services for the vulnerable. The key objectives of the 1990 legislation were:
(a) to promote the domiciliary day and respite services to enable people to live in their own homes whenever possible;
(b) to make proper assessment of need and good care management the cornerstone of high quality care;
(c) to ensure that service providers make practical support for carers a high priority; and
(d) to secure better value for taxpayers' money by introducing a new funding structure for social care.[12]

The National Health Service and Community Care Act 1990, Pt III implements the proposals submitted by *The Griffiths Report* that local social services should 'ensure that the needs of individuals within the specified groups are identified, packages of care devised, and services co-ordinated'.[13] The National Health Service and Community Care Act 1990 imposes a duty upon local authorities to assess and meet any identified needs.[14] This duty only extends to the mentally disordered, elderly or generally vulnerable. For those who suffer from a physical condition, their particular needs are met by the Chronically Sick and Disabled Persons Act 1970, the Disabled Persons (Employment) Act 1958 and the Disabled Persons (Services, Consultation and Representation) Act 1986.

---

11 See Crawford, A & Jones, M 'Inter-agency co-operation and community-based crime prevention' *British Journal of Criminology* 1995, Vol 35, p 17.
12 Fish, D 'Community care: duties towards mentally ill people and their families' *Legal Action* (1995) November, p 20.
13 Griffiths, Sir Roy *Community Care: Agenda for Action* (1988) HMSO, London, p vii.
14 As the duty to provide after-care facilities is founded upon the assessment of patient need, the duty requires discretionary choices to be made.

4 The Role of Housing

(a) Background

Proponents of community care have argued that reliance on the institution to provide psychiatric care merely isolated patients from the rest of society and subjected them to unnecessarily extensive control. Community care, on the other hand, was regarded as a policy that sought to provide a structure of care, which would enable the mentally disordered to have some choice in their care environment and allow the cultivation of important skills for independent living. Therefore, the provision of alternative housing was an inherent aspect of the policy.[15] However, the issue of housing was not incorporated into the preliminary preparations of community care leaving it disorganised and reliant on inter-agency co-operation in the early stages.[16] It has been observed that '[f]undamental divisions remain between the health, social care and housing fields which are having a direct negative impact on users, carers and the community at large'.[17] These divisions are a result of professional, cultural and institutional differences, which have led each department to maintain varying priorities.

The *Confidential Inquiry* concluded that changes in the pattern of care were accepted as a factor which could lead to changes in the patient's mental state.[18] The upheaval associated with leaving institutional care can be minimised by providing a solid base in which the patient can obtain and maintain some roots. The provision of decent housing is therefore vital to ensure community care success. The enactment of the National Health Service and Community Care Act 1990 brought about changes in the attitude towards the role of housing in community care. The debate as to whether there was a role for housing in community care shifted to how housing could be used to improve the lives of the vulnerable. For the first time, in 1993/4, the housing issue was included in the Social Services Conference and the NHS Hospital and Care Premises Management Conference agenda. Also, the Support Force paper

---

15 Department of Health *Caring for People: Community Care in the Next Decade and Beyond* Cm 849 (1989) HMSO, London, and in the joint DOE/DOH Housing and Community Care Circular 10/92 12, (1992) HMSO, London.
16 Pinch, H 'The barriers to homeless people accessing community care' *Community Care, Planning and Management* 1993, Vol 1, No 5, p 131 and Fletcher, P 'Housing and community care: from rhetoric to reality' *Community Care Planning and Management* 1993, Vol 1, No 5, p 137.
17 Palmer, J, Harker, M, Kilgallon, B & Tickell, C *Making Connections* (1996) Unpublished.
18 Ritchie, J et al *Report of the Inquiry into the Care and Treatment of Christopher Clunis* (1994) HMSO, London, p 69.

Implementing Community Care – A Framework for Integrating the Housing Agenda was widely circulated.[19] The Department of the Environment formally acknowledged the social role of housing management, which resulted in an increase in collaboration between agencies.[20]

(b) Types of housing provision

If it is accepted that appropriate housing provision plays a key role in the success of the community care programme, then what types of housing within the community are available to the discharged patient? Mainstream housing may not be suitable for patients who have adapted to institutional life. Although constant supervision is not feasible in the community at large, a level of assistance may still be necessary. The accommodation has to reflect this by providing a measure of support to the patient. Accommodation specifically built or adapted to reflect this need is termed 'special needs' housing.[21] 'Special needs' housing consists of a range of housing, from housing with high-intensity support to accommodation which provides limited support in a flat-share situation for those former patients that have progressed sufficiently to lead relatively independent lives.[22] Although the 'special needs' housing scheme provides step-by-step assistance, a number of problems exist. The main difficulty is the lack of available 'special needs' housing. In addition, the places that do exist are expensive to fund. Those patients that are fortunate enough to receive a place inevitably have the same problem at the end of their short 'special needs' stay. Once out of 'special needs' accommodation they must find shelter in the mainstream housing system. It has been argued by Means and Wheeler that the heavy emphasis of central government on such 'sheltered housing' schemes deflects attention away from the need to provide enough affordable, appropriate and flexible housing within mainstream provision[23] and as a result, only a small percentage of

---

19　Department of Health *Implementing Community Care – A Framework for Integrating the Housing Agenda into Community Care: Community Care Support Force* (1993) HMSO, London.
20　See generally, Cowan, D 'Accommodating community care' *Journal of Law and Society* 1995, Vol 22, No 2, p 212.
21　Dimond, B *Legal Aspects of Care in the Community* (1997) MacMillan, London, particularly pp 530-41.
22　Clapham, D & Smith, S 'Housing policy and needs' *Policy and Politics* 1990, Vol 18, No 3, p 193.
23　Means, R 'Older people in British housing studies' *Housing Studies* 1987, Vol 2, No 2, p 82 and Wheeler, R 'Housing policy and elderly people' in Phillipson, C and Walker, A (eds) *Ageing and Social Policy: A Critical Assessment* (1988) Gower, Aldershot.

discharged psychiatric patients have the housing opportunity they need. Sinclair believes the housing problems faced by discharged psychiatric patients stem from within mainstream housing rather than from restricted 'special needs' housing places.[24] In practice, discharged patients fall into a hierarchy of need: those patients that although discharged will continue to need high-level support and those patients that have progressed enough to live without such intensive support. The latter category of patients can be further sub-divided into patients who are sufficiently capable of living in the community in 'sheltered' housing and patients who are able to live in the community relatively independently in mainstream housing. Although the demand for 'special needs' housing is apparent, the housing available is insufficient and, consequently, released psychiatric patients have had to rely upon mainstream provision. For many released psychiatric patients the mainstream housing system has proved to be too intimidating. For other patients, the mainstream system has failed to meet their needs.

Mainstream housing is limited in supply and determining the availability of such housing cannot be ascertained simply by the number of houses/flats in existence alone. Issues such as the affordability of the property affect such figures as do the areas where such housing is found, the facilities and amenities available and the accommodation's state of repair. There have been a number of studies made to assess the availability of housing, yet none of these studies have emphasised the affect the community care policy has and will continue to have on the housing market. Studies such as the one Niner[25] carried out in 1989 estimated that by the year 2001, an extra 2.2 million to 3 million households would need housing because of an aging population. If community care continues, to what extent will mental health patients be provided with the accommodation they need? The report commissioned by the National Federation of Housing Associations[26] estimated that:

(a) People with learning disabilities in long-stay institutions: 2,000 to 3,000 units per year would be needed over the next decade.
(b) People with mental health problems in hospitals: 2,000 to 3,000 units per year would be needed over the next decade.
(c) Increase in elderly people over 85: about 3,500 new units of supported accommodation required per annum to meet their needs.

24 Sinclair, I 'Residential care for elderly people' in Sinclair, I (ed) *Residential Care: the Research Reviewed* (1988) HMSO, London.
25 Niner, P *Housing Needs in the 1990's: An Interim Assessment* (1989) National Housing Forum, National Federation of Housing Associations, London.
26 Office for Public Management *Assessment of the Housing Requirements of People With Special Needs Over the Next Decade* (1992) National Federation of Housing Associations, London.

(d) Changes in funding of residential and nursing home care: between 2,700 and 6,750 people per year might require alternative housing.
(e) People with mental health problems who are homeless, in temporary accommodation or in prison may require as many as 15,000 units in total.
(f) People with learning disabilities living with families: 2,000 units per year may be needed.

During the past 20 years while governmental policy has encouraged the care of the mentally disordered in the community, it has also emphasised the importance of encouraging owner-occupation to break local authority control over rented accommodation, and to take and maintain comprehensive control over public expenditure. A conflict exists between these two aims, because community care has increased the number of people in the community requiring inexpensive accommodation, while control of public expenditure has led to increases in rental prices. The goal of breaking the housing monopoly initially began by encouraging the sale of council houses and by cutting back the monetary resources placed in housing investment programmes. The Housing Act 1988 and the Local Government and Housing Act 1989 took this further. The objective of the 1988 Act was to 'free' rent levels and allow market forces to set them. Before this, a system of rent regulation existed under the guise of the Rent Act 1965. Rent regulation took place under the concept of the 'fair rent'. The statutory definition of 'fair rent' was then assimilated into the Rent Act 1977. Determining a fair rent depended on the age, character, locality and state of repair of the dwelling house and whether or not the property was furnished.[27]

In *Palmer v Peabody Trust*[28] Lord Widgery LJ observed that 'one must ... have regard to ... factors which tend to push rents up or down in the market' when attempting to establish a fair rent.[29] In 1971, the report of the Francis Committee on the operation of the Rents Acts was published[30] and it observed that when the concept of 'fair rent' was invoked, three elements appeared to play important roles in its determination:
(a) calculating what would be a reasonable rent on the basis of various conventional criteria;
(b) looking at recently registered market rents in respect of which there was no scarcity;
(c) looking at comparables.

---

27 Rent Act 1977, s 70(1).
28 [1975] QB 604 at 608C.
29 See *Metropolitan Property Holdings v Finegold* [1975] 1 WLR 349 at 351F.
30 Cm 4609 (1971) HMSO, London.

The courts' attitude towards playing a role in the assessment of 'fair rent' has been unenthusiastic. Lord Kilbrandon said in *Mason v Skilling*[31] that '[t]he fixing of a fair rent calls for skilled estimates of a hypothetical figure, namely, the rent which a landlord could demand and a tenant would be prepared to pay if the market were roughly in a state of equilibrium ... [it is a] valuation problem rather than a legal question of law'. The task of assessing and determining the rent levels was largely left to the discretion of rent officers. The rent officer and the appeal rent assessment committee, using the criteria in the Rent Act 1977, would establish a 'fair rent' based on a hypothetical market rent for each property, assuming an equilibrium between supply and demand. The 'fair rent' provided a checking mechanism to prevent unnecessarily abusive rent levels and the exploitation of the vulnerable.

However, with the enactment of the Housing Act 1988 and the Local Government and Housing Act 1989, the requirement of determining a 'fair rent' was abolished for most post-Act tenancies and rent levels became subject to market forces. The intention was to allow the market to determine appropriate rent levels and then develop a subsidy system (the creation of housing benefit[32]) for those on low incomes. The administrative and financial context of the legislation suggests that the rent should usually be set at below market level 'within the reach of those in low paid employment'.[33] However, the inevitable result of this legislation has been an increase in rent prices.[34] With the increasing levels of psychiatric patients being released into the community, the high rental demands have inevitably influenced the housing provision available to them. In addition to the cessation of the 'fair rent', the 1988 Act[35] also introduced more deregulation by reducing security of tenure for some forms of tenancy. These measures in the Housing Act 1988 have made the position of the

31 [1974] 1 WLR 1437 at 1443C.
32 It must be noted that rent rebates and rent allowances (for the public and private sector respectively) have been present for many years. However, their take-up rate has grown rapidly since 1989, when subsidies shifted from bricks and mortar to people.
33 Housing Corporation *The Tenant's Guarantee: Guidance on the Management of Accommodation Let on Assured Tenancies by Registered Housing Associations* (1991) Housing Corporation, London, p 6.
34 'Average rents in new lettings rose from £18.16 in the second quarter of 1988 to £31.89 by the second quarter of 1991, an increase of 81%. Rents for lettings of newly developed homes (new lets) increased by 104%. In comparison, the ... [Retail Price Index] ... increased by 26%. Average rents have therefore, risen at three times the rate of general inflation': Randolph, B 'The re-privatisation of housing associations' in Malpass, P & Means, R (eds) *Implementing Housing Policy* (1993) Open University Press, Milton Keynes. See also the Housing and Construction Statistics published quarterly and annually by the Department Of Environment for up to date figures.
35 See also the Housing Act 1996 amendment to the Housing Act 1988.

vulnerable much more problematic. It has made finding affordable accommodation more difficult and has opened up the possibility of vulnerable people being exposed to eviction and tenancy cessation.

As the provision of housing in the rental sector is now the province of market forces, the level of adequately repaired housing has also been influenced because profit margins now take priority over the provision of decently repaired and furnished accommodation. Accommodation that is available to the newly-discharged psychiatric patient, as is noted above, is already limited because such people often need additional facilities, such as nearby shops and medical services. They also need accommodation that is fully repaired, furnished and suited to their needs. Stephen Laudat's needs were overlooked when he was provided with an unfurnished flat and this has since been connected with his violent outburst.[36] Owing to the implementation of community care, the reliance on market forces to establish rental levels and the reduction in good quality housing to meet the needs of vulnerable people, the homelessness problem has become increasingly widespread.

(c) Homelessness

'How can the researcher begin to define it ... writers have used it in almost every conceivable way – from meaning complete shelterlessness to simply having serious accommodation difficulties, from having no fixed abode to living in a hostel or lodging house.'[37]

This quotation highlights the difficulties attached to defining such a social occurrence. Broad definitions of homelessness include living in bed and breakfast accommodation, whereas the narrower definitions look to absolute 'rooflessness' as evidence of homelessness. The importance attached to arriving at a definition is immense because as Greve observes, 'the resources which would be required to tackle and eliminate these problems explains the unwillingness of central and local government to accept the broader definitions of homelessness'.[38] By accepting that

---

36   Woodley Team Report (The) *Report of the Independent Review Panel to East London and The City Health Authority and Newham Council* (1995), London, East London and The City Health Authority and Newham Council, pp 57 and 63.
37   1974 quotation by Brandon in Watson, S & Austerberry, H *Housing and Homelessness and Feminist Perspective* (1986) Routledge and Kegan Paul, London.
38   Greve, J *Homelessness in Britain* (1991) Joseph Rowntree Foundation, London, p 52.

homelessness spans the scope of all temporary and inadequate housing as well as complete 'rooflessness', central government could face social demands that they could not, or would not be willing to meet. With this in mind, the legislative definition of homelessness derives from the Housing (Homeless Persons) Act 1977, which has since been assimilated into the Housing Act 1988 and the Housing Act 1996.[39] The Housing Act 1996, s 175 defines homelessness as having no accommodation, being locked out of accommodation or being forced to leave accommodation because of something beyond a person's control. The present housing legislation, therefore, reflects the narrower definition of homelessness. However, in *Din v Wandsworth London Borough Council*[40] Lord Lowry said:

> 'that to be homeless and to have some temporary accommodation are not mutually inconsistent concepts. Nor does a person cease to be homeless merely by having a roof over his head or a lodging, however, precarious'.[41]

Also, in *R v Ealing London Borough Council, ex p Sidhu*[42] the Court of Appeal, relying upon the *Wandsworth* dictum, found that a woman who left the family home because of violence could still be regarded as homeless even though she had a temporary place in a woman's refuge. Such cases demonstrate the courts' intervention in the homelessness definition, which has gone some way to broaden the statutory interpretation of homelessness. By extending the scope of the Housing (Homeless Persons) Act 1977 definition a larger number of people have managed to fall within the ambits of the concept of homelessness and have been housed. However, since 1995 a more restrictive view has been adopted. In the case of *R v London Borough of Brent, ex p Awua*,[43] the House of Lords held that the Housing Act 1985, Pt III does not place upon housing authorities a duty to provide permanent accommodation. The duty is merely to provide suitable accommodation, which does not have to be of a permanent nature. The implications of this decision for homeless people with mental health problems are vast. Patients who are released into the community may be given temporary accommodation; provided the accommodation satisfies the 'suitability' requirement, the housing authorities will have fulfilled their duty.

---

39 Stewart, A 'Rethinking housing law: a contribution to the debate on tenure' *Housing Studies* 1994, Vol 9, No 2, p 263.
40 [1983] 1 AC 657.
41 [1983] 1 AC 657 at 677F-G.
42 (1983) 2 HLR 45.
43 [1995] 3 All ER 493.

The concern, which is raised by the implementation of community care, is that patients who have been discharged to the community may add to the homelessness problem. Even before community care had been endorsed, the level of homeless people suffering from some mental disturbance was high. For example, in 1991 the Government figures of homeless people considered to have mental health problems in London alone was totalled at 3,000, an increase of 75% over 1990. Since then, such figures have risen considerably.[44] It is agreed[45] that the prevalence of homelessness is increasing, with the percentage of homeless suffering mental health problems being significantly higher than it once was.[46] The side effects of homelessness may also be initiating mental health problems in those who have not previously suffered. Lack of food, warmth and social interaction may be enough to trigger such difficulties.[47]

(d) The link between mental health problems and homelessness

Three years after the passing of the National Health Service and Community Care Act 1990 the operational measures taken to implement the community care policy began in earnest. The era in which institutional care predominated was ending. In 1955 165,000 patients were treated in psychiatric hospitals, whereas 10 years later the patient level had dropped to 120,000. In 1993, it was estimated that there was a patient level of 50,000 in psychiatric units across the country.[48] The use of institutions for the care of the mentally disordered has continued to fall. De-institutionalisation has entailed taking patients with mental health problems away from the traditional method of care and placing them in caring surroundings within the community environment. However, many patients have spent a large proportion of their lives in psychiatric hospitals and such changes have caused high levels of fear in the patient population. It must be acknowledged that feelings of abandonment and rejection are just as commonly associated with patients leaving hospital

---

44 Bean, J & Mounser, P *Discharged From Mental Hospitals* (1993) MacMillan, Basingstoke.
45 Lamb, H et al *The Homeless Mentally Ill* (1984) American Psychiatric Association, New York.
46 Burrows, R, Pleace, N & Quilgars, D *Homelessness and Social Policy* (1997) Routledge, London, p 149.
47 See generally, Davies, HE *Homelessness and its Links with Mental Health Problems: Are There Implications for the Criminal Justice System?* (1990) MA Dissertation, Nottingham University. See also Dyer, O 'More than two million homes are cold enough to cause ill health, Shelter says' *British Medical Journal* 2002, Vol 324, p 634.
48 Bean, J & Mounser, P *Discharged From Mental Hospitals* (1993) MacMillan, Basingstoke, p 19.

as feelings of freedom, release and independence.[49] One apparent fallacy that continues to prevail is that homelessness is a direct result of de-institutionalisation and the community care policy per se. This is too simplistic. The problems have arisen because of practical limitations in the implementation of the policy rather than its notional basis. The community care concept could have provided a structure of care where patients were supervised whilst also maintaining the scope for independence. However, not only has the practical implementation of the concept failed to meet the expectations of the care profession and the patients, but the working of the concept within the housing legislation has left the discharged patient vulnerable. Discharged patients who are homeless could miss out on community care altogether, while already housed people with mental health problems could simply end up homeless because they are unable to hold down a tenancy without support.[50]

Homeless discharged patients suffer from the lack of permanent shelter. The ramifications of being without a home can have far-reaching consequences. Perhaps the greatest cause of distress is the failure to be able to satisfy the basic needs that all individuals require for primary survival, such as food, sleep, security, comfort and positive regard.[51] It is thought that this could either induce mental health problems or hinder the successful improvement of such conditions.[52] Homelessness can create a vicious cycle preventing discharged patients from really benefiting from the community care policy. In the Annual Report of the Medical Campaign Project it was observed that:

'[f]actors such as the need to give an address, inflexible appointment systems and the bureaucracy surrounding claims for exemption from prescription or dental charges will continue to exclude the homeless ... from receiving the services they need'.[53] Therefore, without adequate community provision, patients may find themselves without a home, without connection with the rest of society and with limited access to medical care.

49 Brearley, P *Leaving Residential Care* (1982) Tavistock, Aldershot.
50 Norden, B 'Passed parcel' *Roof* (1993) March/April, p 33.
51 See Fischer, P & Breakley, W 'Homelessness and mental health: an overview' *International Journal of Mental Health* 1986, Vol 14, No 4, p 4.
52 *Housing and Mental Health Policy Paper* (1992) MIND, London, p 4.
53 1991-1992, p 1.

(e) The duty to provide adequate housing

When a patient is discharged from a psychiatric hospital in theory he is left homeless until alternative living arrangements are made. It is therefore necessary to analyse the duty upon the local authority to provide housing within the statutory framework. Initially the patient has to satisfy the homelessness definition.[54] Emphasis is then placed upon whether the applicant for housing has a priority need under the Housing Act 1996, s 189. Owing to the community care policy a discharged psychiatric patient may fall under the Housing Act 1996, s 189(1)(c), which provides for individuals with a 'mental illness'.[55] Applicants for housing under priority need are chosen on the basis of vulnerability. 'Vulnerable' in the context of the Housing Act 1977 means someone who is less able to fend for himself, so that injury or detriment will result in a situation where a less vulnerable man will be able to cope without harmful effects.[56] In addition, Russell LJ observed in *R v Wandsworth London Borough Council, ex p Banbury*[57] that 'whether ... [the condition] ... renders a person vulnerable must be at all times a question of fact and degree'. So consideration must be given to: the creation of detriment to the individual and the influence such a condition could have upon obtaining and maintaining housing.

Upon discharge a patient who becomes homeless may be found to have a priority need under the Housing Act 1996, s 189(1)(c) due to mental illness provided further evidence indicates that the mental illness could lead to vulnerability in the housing market. If this is evidenced it is the duty of the local authority to ensure the discharged patient is housed as quickly as possible. However, what would the local authorities duty be if, upon discharge to the community, the patient was given accommodation, yet either due to his mental disorder, his inability to cope or for some other reason, he left the accommodation with the result that he became intentionally homeless under the Housing Act 1996, s 191? In *R v Salford County Council, ex p Davenport*[58] Fox LJ provided four criteria to be used in order to establish intentional homelessness: the person ceases to occupy accommodation; the accommodation was available for his occupation; it would have been reasonable for him to continue to occupy it; he deliberately did or failed to do something in consequence of which he ceased to occupy it.[59]

54 Knafler, S 'Homelessness update: Housing Act 1996' *Solicitor's Journal* 1996, 6 December, p 1173.
55 This provides for those suffering from 'mental illness'.
56 *R v Waverney District Council, ex p Bowers* [1983] QB 238 per Waller LJ at 244.
57 (1986) 19 HLR 76 at 83.
58 (1983) 8 HLR 54.
59 (1983) 8 HLR 54 at 62.

When an application is made, the local authority must have regard to the applicant's conduct. In *R v North Devon District Council, ex p Lewis*[60] the court examined the behaviour of a man who left his job with the result that he lost his tied cottage. The court found that by leaving his employment the applicant had become intentionally homeless. Furthermore, for a finding of intentional homelessness the homelessness must result from a conscious act, such as purposely failing to pay mortgage instalments.[61] However, if a patient left accommodation, which had been provided as part of a community care package, because of his mental illness, could such an act be considered voluntary? It has been found that a pregnant woman who lost her home because of her condition was not intentionally homeless.[62] Is there any difference between pregnancy and mental illness as regards the deliberation involved? Owing to the symptoms of schizophrenia, a patient may desire solitude. By leaving accommodation, such acts could be considered involuntary and uncontrolled. If this is so, the question remains whether such acts could lead to a finding of intentional homelessness or whether, as in the case of pregnancy, the homelessness is found to be unintentional. In the case of a discharged psychiatric patient who has left accommodation provided as part of his community care plan the local housing authority should pay attention to all the reasons given for leaving the accommodation. The local housing authority should also balance up all the factors involved in the decision made by the applicant to leave the accommodation. *R v Newham London Borough Council, ex p Campbell*, has confirmed this position.[63]

For homeless psychiatric patients there is a conflict between the two central provisions within the Housing Act 1996 relating to homelessness. On the one hand, there is the provision for priority need and on the other, the need to limit the duty on the part of the local authorities to house persons who are intentionally homeless. Which provision is ultimately looked to in the case of a psychiatric patient? Does the local housing authority have to make sure that all those with priority need are catered for even if some intentionally homeless people slip through the net? Housing departments (just like all other local authority departments) are clearly influenced by the level of available resources and this will affect the decision-making process. What may result from a patient leaving accommodation is either homelessness or a perpetual cycle of temporary addresses.

60   [1981] 1 WLR 328.
61   *R v Eastleigh Borough Council, ex p Beattie (No 2)* (1984) 17 HLR 168.
62   *R v Eastleigh Borough Council, ex p Beattie (No 2)* (1984) 17 HLR 168.
63   [1995] 1 FCR 33.

(f) Duties to the homeless

The duty to provide housing is not a duty spanning the entire homeless population but is limited to those applicants that can satisfy the criteria, such as whether they have a priority need and are regarded as vulnerable. For those applicants that are believed to be homeless and fulfil the criteria, the housing legislation does require the local housing authorities to make inquiries and an assessment as to the individual's need. Where applicants do have a priority need and are not intentionally homeless, the local housing authority has a duty to provide accommodation which should preferably be of a long-term nature. Where there is a conflict between priority need and intentional homelessness the local housing authority is under a duty to provide temporary accommodation whilst the applicant finds longer-term housing. In addition, the authority is required to provide advice and assistance in obtaining such housing.

If community care is to have a future, more affordable yet adequate housing must be provided.[64] The housing legislation was not drafted to provide for such people and cannot adequately fulfil their needs. As the level of public housing available is already limited, until the necessary measures are taken to provide the essential housing services and facilities needed by discharged patients, the success of community care may be limited. The difficulty has not been created by the current legislative provision but has resulted rather from the lack of housing set aside as part of the community care policy. The housing authorities have to shoulder the burden of the policy's oversight. If housing had been given greater emphasis within community care provision from the beginning, the homelessness problem in the mentally disordered population might not have been so far-reaching. The legislation has not been drafted with special reference to the needs of this particular group with the result that the housing legislation has not been able to promote patient welfare within the community.

---

64 Department of Environment *Housing and Construction Statistics* 1996, March Quarter, Part I. Just over 900 new lets, categorised as 'specialised dwellings' were started and completed by March 1996. This figure represents the total number of new dwellings, which are designed for the chronically sick, or disabled, in both the mental and physical sense. Such a figure cannot hope to satisfy the needs of the homeless mentally disordered as the housing is for all those considered to be disabled.

5 Establishing Financial Security

(a) Employment

The move from hospital to community for all psychiatric patients represents a significant change in their lives. Although few patients now spend many years confined in a hospital environment, any length of time in a strictly regimented atmosphere can lead to dependency and loss of confidence. One of the key objectives of the community care programme is to minimise the effect that such surroundings can have on patients, by emphasising the importance of normalising techniques and discharging the patient to the community as soon as possible. By the nineteenth century, the importance of employment as a therapeutic 'normalising' tool was recognised by John Connolly, who was the superintendent at the Maudsley Hospital. He wrote:

> '[a]mong the means of relieving patients from the monotony of an asylum, and of preserving the bodily health, and, at the same time, of improving the conditions of the mind, and prompting recovery, employment of some kind or other ranks the highest'.[65]

One benefit that hospitals have over their community counterpart is that they can offer patients a social setting, albeit an artificial one, which forces patients to communicate with others. The community does not offer this in quite the same way, thereby allowing many patients to lose contact with others and become isolated. As such, efforts must be made to ensure the community environment provides alternative opportunities for patients to experience social interaction. Traditionally, employment has been regarded as offering the greatest scope for social dealings.[66] Employment offers two main advantages to the recently discharged psychiatric patient: the first is a similar source of social contact to that found in hospital; the second is that it provides a means of financial security to enable the individual to meet his daily needs.[67] However, despite these clear benefits, the employment market also provides scope for prejudice and discrimination on grounds of disability and mental vulnerability. The work environment is not a particularly sensitive place and it will not always meet the needs of its workforce. However, the

---

65 Connolly, J *The Construction and Government of Lunatic Asylums and Hospitals for the Insane* (1847, republished 1968) Dawsons of Pall Mall, London.
66 Pilling, S 'Work and the continuing care client' in Lavender, A & Holloway, F (eds) *Community Care in Practice* (1988) John Wiley and Sons, London.
67 See generally, Nehring, J, Hill, R & Poole, L *Work, Empowerment and Community* (1993) Sainsbury Centre for Mental Health, London.

enactment of the Disability Discrimination Act 1995[68] provides protection for those in the employment market (whether in employment or looking for employment) from being actively discriminated against. The Disability Discrimination Act 1995 renders it unlawful for most employers[69] to discriminate against anyone owing to present or past disability.[70]

The discharged patient population is increasing with further closures of psychiatric institutions and facilities. Such patients can be grouped into three categories:

(a) those patients who could function adequately enough in the open employment market as long as treatment and supervision continue on a regular basis in the community;
(b) those patients who are only capable of working within a sheltered environment; and,
(c) those patients who will never be capable of work.

Patients falling into the last group are always likely to rely upon other means of financial support such as the social security system.[71] A variety of social security benefits are available to people with psychiatric problems. These include benefits intended to provide financial assistance to people who cannot work because of sickness and/or disability, income replacement benefits and community care grants from the social fund, which are one-off payments to help with the transition between hospital care and community care. The needs of group (b) could be more adequately fulfilled if sufficient resources were provided for sheltered work centres. However, group (a) may receive the greatest assistance from the Disability

68 This Act replaces most of the prior disabled employment law contained in the Disabled Persons (Employment) Acts 1944 and 1958.
69 Disability Discrimination Act 1995, s 7 provides an exemption for those employers who have a workforce of less than 20 employees.
70 Lewis, T & Tsamados, P 'Employment law: practice, guidance and trends' *Legal Action* 1996, May, p 10; O'Dempsey, D, Short, A & Brown, J 'Disability Discrimination Act 1995' *Solicitors Journal*, 1996 16 August, p 814; Korn, A 'Disability discrimination and dismissal for ill health' *Solicitors Journal* 1996, 19 July, p 710; See also, Doyle, B 'Enabling legislation or dissembling law? The Disability Discrimination Act 1995' (1997) 60 MLR 64; and Doyle, B *Disability Discrimination: The New Law* (1996) Jordans, Bristol.
71 See Direction 4, Social Security Advisory Committee, Fourth Report, 1985, paras 3.61-3.62. See also the *Social Fund Guide* para 5140. For general information see, Dimond, B *Legal Aspects of Care in the Community* (1997) MacMillan, London, section E, ch 33, and Ogus, A, Barendt, E & Wikeley, N *The Law of Social Security* (4th edn, 1995) Butterworth, London. The social security system suffers many problems in its dealings with the mentally vulnerable. The system is complex; the understanding of the particular needs of the mentally disordered are limited; and the system has difficulty reacting to the needs of such people: see Zarb, G *Social Security and Mental Health: Defining the Issues* (1996) SSAC, London.

Discrimination Act 1995. If the level of disability discrimination can be reduced by legislative intervention, group (a)'s position in the open employment market may be offered an equal footing with the rest of the working population.

The Disability Discrimination Act 1995 applies to those who can fulfil the definition of disability.[72] Disability amounts to a physical or mental impairment which has a substantial and long-term adverse effect on the individual's ability to carry out normal daily activities. The Disability Discrimination Act 1995, Sch 2 also incorporates those who were disabled but have since recovered. A physical disability can amount to anything that is a result of a serious or long-term complaint, whereas those of a transitory nature are excluded. For the mentally disordered, the impairment has to result from, or consist of, a mental illness which has been clinically recognised.[73] In addition, the mental illness has to be of a chronic nature. The Disability Discrimination Act 1995, Sch 1, para 2 defines long-term as lasting for at least 12 months, likely to last for at least 12 months, or likely to last for the rest of the person's life. This definition also includes those illnesses that follow patterns of recovery and relapse so that consecutive episodes can be included together to form the 12-month requirement. Even where a person with a mental disorder takes regular medication to control the symptoms of the disorder, he will still be considered disabled.[74] The Disability Discrimination Act 1995, Sch 1, para 4 provides that for the disability to have a disabling effect such as to interfere with 'normal day-to-day activities', mobility, manual dexterity, physical co-ordination, continence, ability to lift, carry or otherwise move everyday objects, speech, hearing or eyesight, memory or ability to concentrate, learn or understand, or perception of the risk of physical danger must be affected.[75] For the employer, the Disability Discrimination Act 1995 represents a cause for concern because, before any action can be taken, medical advice has to be sought to decide whether the normal ill-health procedures can be used in the case of any industrial dispute.[76]

72 Disability Discrimination Act 1995, s 1(1).
73 Disability Discrimination Act 1995, Sch 1, para 1.
74 Disability Discrimination Act 1995, Sch 1, para 3.
75 However, the Disability Discrimination (Meaning of Disability) Regulations 1996, SI 1996/1455, para 4 provides that some conditions will not be treated as impairments: (a) a tendency to set fires; (b) a tendency to steal; (c) a tendency to physical or sexual abuse of other people; (d) exhibitionism; and (e) voyeurism. In addition, para 3 provides that addictions to alcohol, nicotine or any other substance will not be considered an impairment.
76 See generally, Gooding, C C 'Disability Discrimination Act 1995' *Legal Action* 1997, January, p 10 and Bryan, N 'Disability rights project' *Legal Action* 1997, Dec, p 6.

The first hurdle faced by discharged patients who are capable of working on the open employment market is discrimination within the applications procedure. The Disability Discrimination Act 1995, s 11 provides that where the employer advertises a job no reference should be made to his particular physical requirements, eg 'no persons with a disability need apply'. Where a disabled person applies for a job and is rejected, the tribunal shall assume that the decision was made with reference to the applicant's disability.[77] The Disability Discrimination Act 1995, s 11 does not provide that all employers should take steps to ensure that disabled persons are employed (positive discrimination[78]) but it ensures that such people are not turned away because of their disability before consideration is given to their skills and the potential contribution they could make to the workforce. If the decision to employ a disabled applicant is affected by the disability, the employer will be regarded as having adopted a discriminatory approach if it leads him to refuse the application.[79] However, if a disabled person is offered employment, an employer is treated as discriminating against the disability if he treats the new employee less favourably.[80]

Discrimination may take two forms: either a person may be treated less favourably[81] or an employer may refuse or fails to make adjustments[82] within the working environment.[83] Discrimination is found to exist where these actions or inactions cannot be justified. Therefore, a finding of discrimination does not emerge because of the employers' actions or attitude alone: there must also be evidence that these actions cannot be justified. Justification is only possible where the reason relied upon is 'both material to the circumstances of the case and ... [is] ... substantial'.[84]

The Disability Discrimination Act 1995 provides that where any arrangements are made by or on behalf of the employer,[85] or where any physical feature of the premises occupied by the employer places the disabled person at a disadvantage, the employer is under a duty to make

77 Disability Discrimination Act 1995, s 11(2).
78 See for example, Fenwick, H 'Perpetuating inequality in the name of equal treatment' *Journal of Social Welfare and Family Law* 1996, Vol 18, No 2, p 263, Squires, J 'Quotas for women: fair representation?' *Parliamentary Affairs* 1996, Vol 49, No 1, p 71.
79 Disability Discrimination Act 1995, s 4.
80 Disability Discrimination Act 1995, s 5(1).
81 Disability Discrimination Act 1995, s 5(1).
82 Disability Discrimination Act 1995, s 5(2) and (6).
83 Disability Discrimination Act 1995, s 5(2)(b).
84 Disability Discrimination Act 1995, s 5(3) and (4). The Draft Code of Practice for the Elimination of Discrimination in the Field of Employment against disabled people suggests that 'material' and 'substantial' refer to the particular case and cannot be 'trivial or minor'.
85 Disability Discrimination Act 1995, s 6(1)(a).

adjustments to relieve that disadvantage.[86] These steps play a key role in providing employment opportunities for both the physically and mentally ill in the open employment market. However, the requirement for adjustments to be made must simply meet the standard of 'reasonableness'. While establishing whether such adjustments are reasonable, the Employment Appeal Tribunal (EAT) must consider the extent to which the steps taken would assist the disabled person at work; the extent to which it would be practicable for the employer to take the steps; the financial cost of such steps and whether this cost could disrupt the rest of the workforce. Regard must also be had to the employer's financial position and how available resources are to finance the adjustment plan.[87]

Although the Code of Practice provides that the employer is justified in terminating the employment of an employee if his disability makes it impossible for him any longer to perform the main functions of his job, this does not provide a blanket cover for the employer.[88] If the disabled employee is unable to perform the main functions of his job, before a dismissal can be justified the employer must consider whether there might be another role for the disabled person. It would then be necessary, under the adjustment requirement, to place the disabled employee in that job if such a transition could be carried out without too much expense or disruption. Therefore, when a patient is discharged from hospital, the Disability Discrimination Act 1995 now provides a structure to prevent discrimination when applying for jobs and when working. Where it appears that an employment decision has been based upon discriminatory criteria, complaints can be made to an employment tribunal which can make a declaration, award unlimited compensation and make recommendations as to how such discrimination can be alleviated.[89]

However, the Disability Discrimination Act 1995, Sch 3[90] provides that no civil or criminal proceedings may be brought against any person in respect of an act merely because the employer's action is unlawful under the Act. In addition, the Disability Discrimination Act 1995 works in relation to the employer alone and not in relation to other employees, so that when a mentally disordered person endures discriminatory behaviour from his colleagues, the Disability Discrimination Act 1995 cannot protect

---

86 Disability Discrimination Act 1995, s 6(1)(b).
87 Disability Discrimination Act 1995, s 6(4). See also in general, the Disability Discrimination (Employment) Regulations 1996, SI 1996/1456.
88 The Draft Code of Practice for the Elimination of Discrimination in the Field of Employment, para 6.21.
89 Disability Discrimination Act 1995, s 8.
90 Disability Discrimination Act 1995, s 2(1) and Sch 3.

him. In *Tower Boot Co Ltd v Jones*[91] the Employment Appeals Tribunal found that a black employee's colleagues were not acting in the course of their employment when they racially harassed him, both verbally and physically, at work. As a result, the employer was not vicariously liable for the harassment. This situation might equally arise where a mentally vulnerable employee is tormented at work. If an employer becomes aware of the harassment, if it is deemed reasonable, the employer may be under a duty to adjust the working structure so that the employee is moved to avoid the harassment. The Disability Discrimination Act 1995 is a step in the right direction but it does not go far enough to minimise the problems faced by many mentally disordered employees.

Half-measures like the Disability Discrimination Act 1995 may afford little protection to those it seeks to assist. A false sense of security is created when some efforts are made, resulting in a less rigid inspection of the problems of discrimination found within the disabled population. Inertia is certainly not required at a time when greater numbers of vulnerable people will be entering the community. However, although there are clear problems and limitations with the Disability Discrimination Act 1995, it should be recognised that it does provide some assistance to those who have returned to the community. Without the legislation, many people with mental health problems who are capable of working within the open employment market would be unable to obtain or maintain employment and inevitably the opportunity to enjoy the benefits associated with employment would be lost.

The positive impact that occupation has on the mentally vulnerable has been recognised by many. Freud believed employment bound 'the individual to reality' while Szasz considered '[i]t ... the closest thing to a genuine panacea known to medical science'.[92] A number of more recent studies have illustrated the positive effects that employment can have. Jahoda[93] groups the different aspects of work into two categories: the manifest and the latent functions of employment. The manifest functions are the basic terms and conditions of employment, whereas the latent

---

91 [1995] IRLR 529, EAT. See also, *Cobham v Forest Healthcare NHS Trust* (1995) 533 IRLB 12, EAT.
92 See also Rowland, L A & Perkins, R E 'You can't eat, drink or make love eight hours a day: the value of work in psychiatry – a personal view' *Health Trends* 1988, Vol 20, p 75.
93 Jahoda, M 'Work, employment and unemployment: values, theories and approaches to social research' *American Psychologist* 1981, Vol 36, p 184.

functions consist of the less overt effects upon the individual, such as the creation of a time structure, the provision of shared experiences, the development of goal achievement, creation of personal status and identity and the enforcement of activity.[94] Regular occupation can create an environment of normality for the mentally vulnerable. Many patients will receive some training while in hospital to aid the therapeutic process. There have been a number of studies, which have analysed the connection (if any) between obtaining work skills in hospital and obtaining employment upon discharge.[95] None of the studies found any connection between the patient having the ability to carry out an industrial task and obtaining open employment upon discharge. However, Watts[96] found that the main benefit of a rehabilitation unit was that it provided the patient with an environment suited to nurturing sociability. If a patient appears to be sociable in these surroundings, this was regarded as a good indicator of the patient's chance of success in finding and maintaining work in the community. Watts also found that for those patients diagnosed as psychotic, a good predictor of their potential success in open employment was their response to supervision in the industrial unit.[97] Although the age of these studies must be recognised, they each have concluded that an increase in occupation can lead directly to an improvement in the patient's clinical state.[98] Anthony et al[99] found in 1972 that for those patients that had left hospital, between 30% and 50% were in employment in the open market within six months of their discharge. However, the position is very different today. Many face unemployment and with the limited availability of permanent jobs, the vulnerable and those considered socially unacceptable are finding work even more difficult to

94 See Pilling, S 'Work and the continuing care client' in Lavender, A & Holloway, F (eds) *Community Care in Practice* (1988) John Wiley and Sons, London.
95 See Wing, J K 'Social and psychological changes in a rehabilitation unit' *Social Psychiatry*, 1966, Vol 1, p 21; Griffiths, D R P, Hodgson, R & Hallam, R 'Structured interview for the assessment of work related attitudes in psychiatric patients: preliminary findings' *Psychological Medicine* 1974, Vol 4, p 326; Griffiths, D R P 'Rehabilitation of chronic psychotic patients: an assessment of their psychological handicaps, an evaluation of the factors which predict outcome' *Psychological Medicine* 1974, Vol 4, p 316. See also Cole, N, Brewer, D, Allison, R & Hardin Branch, C H 'Employment characteristics of discharged schizophrenics' *Archives of General Psychiatry* 1964, Vol 10, p 314.
96 Watts, F N 'A study of the work behaviour in a psychiatric rehabilitation unit' *British Journal of Social and Clinical Psychology* 1978, Vol 17, p 85.
97 As such, units can be ascribed the role of a preliminary predictor of future success within the community.
98 Wing, J K & Brown, G W *Institutionalisation and Schizophrenia* (1970) Cambridge University Press, Cambridge.
99 Anthony, W.A., Buell, G.J., Sharratt, S. & Althoff, M.E. 'Efficacy of psychiatric rehabilitation', *Psychological Bulletin*, 1972, Vol 78, p 447.

find. Carson[100] observed that in a study conducted in a small industrial workshop of 70 members, over 95% had worked before succumbing to mental disorder, but half of the sample had not worked for the last 15 years. Carson contends that without the opportunity for patients to gain some experience in sheltered workshops, 'most would have been unemployed and would be regarded by many employers as unemployable'.[101] However, from the patients' point of view, 38% thought that the work they did in the sheltered workshop could assist them in obtaining work in the open market whereas 44% thought that this experience would not help them, as they would still have to face employer and employee prejudice.[102]

Since employment opportunities are now more limited, some recent studies[103] have focused upon the impact of unemployment. These studies have looked at the effect work deprivation can have upon the individual. Warr[104] identified a severe deterioration in the health of those who could not initially find employment and those who could not maintain a job for any length of time. This deterioration in health amounted to increased distress, lack of confidence, apathy and generally increased nervousness and disquietude. When patients are discharged from hospital, their entire daily routines change. In hospital, days are organised, providing patients with daily contact with others through either industrial or occupational units, whereas in the community, this social setting is not automatic.

100 Carson, J 'Job satisfaction?' *The Health Service Journal* 1991, 1 August, p 21.
101 Carson, J 'Job satisfaction?' *The Health Service Journal* 1991, 1 August, p 21.
102 Leary, J & Johnstone, E et al 'Disabilities and circumstances of schizophrenia: a follow up study' *British Journal of Psychiatry* 1991, Vol 159, Supp, 13, p 7. Penn et al 'Dispelling the stigma of schizophrenia: what sort of information is best?' *Schizophrenia Bulletin* 1994, Vol 20, No 3, p 567 contained a study to establish what level of stigmatisation was faced by people suffering from schizophrenia. It observed that the level of stigma was much higher with people who had had no contact with persons suffering such disorders before and noted that employers faced by such people were much more likely to reject their applications.
103 Warr, R 'Work, jobs, unemployment' *Bulletin of the British Psychological Society* 1983, Vol 36, p 305; Brenner, M H Mortality and the national economy' *Lancet* 1979, Vol ii, p 568; Cook, D G, Bartley, M J, Cumming, R O & Shaper, A G 'Health of unemployed middle aged men in Great Britain' *Lancet,* 1982 Vol. I, p 1290; Fagin, L & Little, M *Unemployment and Health in Families: A Case Study Based on Family Interviews: A Pilot Study* (1981) HMSO, London.
104 War, R 'Work, jobs, unemployment' *Bulletin of the British Psychological Society* 1983, Vol 36, p 305; Brenner, M H Mortality and the national economy' *Lancet* 1979, Vol ii, p 568; Cook, D G, Bartley, M J, Cumming, R O & Shaper, A G 'Health of unemployed middle aged men in Great Britain' *Lancet,* 1982 Vol. I, p 1290; Fagin, L & Little, M *Unemployment and Health in Families: A Case Study Based on Family Interviews: A Pilot Study* (1981) HMSO, London.

Without employment in some form, the discharged patient may suffer from some of the negative aspects of unemployment. With fewer employment opportunities being available, efforts to provide alternative work facilities must be made.

(b) Alternative employment opportunities

Despite legislation to protect the employment rights of those with disabilities, it must be accepted that many mentally disordered people may not be offered genuine employment opportunities. Therefore, alternative work provisions can and should be devised. For example, a Local Exchange Trading System (LETS) creates a non-cash based economy where emphasis is placed upon the exchange of goods and services. These systems have grown in popularity over the last few years owing to the increase in unemployment.[105] A large pool of skills found within the community is formed and reliance is placed upon the barter of goods and services. The LETS system not only provides a way in which people can have a job carried out when they could not afford it in the cash economy but it also provides a source of employment among the unemployed. The mentally disordered population consists of many people with many backgrounds and skills. In the cash economy their disorder may prevent employment, but in a LETS scheme they are able to work and benefit from this system of reciprocity. All the positive aspects of employment can be obtained from the LETS scheme and allow the individual to feel that they are positively contributing to society. Other schemes of 'employment' exist, such as the District Services Centre (DSC), which is attached to the Maudsley Hospital in London. It has three workshops, which provide for differing abilities. In addition, it maintains close links with the hospital and the hospital occupational units so that a community spirit is sustained. The aim of the DSC is to obtain employment for patients outside the whole hospital structure either in open employment or sheltered workshops. Independent sheltered workshops (eg the Camberwell Rehabilitation Association, which works independently but has links with the Maudsley Hospital) work in a similar way, except they are usually located on industrial premises. The workshops provide the scope for many trades to be learnt, with the ultimate aim of creating long-term work opportunities. It is hoped that because such

---

105 'Rebirth of barter economy lifts morale in jobless Britain. How Britons barter their way out of debt', *Observer*, 17 January 1993 and 24 January 1993. See also, Wray, S. 'A community solution to unemployment for mentally ill people', *Mental Health Nursing*, 1995, Vol 15, No 1, p 6.

workshops enjoy a close link with industry employers may lose any preconceptions about people with mental health problems and their abilities to work. Other centres place particular emphasis upon assessing the patient's potential for working within the open market. These centres provide a scheme of work that is aimed particularly at assessing and preparing the patients for work in the outside world.

However, such schemes are beset with problems. With the implementation of community care, the sheltered provision available cannot meet the needs now created and the original goal (that such programmes would encourage employers in the open market to employ discharged patients) has failed to materialise. In the late 1960s and 1970s the sheltered work schemes led to many discharged patients obtaining work, yet with increasing unemployment such expectations have not been realised. Cornes et al[106] reported that in the 1940s up to 84% of all patients that had sheltered workshop training found work or training within society afterwards. However, by the 1970s this figure had dropped to 44% of patients finding some form of occupation with only 25% finding work in the open employment market. This figure has continued to fall. The benefits of employment are increasingly accepted, yet scarce employment opportunities are preventing discharged patients from taking advantage of these. While employment opportunities remain limited, those who are discharged into the community may continue to face a community which fails to offer the same assistance, care or support existing within the psychiatric hospital.

6 Conclusion

The discharged psychiatric patient has many needs that must be met in order for community care to succeed. The provision of adequate community services plays a vital role in the care programme approach and its importance should not be underestimated. Many reports in recent years have highlighted continuing failures in the care policy. These failures have frequently been attributed to inadequate provision of community services, inappropriate housing provision and lack of occupational opportunities.

This chapter has undertaken a review of two factors which have been repeatedly connected with the failure of community care and have ultimately led to a feeling of disillusionment. Discharged psychiatric

---

106 Cornes, P, Alderman, J, Cumella, S & Harradence, J et al *Employment Rehabilitation: The Aims and Achievements of a Service for Disabled People* (1982) Manpower Services Commission, Sheffield.

patients must be provided with accommodation that allows them to establish stability in the community environment. Decent housing is essential, for without it there is a greater risk of the individual becoming lost to the caring system. In the cases of Christopher Clunis and Stephen Laudat, a connection was made between spasmodic homelessness and cessation of medication with the deterioration in their mental state. Consequently, the provision of housing is not a peripheral need and has to be given equal emphasis with medical assistance. The lack of consideration given to the role of housing continues to have significant repercussions. Not enough housing provision has been made either in 'special needs' accommodation or mainstream housing. 'Special needs' housing is limited in availability, whilst mainstream housing is of low quality and the rental prices are high. As a result, few discharged psychiatric patients are being offered the housing provision they need resulting in increasing homelessness within the mentally disordered population.

Occupational opportunities for the former psychiatric patient have also proved to be limited. The benefits of regular activity are clearly documented, yet unfortunately, practice and theory have not converged. Efforts to limit disability discrimination by way of the Disability Discrimination Act 1995 are welcomed, but glaring loopholes exist and the mentally vulnerable may be left with little or no protection. People who are newly discharged from psychiatric institutions have to face a change in their caring environment, an environment which does not guarantee a place to live, a regular income or even an evening meal. While serious practical inadequacies and limited legislative provision to meet the needs of the vulnerable prevail within the care policy, the road to disillusionment seems to be one which will continue to be travelled by those with mental health difficulties, professionals and the wider community.

Chapter 7
Mentally disordered offenders

1 Introduction

This chapter considers the way in which mentally disordered offenders are treated within the criminal justice system, focusing particularly on the diversion policy. The diversion policy seeks to remove mentally disordered offenders from the criminal justice system and provide them with appropriate psychiatric assistance, thereby replacing the notion of punitive sanction with therapeutic intervention. The origins of the diversion policy date back to the Mental Health Act 1959, but it was not until the Conservative Government (1979-97) that more substantial efforts were made to introduce diversionary measures. The current Labour Government continues to support these efforts. The mechanisms for diverting mentally disordered offenders, which are primarily located within the MHA 1983, will be evaluated and consideration will be given to the factors which influence the policy's success or failure, most notably resources and the ability of different agencies to collaborate effectively.

2 Diversion from the Criminal Justice System

Many individuals suffering from mental health problems will face a barrage of prejudice, stigma and discrimination in several areas of their lives. Likewise, the fear that surrounds mental illness has frequently led the public to associate criminality and mental disorder, yet in recent years the official response to mentally disordered offenders has been one of separation from, rather than conflation, with the rest of the criminal population.[1] This move reflects a growing trend to 'divert' such offenders out of the criminal justice system and into the health and social services sector. Yet, despite the recognition that mentally disordered offenders would benefit from a therapeutic rather than a penal environment, much confusion remains as to whether the mentally disordered offender should receive punishment for his actions or whether treatment and psychiatric support should be offered.

The penal environment is one which embraces restrictive practices. The prison system controls the movements, actions and thought processes of the inmates. The purpose of such control is to 'inflict deterrent punishment and suffering' on those who are forced to live within it.[2] Therefore, any attempt to treat and rehabilitate those suffering from mental health problems within prison is likely to be significantly hindered. The prison culture is one of punishment and retribution and it is this that has the most damaging effect on the mentally disordered offender.[3] As Bean points out '[o]ne cannot graft a therapeutic regime onto a punitive one' and while the objective of prison remains, as it must, a place of control and ultimately punishment, therapeutic endeavour will only ever be a secondary objective.[4]

While the prison regime itself poses perhaps the most difficulty, other problems exist within the prison system that prevent rehabilitation and treatment. Woeful levels of over-crowding, mismanagement and under-resourcing are commonplace,[5] while the Health Care Service for Prisoners is restricted in what it can do for prisoners with mental health problems because staff are not adequately trained to deal with them. Neither are the prison hospital facilities satisfactory.[6] In 1986, it was found that the Health Care Service for Prisoners could not provide the appropriate level of care and support to prisoners who needed psychiatric assistance. Indeed, at that time only 40% of medical officers had any training in psychiatry.[7]

1　Home Office *Provision for Mentally Disordered Offenders* circular 66/1990 (1990) HMSO, London. The Department of Health issued similar guidance to all health and social services professionals: NHS Management Executive Letter EL (90) 168, para 1.
2　Gunn, J et al *Psychiatric Aspects of Imprisonment* (1978) Academic Press, Carolina, p 9.
3　Liebling, A & Kramp, H *Suicide Attempts in Male Prisons* (1994) Home Office Research Bulletin 36.
4　Bean, P *Mental Disorder and Legal Control* (1986) Cambridge University Press, Cambridge p 90.
5　Bynoe, I 'The prison medical wing: "A place of safety"?' *Journal of Forensic Psychiatry* 1990, Vol 1, p 251.
6　NACRO *Mentally Disturbed Prisoners at Winson Green* (1993) NACRO, London, pp 5-7.
7　House of Commons Select Committee on Social Services, Third Report Session 1985-6 HC 72, paras 55 and 56.

Training is vital if mental health difficulties in prisoners are to be recognised and dealt with effectively. Yet, while these difficulties could be overcome if more funding was ploughed into the prison health service and greater efforts were made to instruct medical officers, little can be done to ameliorate the penal environment.[8]

As the prison environment is not conducive to treatment and rehabilitation, 'diversion' from the criminal justice system into the mental health system is considered to offer greater therapeutic opportunities for the mentally disordered offender. In 1990, it was stated in a government circular that 'it is government policy that, *wherever possible*, mentally disordered persons should receive care and treatment from the health and social services'.[9] *'Wherever possible'* indicates that the diversion policy is discretionary in nature and since the policy was embraced by the Conservative Government[10] there has been increasing concern about the high numbers of mentally disordered offenders in the penal system and the under-use of therapeutic sentencing powers.[11]

The diversion policy seeks to ensure that at various stages throughout the criminal justice process,[12] decisions are made as to whether the offender

8   Smith, R 'Disorder, disillusion and disrepute' *British Medical Journal* 1983, Vol 287, p 1522, 1787; Gunn, J. 'The role of psychiatry in prisons' in Roth, M & Bluglass, R (eds) *Psychiatry, Human Rights and the Law* (1985) Cambridge University Press, Cambridge.
9   Home Office *Provision for Mentally Disordered Offenders* circular 66/1990 (1990) HMSO, London. The Department of Health issued similar guidance to all health and social services professionals: NHS Management Executive Letter EL (90) 168, para 2 (emphasis added).
10   In 1993 the Conservative Government announced that pump-priming funding would be available in order to establish diversion schemes and encourage ones that were already set up: *Health of the Nation (A Strategy for Health in England)* Session 1992-3 Cm 1986 (1993) HMSO, London.
11   See for example, Home Office and DHSS *Interdepartmental Working Group Report into Mentally Disturbed Offenders in the Prison System* (1987) HMSO, London, para 5.6; NACRO Briefing *The Imprisonment of Mentally Disordered Offenders* (1990) HMSO, London; Mental Health Act Commission *Second Biennial Report 1985-87* (1987) HMSO, London, p 47; Social Services Select Committee *Third Report on the Prison Medical Service* Session 1985-86 HC 72, para 56; *'Legal groups in call for action on remand crisis' The Times* 12 December 1988 p 6; *Report on the Work of the Prison Service 1986 -87* Cm 246, HMSO, paras 34-36.
12   The success of diversion schemes in other countries around the world encouraged the continued support of the policy, see for example, Duff, P & Burman, M *Diversion from Prosecution to Psychiatric Care* (1994) Scottish Office Central Research Unit; Dank, N & Kulihoff, M 'An alternative to incarceration of the mentally ill' *Journal of Prison and Jail Health* 1983, Vol 3, p 95; Cooke, D J 'Treatment as an alternative to prosecution: Offenders Diverted for Treatment' *British Journal of Psychiatry* 1991, Vol 158, p 785; Palermo, G B et al 'Jail versus mental hospitals: The Milwaukee approach to a social dilemma' *International Journal of Offender Therapy and Comparative Criminology* 1991,

should be prosecuted and punished for his actions or treated for his mental condition through the health care system.[13] The diversion of a mentally disordered offender can be achieved in a variety of ways and is dependent on the nature of the disorder and the offence committed. Diversion may take place before prosecution and even arrest by the police. In this case, the individual will be removed from the criminal justice system altogether and immediately directed into health and social services care. Early diversion may occur if the police decide against taking formal action and refer him to mental health services. Likewise, the Crown Prosecution Service (CPS) may decide to discontinue a case if the medical evidence suggests that the individual's mental condition prevented him from being responsible for his actions. Diversion can take place when an offender is being processed within the criminal justice system: instead of being remanded into custody, he is remanded in hospital or required to accept medical treatment as a bail condition. Diversion may also be achieved later on in the criminal justice process. The individual may be prosecuted but may be subject to a therapeutic disposal rather than a custodial sentence.

3 The Role of the Mental Health Act 1983

The diversion policy is implemented in practice through a number of legislative mechanisms, which are largely, though not exclusively, located within the MHA 1983, Pt III.[14] The objective of the provisions is principally to enable the effective treatment of the offender's mental condition and to shield him from unnecessary punishment.[15] Despite some practical difficulties with the policy's execution and some indication that the policy is under-used, it remains well supported and is generally regarded as a 'good thing'.[16]

Vol 35, p 97. See also, Joseph, P *Psychiatric Assessment at the Magistrates Court* (1992) Home Office, London and Tonak, D & Cawdron, G 'Mentally disordered offenders and the courts: co-operation and collaboration of disciplines involved' *Justice of the Peace* 1988, Vol 152, p 504.

13 Blummenthal, S & Wessely, S 'National survey of current arrangements for diversion from custody in England and Wales' *British Medical Journal* 1992, Vol 305, p 1322.

14 As supplemented by the Mental Health Act revised *Code of Practice* (1999) HMSO, London. The MHA 1983, s 118 imposes a duty on the Secretary of State for Health to prepare, publish and revise a *Code of Practice* to guide those who are involved in the detention process of mentally disordered individuals.

15 Department of Health/Home Office *Review of Health and Social Services for Mentally Disordered Offenders and Others Requiring Similar Services* Cm 2088 (1992) HMSO, London.

16 As highlighted by Bartlett, P & Sandland, R *Mental Health Law: Policy and Practice* (2000) Blackstone Press, London, p 154. See also Department of Health

4 Early Diversion

(a) The police

The earliest contact a mentally disordered individual will have with the criminal justice system will be with the police. As growing numbers of mentally disordered patients are released from hospital as part of the ongoing community care policy, the police are increasingly involved with management of the mentally ill who are living in the community.[17] Under the MHA 1983, s 136, police officers are provided with the power to remove to a place of safety a person who is found in a public place and appears to be mentally disordered and in need of care or control. The decision to remove an individual from a public place must be made on the basis that either it is in the interests of the individual concerned or is warranted in order to protect the public. The provision is usually invoked when 'a person's abnormal behaviour is causing nuisance or offence'.[18] The individual may only be detained for a period of 72 hours, at which point he will usually be the subject of alternative provisions within the MHA 1983, be charged by the police or released. Detention to a place of safety under the MHA 1983, s 136 provides sufficient time[19] for the individual to be examined and assessed by a medical practitioner and interviewed by 'an approved social worker'.[20] A 'place of safety' is defined in the MHA 1983, s 135(6) as:

> 'residential accommodation provided by a local social services authority under Part III of the National Assistance Act 1948, ... a hospital ..., a police station, a mental nursing home or residential home for mentally disordered persons or any other suitable place'

The Government's Response to the Health Select Committee's Report into Mental Health Services Cm 4888 (2000) TSO, London, pp 40-42.

17 Teplin, L A & Pruett, N S 'Police as streetcorner psychiatrist: Managing the mentally ill' *International Journal of Law and Psychiatry* 1992, Vol 15, p 139; Fahy, T, Berningham, & Dunn, J 'Police admissions to psychiatric hospitals: A challenge to community psychiatry' *Medicine, Science & Law* 1987, Vol 27, p 263.

18 Department of Health and Social Security *Review of the Mental Health Act 1959* Cm 7320 (1978) HMSO, London, para 2.22.

19 The *Code of Practice* for the Detention, Treatment and Questioning of Persons by Police Officers (known as Code C) which has been issued under the Police and Criminal Evidence Act (PACE) 1984, s 66 states that the person concerned should be assessed as soon as possible: para 3.10.

20 An approved social worker is defined in the MHA 1983, s 145(1) as an employee of a social services authority who is competent and has been appointed to act as an approved social worker to carry out functions given to him or her by the MHA 1983.

which can provide temporary accommodation. While detained under the MHA 1983, s 136, no medical treatment may be administered without the individual's valid consent.[21]

The powers under the MHA 1983, s 136 are not technically diversionary measures, as the police can use them irrespective of whether or not an offence has been committed or suspected of being committed. However, for some mentally disordered people, the MHA 1983, s 136 provides a means of accessing mental health services at the earliest opportunity. Section 136 has been subject to some criticism over the years because research indicates that its use is erratic, more prevalent in large urban conurbations, and practically non-existent in locations that are more rural.[22] However, the use of the MHA 1983, s 136 merely reflects the greater demand for police intervention in large cities. Mentally disordered individuals tend to gather in large cities allowing many to be anonymous and free from interference.[23] Criticism has also been levelled at the police for not being adequately trained to recognise people suffering from psychiatric illness.[24] Yet research suggests that this is not a true reflection of the ability of police officers, as most of the MHA 1983, s 136 cases are shown to be correct decisions when the psychiatrist examines the individual concerned.[25] The difficulty that does exist with the use of the MHA 1983, s 136 is one of resources. As noted above, section 136 provides some people with the opportunity to be received into the mental health service, yet many NHS facilities (even if they have the space) are unwilling to admit such patients, as frequently the individuals are disturbed and volatile. The police are in a difficult position when health care facilities are not forthcoming as it is essential that the individual concerned be assessed as soon as possible. When the police decide against bringing charges, it frequently results in police officers becoming involved in arduous discussions in order to gain access to the health care system and to procure the appropriate care and support.[26] As Bartlett and Sandland note 'early diversion is something of a lottery' and is dependent

21 The MHA 1983, s 56(1)(b).
22 For example, see Bean, P *Mental Disorder and Legal Control* (1986) Cambridge University Press, Cambridge.
23 Weller, M et al 'Psychosis and destitution at Christmas: 1985–88' *The Lancet* 1989, Vol 2, p 1509.
24 Laing, J 'The mentally disordered suspect at the police station' *Criminal Law Review* 1995, p 371.
25 Kelleher, M J & Copeland, J R 'Compulsory psychiatric admissions by the police: A study of the use of section 136' *Medicine, Science & Law* 1972, Vol 12, p 220 and Fahy, T 'The police as a referral agency for psychiatric emergencies: A review' *Medicine, Science & Law* 1989, Vol 29, p 315.
26 Dunn, J. & Fahy, T 'Section 136 and the police' *Bulletin of the Royal College of Psychiatrists* 1987, Vol 11, 224-25.

on the availability of facilities.[27] However, if 'greater local consultation and mutual understanding' could be fostered between the police, health and social services authorities some of the negative images commonly associated with the MHA 1983, s 136 cases would undoubtedly be dispelled.[28] Yet even where such collaboration is cultivated, the availability of facilities, appropriately trained personnel and inter-agency cooperation remains crucial.[29]

The MHA 1983, s 136 provides the police with powers to remove an individual from a public place, thereby protecting the public and/or the welfare of the individual concerned. The MHA 1983, s 135 gives the police powers to gain entry to a private place when the police have reason to believe that a mentally disordered individual is at risk. In order to gain entry to the premises, the police much first obtain a warrant issued by a magistrate. The warrant must clearly specify the premises concerned and will authorise a police officer to enter the premises (using reasonable force) to remove the mentally disordered individual to a place of safety for up to 72 hours. The MHA 1983, s 135 is used as a means of protecting the individual from self-harm rather than as a means of protecting others. However, the provision is rarely used, as there are other, less complicated, ways of obtaining access to a mentally disordered individual, usually through the assistance of a relative or friend or by persuasion.

(b) The appropriate adult scheme

Despite the obvious advantages of diverting mentally disordered offenders/individuals from the criminal justice system by way of the MHA 1983, s 136, a considerable number of individuals are diverted later on in the process. The decision to divert an individual immediately or to prosecute is one for the police. The decision will be influenced by numerous factors, not least whether the evidence against them is strong enough and what is gleaned from the interview. Under the Police and Criminal Evidence Act 1984 (PACE), s 66 special safeguards are provided in relation to the questioning and interviewing of persons with mental

---

27   Bartlett, P & Sandland, R *Mental Health Law: Policy and Practice* (2000) Blackstone Press, London, p 155.
28   *Report of the Committee on Mentally Abnormal Offenders* Cm 6244 (1975) HMSO, London, p 141. However, it is worth noting that where there is evidence of a serious crime then the MHA 1983, s 136 is rarely used, as the police prefer to leave the question of diversion to the court: see Robertson, G, Pearson, R & Gibb, R 'The entry of mentally disordered people to the criminal justice system' *British Journal of Psychiatry* 1996, Vol 169, p 172.
29   See further chs 5 and 6 above.

impairment, the mentally ill and juveniles.[30] Code C ensures that the evidence the police assemble against the suspect can meet any challenges in court. PACE provides that evidence must meet certain criteria.[31] PACE, s 76(2)(a) requires a court to exclude evidence that was obtained by oppression or duress. PACE, s 76(2)(b) requires that evidence that was obtained in circumstances likely to render any confession unreliable be excluded. PACE, s 78(1) allows discretion to exclude evidence that would adversely affect the fairness of the proceedings if admitted and PACE, s 77(1) places a duty on a trial judge to warn the jury about relying on the uncorroborated confession of a mentally handicapped or impaired (though not disordered) offender.

In addition to the safeguards outlined above, Code C also requires the police, when detaining someone whom they believe to be mentally impaired or mentally ill, to ensure an 'appropriate adult' is present to assist the suspect.[32] The role of the appropriate adult scheme is to protect the rights of vulnerable suspects and to prevent exploitative tactics being adopted by the police. This protective mechanism is considered particularly necessary because vulnerable suspects are highly susceptible to pressure.[33] The appropriate adult is expected to be pro-active in the interview process rather than to act as a mere observer of the proceedings. He must explain the procedure to the suspect, facilitate communication between the suspect and the police and make sure the interview process is conducted properly. The appropriate adult does not need special training and is usually a relative or guardian of the suspect. If a relative or guardian is not available then a person with experience in mental impairment or mental illness or some other responsible person can assume the role of appropriate adult. However, a police officer may not be an appropriate adult because of the clear conflict of interest generated by such a dual role.

As the decision to call in an appropriate adult is made by the police officers involved in the case, they must have the ability to identify which suspects

---

30 The *Code of Practice* for the Detention, Treatment and Questioning of Persons by Police Officers (known as Code C) issued under the Police and Criminal Evidence Act (PACE) 1984, s 66.
31 PACE 1984, ss 76, 77 and 78.
32 Littlechild, B 'Reassessing the role of the appropriate adult' *Criminal Law Review* 1995, p 540; Hodgson, J 'Vulnerable suspects and the appropriate adult' *Criminal Law Review* 1997, p 785; Pearse, J & Gudjonsson, G 'How appropriate are appropriate adults?' *Journal of Forensic Psychiatry* 1996, Vol 7, No 3, p 570.
33 Gudjonsson, G H *The Psychology of Interrogations, Confessions and Testimony* (1992) John Wiley, Chichester; Royal Commission on Criminal Justice *Report of the Royal Commission on Criminal Procedure* Cm 8092 (1993) HMSO, London.

are vulnerable as a result of mental impairment or mental disorder. The Runciman Commission on Criminal Justice, which reported in 1993, recognised that greater efforts should be made to protect vulnerable suspects in police custody.[34] Research conducted for the Commission by Gudjonsson et al found that of a sample group over 20% of suspects needed the presence of an appropriate adult although only 4% of the same sample actually received one.[35] Therefore, the presence of an appropriate adult is dependent on the ability of the police officer (frequently the custody officer) to detect mental impairment or disorder.[36] Concerns raised by the Runciman Commission led to the establishment of the Working Party on Appropriate Adults, which looked into the workings of the appropriate adult scheme and reported in 1995. It recommended that clearer guidelines should be laid down defining the role of the appropriate adult and the remit of his power. However, none of these recommendations were followed. Confusion as to the appropriate adult's role remains and it is questionable as to how worthwhile it is. Evidence suggests that most appropriate adults merely observe the proceedings.[37] Observation alone cannot protect the rights of vulnerable suspects.[38] Yet the notion behind the appropriate adult scheme is a valid one. The presence of a person to ensure the interview process is carried out correctly and fairly is needed despite the current problems. Alternatives to the appropriate adult have been suggested. Fennell proposes the abolition of the appropriate adult scheme, replacing it with 'fully qualified solicitors with special training in advising mentally disordered clients'.[39] While Laing notes 'the overall shortcomings of the treatment of the mentally ill whilst in police custody

34 Royal Commission on Criminal Justice *Report of the Royal Commission on Criminal Justice* Cm 2263 (1993) HMSO, London.
35 Gudjonsson, G, Clare, I, Rutter, S & Pearse, J *Persons At Risk During Interviews in Police Custody: The Identification of Vulnerabilities* (1993) Royal Commission on Criminal Justice research study No 12.
36 Interestingly, with the use of the MHA 1983, s 136, research suggests that the police use their powers effectively and are often able to accurately assess whether a mental disorder is present, yet the same ability to identify mental health difficulties for the purpose of the appropriate adult scheme seem to be lacking: see Laing, J M *Care or Custody?* (1999) Oxford University Press, Oxford, p 95.
37 Nemitz, T & Bean, P 'The use of appropriate adult scheme (a preliminary report)' *Medicine, Science & Law* 1994, Vol 34, p 161, Nemitz, T & Bean, P 'The effectiveness of a volunteer appropriate adult scheme' *Medicine, Science & Law* 1998, Vol 38, No 3, p 251.
38 Littlechild, B 'Reassessing the role of the appropriate adult' *Criminal Law Review* 1995, p 540; Hodgson, J 'Vulnerable suspects and the appropriate adult' *Criminal Law Review* 1997, p 785; Pearse, J & Gudjonsson, G 'How appropriate are appropriate adults?' *Journal of Forensic Psychiatry* 1996, Vol 7, No 3, p 570; and Palmer, C 'Still vulnerable after all these years' *Criminal Law Review* 1996, p 633.
39 Fennell, P 'Mentally disordered suspects in the criminal justice system' *Journal of Law and Society* 1994, Vol 21, p 57 at p 67.

serve to strengthen the argument for greater medical involvement'.[40] While each suggestion is clearly laudable, neither truly circumvents the problem of relying on the abilities of police personnel to recognise and to act on the presence of mental health difficulties in the suspect. If more police officers were given the necessary training, early diversion from the criminal justice system could be a more easily attained goal and fewer mentally disordered offenders would then filter through to the courts.

5 Diversion Before Sentencing

(a) Proceeding with the prosecution

Once the police decide to bring charges against the suspect, the CPS must assess the case to decide whether to continue with the prosecution or to drop the case. Its decision will largely be influenced by the 'evidential sufficiency' of the case and the 'public interest' issues. Once the decision to proceed with the prosecution is made, the next step in the criminal justice process is the court appearance. Diversion of mentally disordered offenders from the judicial process is possible before conviction and sentencing, as there are a number of legal mechanisms available. However, these diversionary measures are primarily intended to assist the trial process, as an information collecting exercise or to ensure the accused individual is mentally fit for trial, rather than to make sure the mentally disordered offender receives the psychiatric support he needs.

(b) Bail

All accused individuals have a right to bail under the Bail Act 1976, s 4(1). However, since the enactment of the Criminal Justice and Public Order Act 1994, the presumption in favour of bail has been removed from individuals who are accused of committing an offence while on bail for a previous offence[41] or when accused of murder, manslaughter or rape and they have similar previous convictions.[42] The presumption can also be rebutted if the accused is likely to re-offend while on bail, abscond or interfere with witnesses. Likewise, '[t]he most serious cases of violence would ... be remanded into custody for reasons of public safety'.[43]

40   Laing, J M *Care or Custody?* (1999) Oxford University Press, Oxford, p 96.
41   Criminal Justice and Public Order Act 1994, s 26.
42   Criminal Justice and Public Order Act 1994, s 25.
43   James, D, Cripps, J, Gilluley, P & Harlow, P 'A court-focused model of forensic psychiatry provision to central London: abolishing remands to prison?' *Journal of Forensic Psychiatry* 1997, Vol 8, No 2, p 390 at p 390.

It is possible to attach conditions to the bail order. Where the accused needs medical treatment or the court requires medical reports on the accused's psychiatric state, bail can be granted with the requirement that the accused resides at a specified hospital/unit or attends an outpatient clinic for the purposes of assessment and treatment.[44] Frequently, the court needs more information about the state of the accused's health than it actually possesses, therefore obtaining medical reports is essential in order for the court to act appropriately and to direct the right disposal. Despite the need for more information, the Butler Committee[45] acknowledged that often the psychiatric needs of defendants were not recognised by the courts.[46] Yet, when a medical report is considered necessary, bail is often abandoned, as custody may be seen as being in the interests of the accused's protection[47] or to prevent the accused absconding if he is homeless.[48] The difficulties associated with the court gaining information about the accused's state of mind poses further problems in relation to the use of the diversion policy. The court can only act on the information it has and if this is inaccurate or limited, it is likely that a custodial penal sentence will be the preferred option.[49]

(c) Remand to hospital for report or treatment

It has been shown above that bail may be considered undesirable owing to shortages in information concerning the accused's mental condition, fear that the individual might abscond or because the offence was too severe and the individual might pose a threat to the public. Instead of bail, the court may remand the accused directly to hospital for assessment and treatment under the MHA 1983, ss 35 and 36. For each provision, the court must be provided with evidence that a bed is available in a hospital for the defendant within the next seven days. The individual may be remanded under each provision for up to 28 days[50] and this period can be

---

44   Bail Act 1976, s 3(6).
45   Lord Butler *Report of the Committee on Mentally Abnormal Offenders* Cm. 6244 (1975) HMSO, London.
46   Donovan, W M & O'Brien, K P 'Psychiatric court reports: Too many or too few?' *Medicine, Science & Law* 1981, Vol 21, p 153.
47   See Bail Act 1976, Sch 1, Pt I.
48   Hylton, J J 'Care or control? Health or criminal justice options for the long term seriously mentally ill in a Canadian Province' *International Journal of Law and Psychiatry* 1995, Vol 18, No 1, p 45.
49   Allam, D P 'Sentencing of the mentally disordered' *The Mag* 1990, Vol 46, p 176.
50   The MHA 1983, ss 35(7) and 36(6).

renewed if further time is needed.[51] Remand to hospital for medical reports or treatment cannot exceed 12 weeks in total.[52]

The MHA 1983, s 35 provides a general power to remand a defendant by a magistrates' court or the Crown Court to hospital 'for a report on his mental condition'. As the provision is applicable to an accused individual,[53] a magistrates' court can remand the person in hospital for assessment without being certain that he has carried out the alleged offence. Despite the human rights implications, individuals are at least protected from being treated without their consent.[54] Lord Belstead observed in 1982 that 'there is no intention that a person remanded under [the MHA 1983, s 35] should be regarded as detained for treatment,' and therefore, should not be at risk of receiving non-consensual medical treatment.[55] However, where the individual does not consent, he will usually be detained for treatment under the MHA 1983, s 3 civil powers, thereby circumventing the need for patient consent.[56] The Court of Appeal has ignored concerns raised over individuals being subject to both the civil and criminal provisions of the MHA 1983. In *Dlodlo v Mental Health Review Tribunal for the South Thames Region*,[57] and *R v North West London Mental Health NHS Trust, ex p S*,[58] it was found that application of the provisions in one part of the MHA 1983 could be used in relation to an individual who was already detained under another part.

As Bartlett and Sandland clearly point out, the decision can be strongly argued against.[59] If individuals who are remanded under the MHA 1983, s 35 for assessment can be detained for treatment under the MHA 1983, s 3 if they do not consent to treatment, it begs the question as to why the MHA 1983, s 36 exists. Section 36 confers a power, exercisable only by the Crown Court, to remand the accused to hospital for treatment. The Crown Court must be satisfied with medical evidence that the accused is 'suffering from mental illness or severe mental impairment of a nature or

51 The MHA 1983, ss 35(5) and 36(4).
52 The MHA 1983, ss 35(7) and 36(6).
53 The MHA 1983, s 35(2)(b): an accused person is 'any person who has been convicted by the court of an offence punishable on summary conviction with impairment and any person charged with such an offence if the court is satisfied that he did that act or made the omission charged or has consented to the exercise by the court of the powers conferred by this section'.
54 The MHA 1983, s 56(1)(b).
55 HL Deb vol 426, cols 769-770, 25 January (Lord Belstead).
56 Doubts about the risk of 'double detention' exist, as articulated by Fennell, P 'Double detention under the Mental Health Act 1983 – A case of extra-Parliamentary legislation' *Journal of Social Welfare and Family Law* 1991, p 194.
57 (1996) 36 BMLR 145.
58 [1998] QB 628.
59 Bartlett, P & Sandland, R *Mental Health Law: Policy and Practice* (2000) Blackstone Press, London, pp 168-69.

degree which makes it appropriate for him to be detained in a hospital for treatment'. However, a person who is diagnosed with a psychopathic disorder or mental impairment cannot be remanded in hospital for treatment under the MHA 1983, s 36.

Research suggests that remand to hospital for assessment and treatment has been under-used.[60] Instead, many mentally disordered offenders are regularly remanded in custody, an environment that offers little chance of a proper psychiatric assessment. The fault for this under-use cannot be directed solely at the courts. In order to remand individuals to hospital there must be clear assurance that a hospital bed can be obtained quickly. Where there are no beds available the courts have little choice but to remand the individual to prison. Many NHS facilities are reticent to accept the MHA 1983, ss 35 and 36 cases. As noted earlier, such individuals are frequently perceived as threatening and unpredictable with the result that little effort is made to stretch already over-stretched resources to facilitate the needs of the court. Owing to these difficulties, mentally disordered offenders who would benefit from a more therapeutic environment are finding themselves in prison.

(d) Other criminal law provisions

(i) UNFITNESS TO STAND TRIAL

Trial stage diversionary measures also exist outside the MHA 1983. An accused person may avoid trial by being found unfit to plead. Where an individual is found to be so unfit, the court will ensure a therapeutic order is made.[61] There is no statutory definition of 'unfitness to plead'. *R v Pritchard*[62] remains the leading case. Baron Alderson found that a defendant could be said to be unfit for trial if he is not 'of sufficient intellect to comprehend the details of the evidence'. The jury must decide whether a defendant is unfit for trial.[63] Use of the unfitness to plead

60 Exworthy, T & Glenn, C 'A case for change: Section 35, Mental Health Act 1983' *Justice of the Peace* 1992, Vol 156, p 663; and Robertson, G et al *Mentally Disordered Remand Prisoners* (1992) Home Office Research and Statistics Department Bulletin, No 32.
61 Such therapeutic orders include a guardianship order, a hospital order and a supervision and treatment order, all of which are governed by the Criminal Procedure (Insanity and Unfitness to Plead) Act 1991, ss 3 and 5. See Fennell, P 'The CP (I and UP) Act 1991' *Modern Law Review* 1992, Vol 55, p 547.
62 (1836) 7 C & P 303.
63 Criminal Procedure (Insanity) Act 1964, s 4(5) as substituted by the Criminal Procedure (Insanity and Unfitness to Plead) Act 1991, s 2. See also, Mackay, R *Mental Condition Defences in the Criminal Law* (1995) Clarendon Press, Oxford, p 225.

provision was rare before the Criminal Procedure (Insanity and Unfitness to Plead) Act 1991 because the consequences were harsh.[64] If a defendant was found unfit to plead, he would be subject to an indefinite hospital order that could be ended by the Home Secretary alone (an order for detention during Her Majesty's Pleasure). Since the enactment of the Criminal Procedure (Insanity and Unfitness to Plead) Act 1991, more cases of unfitness to plead have emerged, as more flexible disposal powers are now available.[65] Indefinite hospitalisation was the only option before 1991: now a range of different disposals can be used, such as guardianship orders, hospital orders, and supervision and treatment orders.

(II) INSANITY: THE SPECIAL VERDICT

Finally, there is the 'psychiatric defence'[66] of insanity, which is available to defendants who plead not guilty to the offence. The special verdict of insanity provides an alternative to conviction when the defendant is proved to have been insane at the time of the alleged offence. The defendant will then be found 'not guilty by reason of insanity'. The special verdict is governed by the Trial of Lunatics Act 1883, s 2.[67]

The insanity defence is defined in the *M'Naghten Case*.[68] Tindal CJ observed that in order to establish insanity, 'it must be clearly proved that, at the time of committing the act, the party accused was labouring under such a defect of reason, from disease of the mind, as not to know the nature and quality of the act he was doing; or if he did know it, that he did not know that what he was doing was wrong'.[69] The special verdict is rarely used despite the greater flexibility, which was introduced by the Criminal Procedure (Insanity and Unfitness to Plead) Act 1991. As with unfitness to plead cases, the only disposal, which was available to the court before the 1991 Act, was indefinite detention in hospital. Now a range of disposals is available.[70] Bartlett and Sandland note that the special verdict's use is infrequent because it has been 'superseded by the

64 Mackay, R 'The decline of disability in relation to the trial' *Criminal Law Review* 1991, p 87.
65 Mackay, R & Kearns, G 'The continued underuse of unfitness to plead and the insanity defence' *Criminal Law Review* 1994, p 576.
66 See Laing, J M *Care or Custody?* (1999) Oxford University Press, Oxford, p 121.
67 The special verdict under the 1883 Act must been seen in conjunction with the Criminal Procedure (Insanity) Act 1964 and the Criminal Procedure (Insanity and Unfitness to Plead) Act 1991.
68 (1843) 10 Cl & Fin 200.
69 (1843) 10 Cl & Fin 200 at 210.
70 Tomison, A 'McNaughton today' *Journal of Forensic Psychiatry* 1993, Vol 4, p 371.

defence of diminished responsibility that was introduced in 1957'[71] and 'the abolition of the death penalty in 1965' means that it is no longer clear that indefinite detention in a psychiatric hospital is preferable to a criminal disposal.[72] Where the defence of diminished responsibility is successful, statistics indicate that the defendant will typically receive a therapeutic disposal, such as a hospital order or a supervision order, rather than a penal one.[73]

6 Diversion at Sentencing Stage

(a) Medical and pre-sentence reports

The diversion policy provides an opportunity to redirect mentally disordered offenders away from the criminal justice system and towards the health care system, thereby affording the defendant the means of receiving therapeutic assistance. Diversion should be sought at the earliest moment, yet some offenders will continue right through to the final stages of the criminal process. Having been found guilty of the offence, it will then be a matter for the court to decide on sentencing. Various therapeutic disposals are available to the court, primarily under the MHA 1983, and these offer an alternative to punitive sanctions.

If a therapeutic disposal is being actively considered, the court must obtain a medical and pre-sentence report as required by the Criminal Justice Act 1991.[74] The pre-sentence report provides detailed information, including any information regarding the nature and circumstances of the offence, which could assist the court in determining the best method of dealing with the offender. The medical report outlines the offender's mental state, the possible effect a custodial sentence in prison might have on the condition and any possible treatment options. Obtaining these reports serves one purpose: to ensure the court has all the pertinent information necessary in order to sentence the offender appropriately. Before the enactment of the Criminal Procedure (Insanity and Unfitness to Plead) Act 1991, it was commonly recognised that there had been a decline in the use of medical and other relevant information in the sentencing

---

71 This partial defence reduces a murder charge to one of manslaughter.
72 Bartlett, P & Sandland, R *Mental Health Law: Policy and Practice* (2000) Blackstone Press, London, p 178.
73 Home Office *Criminal Statistics England and Wales 1995* Cm 3421 (1996) HMSO, London.
74 Criminal Justice Act 1991, s 3. See also, Wasik, M & Taylor, R *Blackstone's Guide to the Criminal Justice Act 1991* (1994) Blackstone Press, London.

process.[75] The mandatory nature of these reports acknowledges the important role psychiatric care and treatment has to play in the management of mentally disordered offenders.

(b) Therapeutic disposals

(I) HOSPITAL ORDER

Once the medical evidence is gathered, if hospital care is thought necessary the court can make a hospital order. This power is contained in the MHA 1983, s 37. The court must consider whether punishment or treatment is most appropriate and what risk the mentally disordered offender might pose to others.[76] The order offers an alternative to imprisonment and, once it is made, the defendant will leave the criminal justice system and cannot be brought back into it. The hospital order

> 'is intended to be humane by comparison with a prison sentence. A hospital order is not a punishment. Questions of retribution and deterrence ... are immaterial. The offender who has become a patient is not kept on any kind of leash by the court'.[77]

Before a hospital order is made, the court must be satisfied with the written or oral evidence of two doctors (of which one must be approved) that the defendant is suffering from mental illness, psychopathic disorder, severe mental impairment or mental impairment, of a nature or degree which makes it appropriate for him to be detained in a hospital for treatment.[78] If the individual is suffering from a psychopathic disorder or a mental impairment, the condition must be treatable if a hospital order is to be imposed.[79] The hospital order therefore offers the court the means of facilitating treatment and care rather than being restricted to giving mentally disordered offenders penal sentences.[80] Yet, despite the obvious benefits associated with hospital orders, their use has been limited owing to shortages in hospital facilities. The courts can only grant therapeutic disposals when the beds, professional staff and community psychiatric

75 Donovan, W & O'Brien, K 'Psychiatric court reports: Too many or too few?' *Medicine, Science & Law* 1981, Vol 21, p 153 and Mackay, R 'Psychiatric reports in the Crown Court' *Criminal Law Review* 1986, p 217.
76 *R v Gunnell* (1966) 50 Cr App R 242; *R v Higginbotham* [1961] 1 WLR 1277.
77 (1989) 11 Cr App Rep (S) 202, per Mustill LJ at 210.
78 MHA 1983, s 37(2)(a).
79 A condition is 'treatable' if it is likely to be alleviated or prevented from deteriorating with appropriate treatment.
80 Robertson, G et al 'A follow-up of remanded mentally ill offenders given court hospital orders' *Medicine, Science & Law* 1994, Vol 34, p 61.

facilities are available. When they are lacking, the courts have no option but to sentence the offender to a term in prison irrespective of medical recommendations to the contrary.[81] The problem is partly founded on inadequate collaboration and co-operation between the courts and hospitals.[82] Quite often, the courts cannot acquire sufficient information regarding the availability of hospital beds or they are faced with increasing unwillingness on the part of medical personnel to deal with patients under the MHA 1983, s 37 hospital orders, which are perceived to be too dangerous and unpredictable. The problem of limited hospital beds remains, as does the reticence of nursing staff to deal with such patients, but the MHA 1983, s 39 enables the court to obtain more easily information about bed availability and other psychiatric care facilities. The MHA 1983, s 39 obliges health authorities to inform the court as to the facilities they provide, yet there is no requirement for them to provide such services to specific patients under order from the court. Provision remains subject, therefore, to clinical discretion, and the court at this point is wholly reliant on this in order to divert the mentally disordered offender away from the criminal justice system.[83]

(II) THE PSYCHIATRIC PROBATION ORDER

The medical report may not indicate the need for inpatient hospital treatment but may suggest the need for some form of supervision. Where this is the case, bearing in mind the difficulties faced by the court in locating hospital beds, the court can consider the use of a psychiatric probation order instead. Both magistrates' courts and the Crown Court can impose a psychiatric probation order for any offence (with the exception of murder as this has a mandatory sentence). Under probation, a probation officer will supervise the mentally disordered offender for a period between six months and three years. This order may be accompanied by certain requirements, such as the provision of treatment

81 The difficulty of locating hospital beds is a continuing source of frustration for the courts. See for example *Officer* (1976) Times, 20 February; *R v McFarlane* (1975) 60 Cr App Rep 320; and *Gordon* (1981) 3 Cr App Rep(S) 352. In each of these cases, it was recommended that the defendant receive psychiatric care and treatment in a hospital environment, yet the lack of facilities forced the court to sentence the defendant to a term of imprisonment.
82 This has been a recognised problem since the work of Larry Gostin for MIND in the 1970s: see Gostin, L *A Human Condition, Volume II, The Law Relating to Mentally Abnormal Offenders: Observations, Analysis and Proposals for Reform* (1975) MIND, London.
83 Verdun-Jones, SN 'Sentencing the partly mad and the partly bad: The case of the hospital order in England and Wales' *International Journal of Law and Psychiatry* 1989, Vol 12, p 1.

in order to improve and/or prevent deterioration of the offender's mental condition or to require the submission of the offender to psychological assessment and therapy. Psychiatric probation orders are only suitable for offenders who are not thought to present a risk to others. Where such risks exist, the court will err on the side of caution and direct a custodial sentence. The probation order enables the court to exert some discretion and flexibility in terms of the treatment and care the offender should receive. The order can require the offender to reside at a hospital (although not a special hospital) for assessment and treatment, to attend occupational and other therapy sessions or to submit to psychological treatment. Some latitude even exists as to the length of time such treatment should be administered if the doctor involved considers the treatment should continue for longer than the specified probation period.[84] This scope for amendment has naturally led this order to be popular among the courts and those who endeavour to implement it in practice. However, despite the healthier 'balance of care and control',[85] with the emphasis shifting away from detention, the probation order is nevertheless regarded by some commentators as increasing the likelihood of repeat offending.[86] For those offenders with mental health problems, a psychiatric probation order can only be worthwhile if the necessary care and support within the community is available. Unfortunately, evidence suggests the level of actual support is far from satisfactory and that the usefulness of psychiatric probation orders has been marginalised as a consequence of this.[87]

(III) GUARDIANSHIP ORDER

The guardianship order is governed by the MHA 1983, s 37. The requirements of the provision are identical to that of the hospital order (which is also governed by the MHA 1983, s 37), except treatability for individuals with a mental impairment or a psychopathic condition is not necessary and, rather than inpatient hospital care, the individual is placed under the control of the local social services authority or an approved guardian. As with the hospital order, the court must have adequate

84 Powers of Criminal Courts Act 1973, s 3(5), (6), also Sch 1, para 4.
85 Peay, J 'Mentally disordered offenders' in Maguire, M, Morgan, R & Reiner, R (eds) *The Oxford Handbook of Criminology* (1994) Oxford University Press, Oxford, p 1135.
86 Lewis, P *Psychiatric Probation Orders: Roles and Expectations of Probation Officers and Psychiatrists* (1980) Institute of Criminology, Cambridge, p 36.
87 Mustill, M 'Some concluding reflections', in Herbst, K & Gunn, J (eds) *The Mentally Disordered Offender* (1991) Butterworth-Heinemann, London, p 244.

information about the availability of services when considering whether to impose a guardianship order. The MHA 1983, s 39A, which was inserted by the Criminal Justice Act 1991, s 27(1), enables the court to seek information from the local social services authority about the facilities needed for guardianship and whether it would be willing to act as guardian to the offender. As with guardianship under the MHA 1983, s 7 within the civil provisions, the guardian has specified powers. He may determine a place of residence, decide when and where the offender should go to receive treatment, occupational therapy and so forth, and he may insist on contact between the offender and a named doctor and social worker.[88]

The guardianship order suffers from the same practical problems associated with the psychiatric probation order, but does not have the same advantages. Clearly, as with the psychiatric probation order, the success of a guardianship order will depend on the community facilities and support that can be provided. Without such support, the offender will inevitably break the conditions of the order or re-offend. Under probation, when the offender breaches a condition of the order, suitable sanctions exist which penalise him and deter others from doing the same. Guardianship has no formal sanctions with which to control uncooperative offenders, making the order an ineffectual tool. The lack of sanctions has resulted in guardianship being underused, because without the means to control the offender's activities in the community, the benefits of guardianship are overshadowed by the potential risk to third parties.[89]

(IV) INTERIM HOSPITAL ORDER

The notion of the interim hospital order, which is governed by the MHA 1983, s 38, was introduced by the Butler Committee[90] to overcome the challenge of choosing whether to '[treat] an offender as mad or bad' at an early stage.[91] In the event that the offender is not co-operating with treatment, there has been a mistaken diagnosis or there are no obvious

88 MHA 1983, s 8.
89 See Fisher, M 'Guardianship under the mental health legislation: A review' *Journal of Social Welfare Law* 1988, p 316; Wattis, J P, Grant, W, Traynor, J & Harris, S 'Use of guardianship under the 1983 Mental Health Act' *Medicine, Science & Law* 1990, Vol 30, p 313.
90 The *Butler Committee* gained 'the impression that many doctors found it difficult to decide whether to recommend that a hospital order should be made where they have been able to examine the patient only briefly in a prison hospital under the pressure of impending court proceedings': para 12.5.
91 Hoggett, B *Mental Health Law* (4th edn, 1996) Sweet & Maxwell, London, p 121.

treatment options for the condition, the interim hospital order provides the opportunity to return the offender to court in order to consider whether a different, 'more suitable disposal' should be invoked.[92] Where such an order is imposed by the court, 'the offender's response in hospital can be evaluated without any irrevocable commitment on either side to this method of dealing with the offender if it should prove unsuitable'.[93] The court must have convicted the accused of an imprisonable offence and there must be written or oral evidence of two registered medical practitioners that the accused is suffering from mental illness, psychopathic disorder, severe mental impairment or mental impairment, of a nature or degree which makes it appropriate for him to be detained in a hospital for treatment.[94] Therefore, treatment for the mental condition is an intrinsic part of the order and the offender will be subject to the consent to treatment provisions contained in the MHA 1983, Pt IV. As with the hospital order, there must also be evidence that a bed will be available for the accused in the next 28 days.[95] The stay in hospital can last for up to 12 weeks, followed by a monthly renewal for a maximum period of 12 months.[96] The MHA 1983, s 39 also applies, enabling the court to seek information regarding the availability of hospital beds.

The use of interim hospital orders has been limited since its introduction despite the Butler Committee's recognition that the court and medical personnel working with mentally disordered offenders often faced difficulties deciding upon the most appropriate disposal. The Working Group on Psychopathic Disorder, which reported in 1994,[97] suggests that its underuse might have arisen because of the courts' being unacquainted with the value of the provision. In 1994 Kaul's work on the use of the interim hospital order in the Trent Regional Secure Unit highlighted the usefulness of the order. It found that when the order was imposed its use was primarily as a means of assessing the treatability of patients with psychopathic conditions.[98] If nothing else, any opportunities to assess a

---

92 Laing, J M *Care or Custody?* (1999) Oxford University Press, Oxford, p 134.
93 Home Office *Home Office Circular No 71/1984* Annex, para 15.
94 MHA 1983, s 38(1).
95 MHA 1983, s 38(4).
96 The Crime (Sentences) Act 1997, s 49 extended the time limit for an interim hospital order from six months to twelve months.
97 Department of Health/Home Office *Report of the Department of Health and Home Office Working Group on Psychopathic Disorder* (1994) Home Office, London.
98 Kaul, A 'Interim hospital orders: A regional secure unit experience' *Medicine, Science & Law* 1994, Vol 34, p 233.

mentally disordered offender's condition must be embraced and use of the interim hospital order should therefore be encouraged.[99]

(v) RESTRICTION ORDER

A restriction order is governed by the MHA 1983, s 41 and is added to a hospital order when an additional level of control and security is needed. The restriction order ensures that the offender is no longer

'regarded simply as a patient whose interests are paramount ... . Instead, the interests of public safety are regarded by transferring the responsibility for discharge from the Responsible Medical Officer and the hospital ... to the Secretary of State and the Mental Health Review Tribunal. A patient who has been subject to a restriction order is likely to be detained in hospital for much longer than one who is not, and will have fewer opportunities for leave of absence'.[100]

When considering whether to impose a restriction order, the court must have regard to the nature of the offence, the history of the offender and whether he has any past convictions, the likely risk that he might re-offend and whether the public would be exposed to danger. The Butler Committee recommended that restriction orders should be viewed as a last resort in very serious cases and when it was necessary to protect the public.[101]

The restriction order can be of limited duration.[102] However, this option is rarely used, as the purpose of the order is to ensure the mentally disordered offender receives the psychiatric care and support he needs and is discharged only when he is ready.[103] Inevitably, predicting a date of recovery is plagued with difficulty therefore the courts are reticent to impose time-limited orders.[104] Imposing orders without limit of time gives clinicians sufficient flexibility in the care and treatment of the offender. During the period of the order the offender cannot be given leave of

---

99 See also, Eastman, N & Peay, J 'Sentencing psychopaths: Is the Hospital and Limitation Direction an ill-considered hybrid?' *Criminal Law Review* 1998, p 93.
100 *R v Birch* (1989) 11 Cr App Rep (S) 202 at 211, CA per Mustill LJ. See also, Andoh, B 'The hospital order with restrictions' *Criminal Law Review* 1994, Vol 58, p 97.
101 *R v Courtney* (1987) 9 Cr App Rep (S) 404.
102 MHA 1983, s 41(1).
103 Robertson, G 'The restricted hospital order' *Psychiatric Bulletin* 1989, Vol 13, p 4.
104 *R v Gardiner* (1967) 51 Cr App Rep 187.

absence, be transferred or discharged without the consent of the Secretary of State[105] and, while subject to restriction, the offender will be under constant scrutiny.[106] However, despite these restrictions, since the decision of *X v United Kingdom*,[107] restricted patients are now able to seek a review of their position by a Mental Health Review Tribunal.

Restriction orders without limit of time have been subject to criticism as it has been argued that such orders are 'used more often as a covert way to introduce a punitive element into a treatment order in a way which departs from the spirit of the general policy of diversion'.[108] As the 'discharge' decision is delayed to 'sometime in the future', it can result in many patients being subject to unnecessarily long periods of detention. Furthermore, the decision to restrict the offender without limit of time is one for the court and as the judiciary are not qualified to formulate a prognosis about the offender's mental condition, it would seem that such discretion could be ill placed.[109] Despite concerns that use of the restriction order could lead to many individuals spending long periods in hospital before consideration is given to possible release, the restriction order at least enables responsibility for their care and control to be shared by medical and social services personnel and the prison service. However, in practice the court's decision to impose a particular disposal continues to be influenced by the available resources. If a restriction order is to be used, there must be a bed for the offender in a psychiatric unit, appropriately trained staff and facilities to cope with his needs. The reality is that in many cases inadequate provision has forced the court to impose a prison sentence in place of a restriction order and, once again, the diversion policy is swept aside.

(VI) HOSPITAL DIRECTION

Under the Crime (Sentences) Act 1997 a new disposal has been introduced whereby the Crown Court can impose a hospital direction. The hospital direction resulted after numerous calls were made for greater flexibility to be injected into the current system for dealing with offenders suffering

---

105 MHA 1983, s 41(3).
106 This monitoring is carried out by the Mental Health Unit (MHU) of the Home Office. Annual reports are made to the MHU by the restricted patient's responsible medical officer (MHA 1983, s 41(6)).
107 (1981) 4 EHRR 188.
108 Bartlett, P & Sandland, R *Mental Health Law: Policy and Practice* (2000) Blackstone Press, London, p 189.
109 Walker, N 'Fourteen years on', in Herbst, K & Gunn, J (eds) *The Mentally Disordered Offender* (1991) Butterworth-Heinemann, London.

from a mental disorder.[110] Once the mentally disordered offender has been diverted out of the criminal justice system to hospital, he cannot return to prison. This inflexibility, combined with increasing concerns about the particular challenges brought about by the psychopathically disordered individual, led to the reforms, which were introduced in the Crime (Sentences) Act 1997. The treatability issue presents a problem here for whether psychopathic conditions can actively be treated remains a live debate. Owing to this, the use of therapeutic disposals such as hospital orders under the MHA 1983, s 37 may not be particularly appropriate. In these cases the offender may be released from hospital early because of the lack of treatment options available or he will be given a punitive disposal. Neither case is ideal as the true needs of the individual are not dealt with and re-offending is often an inevitable consequence.[111]

The Crime (Sentences) Act 1997, s 46 inserted sections 45A and 45B into the 1983 Act (MHA 1983, ss 45A and 45B) which provides for 'hospital and limitation directions' to be made by the Crown Court. The MHA 1983, s 45A(3)(a) defines a hospital direction as being 'a direction that, instead of being removed to and detained in a prison, the offender may be removed to and detained in such hospital as may be specified in the direction'. The Crime (Sentences) Act 1997, s 47 stipulates the need for naming the particular hospital where the offender will be admitted. In practice, this disposal allows the court to direct an immediate admission to hospital when also imposing a prison sentence.[112] A hospital direction can be given by the Crown Court if it has sufficient medical evidence to suggest that such a disposal would be appropriate and in circumstances where the court has actively considered giving a hospital order under the MHA 1983, s 37.[113]

The conditions, which need to be met before a hospital direction is imposed, are the same as for the hospital order. There must be evidence from two doctors that the mental disorder is of a nature or degree that warrants detention in a hospital for medical treatment and that this treatment is likely to alleviate, or at least prevent deterioration of, the condition. The hospital direction may also be made with a 'limitation direction', which is introduced in the MHA 1983, s 45A. A limitation

---

110 Home Office/Department of Health *Mentally Disordered Offenders – Sentencing and Discharge Arrangements: A Discussion Paper on a Proposed New Power for the Courts* (1996) Home Office/Department of Health, London.
111 Home Office/Department of Health *Mentally Disordered Offenders – Sentencing and Discharge Arrangements: A Discussion Paper on a Proposed New Power for the Courts* (1996) Home Office/Department of Health, London, paras 10.24-10.26.
112 MHA 1983, s 46.
113 Home Office Circular 54/1997, para 62.

direction is a direction that the offender be subject to the special restrictions contained in the MHA 1983, s 41.

The hospital direction was originally intended for the psychopathically disordered alone.[114] This direction was the result of concerns relating to the care and control of those with psychopathic conditions and the difficulty associated with treatment. However, in order for a hospital direction to be given, the court must have evidence that the condition necessitates treatment in a hospital environment and that the treatment is likely to have some effect on the condition. Therefore, treatability must still be evidenced!

The offender will stay in hospital while he continues to need treatment. If the treatment is not successful, there are no treatment options available, or his condition improves before the sentence term has ended, he will be sent to prison to serve the remainder of the sentence.[115] The same safeguards as given to prisoners who are transferred to hospital under the MHA 1983, ss 47 and 48 (see below) will be accorded to offenders who are subject to a hospital direction, including the right of access to a Mental Health Review Tribunal, thereby ensuring compatibility with the European Convention on Human Rights.[116]

Despite these safeguards, the hospital direction has faced criticism. Initially, this 'hybrid' order was intended to apply to offenders with psychopathic conditions alone.[117] However, the hospital direction's application is far more extensive and can apply to offenders diagnosed with any of the other categories of mental disorder under the MHA 1983, s 1. The use of this disposal has been broadened to deal with the difficulties associated with accurate diagnosis of psychiatric conditions and the problems of dual diagnoses. Yet it is argued that when an offender has benefited from the therapeutic hospital environment and their mental condition has improved, they should not then be remitted back to the

---

114 However, the hospital direction can be extended to other categories of mental disorder by the Secretary of State under the MHA 1983, s 45A(10). Home Office Circular 54/1997, para 62.
115 MHA 1983, s 50(1).
116 For a detailed review of the Human Rights Act 1998, see Wadham, J & Mountfield, H *Blackstone's Guide to the Human Rights Act 1998* (1999) Blackstone, London.
117 Department of Health and Social Security/Home Office *Offenders Suffering from Psychopathic Disorder* Joint DHSS/HO Consultation Document (1986) DHSS/HO, London and Home Office/Department of Health *Mentally Disordered Offenders – Sentencing and Discharge Arrangements: A Discussion Paper on a Proposed New Power for the Courts* (1996) Home Office/Department of Health, London.

harsh prison regime.[118] Indeed, the Mental Health Act Commission have called such practices 'anti-therapeutic' which 'could lead sour relations between patients and staff' to surface and prevent patients from 'confronting their problems by engineering a retreat to prison'.[119] The prison system cannot offer the care and support that many of these offenders need. The added flexibility of this disposal is wasted if the positive work, which is carried out in hospital, is lost once the offender is then restored to prison. It is further argued that the hospital direction flouts the underlying ideology of the mental health legislation, which focuses on timely psychiatric intervention and disregards the recognised diversion policy. In many ways, the hospital direction suggests a positive return to retributive justice.[120]

7 The Transfer of Prisoners to Hospital

(a) Introduction

Despite efforts to divert mentally disordered offenders out of the criminal justice system at the earliest opportunity, many such offenders will still find themselves in prison. This may occur because of failures in mental health screening programmes or prison conditions may adversely affect the prisoner's mental condition.[121] Where prisoners are found to exhibit symptoms of mental disturbance mechanisms exist to transfer such persons from prison to hospital. The current law with respect to the transfer of a person from prison to hospital can be found in the MHA 1983, ss 47 to 49.

(b) Transfer of sentenced prisoners

The MHA 1983, s 47 provides for an offender who has been sentenced to a term in prison, but who has later been found to exhibit symptoms of

118 Ashworth, A 'Sentencing mentally disordered offenders' *Criminal Law Review* 1996, p 457.
119 Mental Health Act Commission *Sixth Biennial Report, 1993–1995* (1996) HMSO, London, p 72.
120 Home Office/Department of Health *Mentally Disordered Offenders – Sentencing and Discharge Arrangements: A Discussion Paper on a Proposed New Power for the Courts* (1996) Home Office/Department of Health, London, para 10.24.
121 Birmingham, L, Mason, D & Grubin, D 'Prevalence of mental disorder in remand prisoners: Consecutive case study' *British Medical Journal* 1996, Vol 313, p 1521; Hardie, T, Bhui, K, Brown, P, Watson, J & Parrott, J 'Unmet needs of remand prisoners' *Medicine, Science & Law* 1998, Vol 38(3), p 233. See also, Gostin, L *Mental Health Services: Law and Practice* (1986) Shaw & Sons, London, para 16.01.

mental disturbance, to be transferred to hospital. The offender must be examined by two doctors (of which one has to be approved) and they must agree that he is suffering from one or more of the four forms of mental disorder as defined in the MHA 1983, s 1. If the offender is diagnosed as suffering from a psychopathic disorder or is mentally impaired, it must also be shown that inpatient hospital treatment will improve, or at least prevent further deterioration of, the condition. Once a diagnosis is made, the Home Secretary can direct his transfer to hospital. A transfer direction has the same effect as a hospital order and can be made with or without restrictions.[122]

The application of the MHA 1983, s 47 has steadily increased since 1984, but its use has been hampered by practical difficulties.[123] Considerable delays from the initial decision to transfer a prisoner to hospital and the actual transfer are commonplace.[124] These delays surface because of inadequate hospital services, lack of beds and reluctance on the part of many psychiatric facilities to admit such patients.[125] Concerns have also been raised as to the possible abuse arising from the transfer of a prisoner in the closing stages of his prison sentence, as prisoners may find themselves detained in hospital after their prison sentence has elapsed.[126] However, research indicates that these fears are unfounded.[127]

(c) Transfer of unsentenced prisoners

There is also provision for the transfer of prisoners who have not yet been sentenced. If a mentally disordered person is currently awaiting trial or sentence and has been remanded in custody, the Home Secretary has the power to transfer the prisoner to hospital for 'urgent treatment' under the MHA 1983, s 48. The use of this provision only applies to prisoners who are suffering from 'mental illness or severe mental impairment of a nature or degree which makes it appropriate for him to be detained in hospital for medical treatment and is in urgent need of such treatment'.[128] This

122 MHA 1983, s 47(3).
123 HO *Statistical Bulletin* 01/95. In 1984, there were 108 section 47 transfers, in 1987, 127 transfers and by 1990, there were 156 transfers.
124 See 54 HC Official Report, para 4.26, Session 1991-2.
125 Grounds, A 'Transfer of sentenced prisoners to hospital' *Criminal Law Review* 1990, p 544. See also, Dolan, M & Shetty, G 'Transfer delays in a special hospital population' *Medicine, Science & Law* 1995, Vol 35, No 3, p 237.
126 Grounds, A 'The transfer of sentenced prisoners to hospital 1960-1983: A study in one special hospital' *British Journal of Criminology* 1991, Vol 31, p 54.
127 Huws, R et al 'Prison transfers to special hospitals since the introduction of the Mental Health Act' *Journal of Forensic Psychiatry* 1997, Vol 8, No 1, p 74.
128 The written or oral evidence of two registered medical practitioners must endorse the need for transfer to hospital: the MHA 1983, s 48(1).

power is, therefore, regarded as being one of last resort to deal with emergencies. Having established the need to transfer the prisoner to hospital, the transfer must be carried out within 14 days of the order being made and the duration of the hospital stay is of no fixed time.

As with the MHA 1983, s 47, the use of the MHA 1983, s 48 has been on the increase since the 1980s. This increase reflected growing concerns that too many mentally ill offenders were being imprisoned when they should have been in receipt of therapeutic intervention. In the 1980s, it was recognised that every effort should be made to 'enable appropriate mentally disordered persons to be taken into the health system rather than the penal system'.[129] However, as with the MHA 1983, s 47, its use has been hampered by inadequate hospital facilities and unwillingness on the part of nursing staff to deal with the MHA 1983, s 48 cases.[130] Yet, despite logistical problems in acquiring hospital beds within 14 days of the order being made, the Home Office has indicated that greater use of the provision should be made where possible.[131]

The transfer of prisoners to hospital should be encouraged where there is evidence to suggest that they are suffering from a mental disorder. However, the need to transfer prisoners also indicates a failure to detect the problem sooner and to divert the offender out of the criminal justice system earlier. The prison environment and regime can have a detrimental effect on an individual with mental health problems. Any time that is spent in such surroundings when psychiatric assistance is more appropriate is a failure in the diversion policy. While it seems that greater hurdles need to be overcome in order to transfer a prisoner to hospital, efforts should be made to ensure mental health difficulties in those who encounter the criminal justice system are detected much earlier, thereby enabling the offender to receive the care and support he needs.

8 Difficulties with the Diversion Policy

This chapter has outlined the source of the diversion policy and considered its practical implementation. The benefits of the policy have been acknowledged, as has the detrimental effect prison can have on

---

129 Home Office/Department of Health and Social Security *Report of an Interdepartmental Working Group of Home Office and DHSS Officials on Mentally Disordered Offenders in the Prison System in England and Wales* (1987) DHSS/ HO, London, para 62.
130 *Report of a Review in Prison Service Establishments in England and Wales* Cm 1383 (1990) HMSO, London, paras 3.64, 3.58, 7.94.
131 Mackay, R & Machin, D *Transfers from Prison to Hospital: The operation of section 48 of the Mental Health Act 1983* (1998) Home Office, London.

vulnerable individuals with mental health difficulties. However, the diversion policy is far from perfect and many offenders slip through the net and find themselves in prison. In addition many recurring problems exist, all of which combine to prevent the policy from being wholly effective.

The most palpable difficulty is the inadequate levels of funding to establish an operational diversion policy. So far, the policy has been financed in a rather haphazard fashion, relying on initial pump priming from the Mental Health Foundation and central Government to get the system started. This money cannot maintain a well-developed national system of diversion and a long-term funding source will need to be found. It has been shown above that use of the diversionary disposals within the MHA 1983 has been somewhat dependent on whether suitable facilities can be obtained. Where such support has not been forthcoming, courts have had little choice but to sentence the offender to a prison term.

Combined with the constant strain of limited resources, other practical problems exist which make diversion difficult to implement. Arranging transport, the sharing of information on the availability of hospital beds and other facilities, the management of individuals with numerous care needs and the assumption of responsibility all hinge on inter-agency communication and co-operation. Each agency has its own objectives and methods. Yet in order for a policy like diversion to be effective these agencies must collaborate. Likewise, without clear and coherent central guidance as to how the diversion policy is to work at a national level, implementation of the policy can suffer through miscommunication, rather than a lack of it. The notion of diverting mentally disordered offenders out of the criminal justice system has, as Bartlett and Sandland point out, 'been left to a large extent to those working at local level, and the result is service provision that is patchy both in terms of geographical spread and of quality'.[132]

These logistical complications have made the implementation of the diversion policy difficult and at times impossible. Yet, even if these problems did not exist, the potential for early diversion has been limited by some of the legal provisions within the MHA 1983. For certain offenders, most notably those who are diagnosed with a psychopathic condition, the diversion opportunities available to them are restricted because of the need to evidence treatability. Hospital and limitation directions can only be applied to those with conditions that are likely to

---

132 As highlighted by Bartlett, P & Sandland, R *Mental Health Law: Policy and Practice* (2000) Blackstone Press, London, p 199.

be improved by medical treatment or at least prevented from deteriorating. Therefore, the ability to shield some mentally disordered offenders from punitive sanction has been lost. The diversion policy has attempted to distinguish between the 'mad' and the 'bad' but the provisions within the Crime (Sentences) Act 1997 that are directed at mentally disordered offenders reveal a possible shift in policy aims. The hospital and limitation direction attempt to combine both corrective and therapeutic objectives but it would seem that, combined with the real difficulties in obtaining the necessary health care facilities and support in order to divert offenders, the punitive role is becoming ever more prominent.

Chapter 8
Mental health law and policy: future directions

I Introduction

The MHA 1983 has dominated the provision of mental health services for nearly two decades. However, during this period there has been a significant upheaval in policy in relation to the care and control of the mentally ill.[1] The provision of hospital-based psychiatric care for patients has gradually been set aside as the potential benefits of community care have emerged. However, as previous chapters have indicated, early preferences for the community care policy quickly faded as serious failings in the policy's practical implementation began to surface throughout the 1990s.[2] Makeshift attempts at community care have failed to meet the needs of patients and professionals alike. Numerous sources suggest that community care is failing vulnerable individuals.[3] The

1   McCulloch, A, Muijen, M & Harper, H, 'New Developments in Mental Health Policy in the United Kingdom' *International Journal of Law and Psychiatry* 2000, p 261 at p 276.
2   See for example, The Woodley Team Report *Report of the Independent Review Panel to East London and The City Health Authority and Newham Council* (1995) East London and The City Health Authority and Newham Council, London; Steering Committee *Report of the Confidentiality into Homicides and Suicides by Mentally Ill People* (1996) Royal College of Psychiatrists, London; Ritchie, J et al *Report of the Inquiry into the Care and Treatment of Christopher Clunis* (1994) HMSO, London.
3   Eg The Woodley Team Report *Report of the Independent Review Panel to East London and The City Health Authority and Newham Council* (1995) East London and The City Health Authority and Newham Council, London; Steering Committee *Report of the Confidentiality into Homicides and Suicides by Mentally Ill People* (1996) Royal College of Psychiatrists, London; Ritchie, J et al *Report of the Inquiry into the Care and Treatment of Christopher Clunis* (1994) HMSO, London.

policy's practical implementation has suffered from a lack of inter-agency co-operation, communication failures and the unwillingness of various agencies to take responsibility for service provision. Intense scrutiny of these services was therefore, inevitable, as were continued demands for reform. Yet, despite its problems, community care continues to be supported by the current Labour Government. The possibility of returning to the traditional mode of psychiatric care – 'the carceral era' – has been utterly rejected.[4] The likelihood of institutional care re-establishing itself as the main approach to psychiatric care is limited for a variety of reasons. Facilities were widely decommissioned throughout the 1980s and 1990s thereby making such a retrograde step highly expensive. In addition, social attitudes have, overall, firmly embraced the more humanitarian ideal of the least restrictive environment of care. In 1998, the Government outlined a new approach, the 'third way', which aims to offer patients greater support while ensuring the public are fully protected from risk.[5]

Reform of the mental health legislation in England and Wales is much needed. Confidence in the mental health system has plummeted as negative images of psychiatric patients are frequently portrayed through the media. In 1998 the Government appointed an expert committee to review the MHA 1983 and consider proposals for reform.[6] Following the Committee's report, the Government published a Green Paper outlining its own model for reforming the MHA 1983.[7] The proposals were intended to develop a more comprehensive mental health service and included: the use of general guiding principles in the new legislation; a re-examination of the definition of mental disorder; the introduction of a new compulsory power in hospital and in the community with amended criteria for compulsory commitment; new provisions regulating compulsory treatment; and the introduction of a new independent Mental Health Tribunal. This lengthy and wide-ranging process of review and consultation culminated in December 2000 when the Government published its White Paper *Reforming the Mental Health Act*.[8] The White

4 Unsworth, C *The Politics of the Mental Health Legislation* (1987) Oxford University Press, Oxford.
5 Department of Health Press Release 98/311, 1998 and 98/580, 1988; Department of Health *Modernising Mental Health Services: Safe, Sound and Supportive* (1998) HMSO, London.
6 Department of Health *Report of the Expert Committee, Review of the Mental Health Act 1983* (1999) HMSO, London.
7 Department of Health *Reform of the Mental Health Act 1983 – Proposals for Consultation* Cm 4480 (November 1999) TSO, London. See Laing, J M 'Reform of the Mental Health Act 1983' *Medical Law Review* 2000, p 210; Walton, P 'Reforming the Mental Health Act 1983: An Approved Social Worker Perspective' *Journal of Social Welfare and Family Law* 2000, p 401.
8 Department of Health *Reforming the Mental Health Act* Cm 5016–I (December 2000) TSO, London.

Paper is divided into two parts. Part One sets out a new legal framework for when and how care and treatment should be provided without the consent of a person with a mental disorder. Part Two outlines how laws and services will be strengthened to safeguard the public against those who pose the greatest risk, including those who are classified as dangerous and severely personality disordered.[9]

The purpose of this chapter is to examine critically the recent policy initiatives, which outline the Government's forthcoming reform plans. The Government has clearly acknowledged the need to modernise the nation's mental health services. It is recognised that patterns of care and treatment for mental disorders over the past 40 years have radically altered. Long spells of inpatient treatment in a hospital setting are often no longer necessary or desirable yet the current legislation does not offer sufficient flexibility for care and treatment in a less restrictive environment. Efforts have been made to '[break] ... the automatic link between compulsory care and treatment and detention in hospital'.[10] In this chapter, a detailed examination of the Government's aims for a new Mental Health Act, which is contained in the White Paper *Reforming the Mental Health Act*, will be made.

2 The White Paper

(a) The reform plans

The White Paper, *Reforming the Mental Health Act*, is the culmination of a wide-ranging review of the current mental health system. It attempts to respond to and resolve some of the more pressing difficulties associated with contemporary mental health provision. The White Paper describes how improvements are to be made to the system by introducing certain reforms to mental health law. These reforms are to go hand-in-hand with extra investment, which has been committed to improving and modernising mental health services. In April 2001, nearly 500 new secure beds were promised and over 320 24-hour staffed beds, 170 assertive outreach teams and access to services 24 hours a day, 7 days a week are to be made available. A further £330 million investment over the next three years has been promised to ensure adequate care and treatment provision for the most vulnerable.[11] These improvements are to work in conjunction

---

9 Department of Health *Reforming the Mental Health Act* Cm 5016–I (December 2000) TSO, London.
10 Department of Health *Reform of the Mental Health Act 1983 – Proposals for Consultation* Cm 4480 (November 1999) TSO, London, p 10.
11 Department of Health *The NHS Plan – A Plan for Investment, A Plan for Reform* Cm 4818-I (2000) TSO, London.

with the new Mental Health National Service Framework,[12] which introduces new national standards for the care and treatment of mental illness. These new standards include: the promotion of mental health in the general provision of care; the identification and assessment of mental health needs and the provision of suitable treatment where necessary; the promotion of accessible local services; the reduction of risk; accessibility to hospital inpatient facilities when necessary; regular review of care and treatment plans; and finally, efforts are to be made to reduce the risk of suicide in the mentally vulnerable community.

The reform plans within the White Paper recognise that much has changed in terms of how psychiatric care is provided. Likewise, it is also recognised that, despite the emphasis shifting towards community based care, many patients with mental health difficulties do not always comply with treatment within a less restrictive environment. The majority of patients receive care and support on a voluntary basis but a proportion of patients remain unable or unwilling to seek and receive the help they need. As such, the Government considers it necessary to put in place a system that can counter the difficulties associated with these particular patients. However, as mental health legislation necessarily includes powers which remove personal liberty, the introduction of all new provisions must be compatible with the European Convention on Human Rights. The Human Rights Act 1998, which came into force in October 2000, requires the Government to ensure as far as possible that legislation which it places before Parliament is compatible with the Convention Rights.[13] Ministers are required to make a statement before Parliament about the compatibility of new legislation with the Convention Rights.[14] With this in mind, the introduction of a new right to independent advocacy, use of a new Mental Health Tribunal to determine all longer-term use of compulsory powers and the new Commission for Mental Health (which will be charged with overseeing the way in which the new legislation is used) are thought likely to offset any difficulties concerning human rights legislation compatibility. In an effort to comply with human rights needs, the new legislation is to be more 'patient-focused'. To achieve this, the Government has recognised the importance of making sure the purpose and scope of any new legislation in this area is clearly understood by those who are involved in the provision and receipt of mental health care and treatment. Clear guiding principles will be incorporated in to the legislation to ensure equality of treatment and transparent decision-making. These are:
(a) compulsory powers will be limited to situations of last resort and only

12 Department of Health *Mental Health National Service Framework* (September 1999) TSO, London.
13 Human Rights Act 1998, s 19.
14 Human Rights Act 1998, s 3.

when it is necessary for the patient's health or safety or the safety of others and after alternative options have been considered;
(b) people with mental disorder should be involved in the process of developing care and treatment plans, thereby promoting self-determination as far as possible; and,
(c) such care and treatment should involve the least degree of compulsion and where possible be provided in the least restrictive environment.

(b) The definition of mental disorder

Use of the provisions within the new legislation will be dependent on whether the definition of mental disorder is met by the individual concerned. The White Paper confirms the proposed amendment to the definition of mental disorder, which was outlined by the Green Paper in 1999. Currently, under the MHA 1983 the definition of mental disorder, which includes mental illness, is open to broad interpretation.[15] After successive invitations for further views and comments during the consultation process, the Government has opted to keep a broad definition of mental disorder. The adoption of a narrower definition has been rejected on the basis that it could exclude some individuals whose conditions would benefit from compulsory care and treatment. Mental disorder will amount to any disability or disorder of mind or brain, whether permanent or temporary, which results in an impairment or disturbance of mental functioning. This definition originates from that recommended by the Law Commission in 1995.[16] Under the MHA 1983 specified categories of mental disorder exist that have been used to limit the scope of the civil commitment powers. The new definition of mental disorder will contain no particular diagnosis requirements. It is thought that this change will ensure the flexibility needed for compulsory powers to be used in the most appropriate way. Physical illness affecting the mind would seem to fall clearly within the definition, but the 'treatability' criterion, which currently plays a crucial role in the MHA 1983, has been abandoned and there will no longer be a need for evidence that compulsory care and treatment will improve or prevent deterioration of the patient's mental or physical condition. This will mean that any individual with a personality disorder who poses a serious risk of harm to others may be subject to the legislation despite the marginal effect of treatment on his or her condition.[17]

---

15 See, ch 2 above.
16 Law Commission Report No 231 *Mental Incapacity* (1995) HMSO, London. See also Lord Chancellor's Department of Health *Making Decisions* Cm 4465 (1999) TSO, London.
17 Royal College of Psychiatrists *Response to Reform of the Mental Health Act 1983* para 3, at http://www.critpsynet.freeuk.com/RCPsych.htm.

(c) A new care and treatment order

Flexibility within the new compulsory powers will play a key role. Currently, under the MHA 1983, care and treatment of a patient is heavily linked to detention within hospital. As reliance on hospital care no longer reflects contemporary psychiatric practice, the legal provision as it stands is inadequate. The MHA 1983 does not have the necessary flexibility to enable compulsory treatment to be carried out in the community, neither does it support the ideal of the least restrictive environment of care. At present, deterioration of an individual's mental condition is necessary before medical intervention is justifiable. Therefore, mental health provision teeters from one extreme to the other: from crisis level to complete health, a situation which certainly does not reflect the experiences and desires of most mentally vulnerable people. Prevention of relapse by readmitting a patient to hospital is not possible at present. Inevitably, this exposes the mentally disordered individual to an unnecessary level of distress and third parties to a greater risk of harm. The White Paper proposes new provisions so that compulsory care and treatment may apply to patients within hospital and in the community. It is hoped that these provisions will significantly reduce the 'revolving door syndrome' whereby patients are frequently brought into hospital to deal with acute phases of their condition and then discharged.[18]

A new three-stage process is to be introduced which will apply to *all* cases. Stage one will involve a preliminary examination by two doctors and a social worker or another mental health professional with specific training. Upon examination, they must all agree that the conditions for the application of compulsory powers are met. The two preliminary conditions are that the patient is suffering from a mental disorder that is sufficiently serious to warrant further assessment or urgent treatment by specialist mental health services. The second condition is that without such intervention the patient is likely to be at risk of serious harm or pose a significant risk to others. Where the patient is compliant and willing to receive care and treatment without compulsion, this will be encouraged. Use of the compulsory powers will generally only be appropriate where the patient is resistant to psychiatric intervention.

Once the decision to employ the compulsory powers is made, the patient will enter the second stage of the process. The patient will undergo a full assessment to establish what his healthcare needs are and whether continued use of formal powers are needed. Assessment and initial

---

18 See Payne, S 'The Rationing of Psychiatric Beds: Changing Trends in Sex-Ratios in Admission to Psychiatric Hospital' *Health and Social Care in the Community* 1995 p 300; Jones, K *Asylums and After* (1993) The Athlone Press, London, p 188.

treatment is carried out under a 'provisional order', which lasts up to 28 days. Details of the proposed care and treatment are to be outlined in a formal care plan. Continued compulsion under the provisional order may only be justified if the patient is diagnosed as suffering from a mental disorder within the meaning of the new legislation; the mental disorder is of such a nature or degree as to warrant specialist care and treatment; and the care plan can address the needs of the mental disorder.

The third stage of the process marks the greatest departure from the compulsory powers that are currently in operation. Continuing care and treatment proposals, which go beyond 28 days, will be subject to independent scrutiny. A Mental Health Tribunal will make a care and treatment order, which authorises the proposed care and treatment regimes, specified in the care plan if the criteria are met. The Tribunal members will consult an expert panel, which are to be appointed to provide expert evidence when necessary. The first two care and treatment orders can be for a period of up to six months and subsequent orders may last for periods of up to twelve months. The introduction of these orders is remarkable in two ways. First, as the decision to grant a care and treatment order is to be made by an independent tribunal, the power to impose long-term compulsory treatment will be removed from the medical profession. This heralds the advent of greater legalistic involvement in the application of mental health legislation since the Lunacy Act 1890. Secondly, the care and treatment order introduces flexibility by allowing its use in both hospital and community environments thereby reflecting more accurately the modern shift towards community care. As with the MHA 1983, certain forms of treatment will be subject to additional safeguards. Psychosurgery will continue to require the consent of the patient and second medical opinion in favour of the treatment. However, currently when patients lack the capacity to provide a valid consent, psychosurgical treatment cannot proceed. In the new legislation where patients lack capacity, the case can be referred to the High Court for approval if there is clear evidence that such treatment would be beneficial to the patient. ECT and polypharmacy will be authorised with either patient consent or a second medical opinion in favour of the proposed treatment. Furthermore, for patients with long-term mental incapacity who need care and/or treatment for a mental disorder new safeguards are proposed in the White Paper.[19] Once a full assessment has been undertaken of the mentally incapacitated person, a care plan will be created. The newly created Commission for Mental Health

---

19   The special needs of this group were highlighted in *R v Bournewood Community and Mental Health NHS Trust, ex p L* [1999] 1 AC 458. See also Glover, N 'L v Bournewood Community and Mental Health NHS Trust' *Journal of Social Welfare and Family Law* 1999, p 151 at p 157. For further details, see ch 4 above.

must be notified that a care plan is being drawn up. The individual's clinical supervisor must certify that in his opinion the care and treatment plan is in the patient's best interests, that he is not actively dissenting, and does not pose a significant risk of serious harm to others.

All patients that are subject to a care and treatment order can challenge its existence. The Mental Health Tribunal, at the patient's request, can review any order for compulsory care and treatment lasting longer than three months. A patient will, however, only be able to request one review during the period of any order. As with current practice, patients will have the right to free legal representation in the event that they wish to challenge the use of compulsory powers against them. Yet, for many patients advice and support are needed at other times. Under the White Paper, it is intended that specialist advocacy services will be made available to patients who are subject to compulsory powers. These advocates will be able to help represent any concerns that a patient might have regarding his care and treatment. The views of those with a significant interest in the operation of the mental health legislation will also be taken into account by the Secretary of State for Health who will be required to provide guidance on the use of the new legislation in the form of a Code of Practice. In addition, the newly created Commission for Mental Health, which will replace the Mental Health Act Commission, will have specific duties to monitor the use of formal powers against individuals. Once discharge from the care and treatment order becomes possible, a written plan setting out the patient's continuing aftercare needs must be created. This plan must be provided, along with notification of discharge, to the Commission for Mental Health.

A care and treatment order may also be available to a mentally disordered offender but only if, based on a full assessment by specialist mental health services, the clinical supervisor recommends continuing care and treatment and the court considers is appropriate to make a care and treatment order. Currently, a range of therapeutic disposal options is available to mentally disordered offenders. This will continue. At any stage of the trial, the court may obtain an assessment of the offender's mental state. The power to remand the offender for assessment will allow the court to detain the individual in hospital for assessment or to grant bail so that the assessment can be carried out in the community. If the individual is convicted, once the court is in receipt of the psychiatric assessment, a number of disposal options are available. A criminal justice disposal may be granted. This is a discretionary disposal and the decision to grant it is dependent on the nature of the offence, the medical evidence, the offender's offending history and the facilities available to manage the needs of the offender. A criminal justice disposal may involve a life sentence, which is mandatory for murder or discretionary for other offences where the offence and evidence of the offender's dangerousness justifies such a step. A criminal justice disposal may also be a prison sentence which is time limited. If the court grants such a disposal, detention under the mental health legislation ends unless a hospital and limitation direction is granted. This option combines both a criminal justice tariff and a care and treatment order. The offender will be required to stay in hospital and receive treatment until the offender's mental condition is stabilised. At this point, the offender will then be transferred to prison, by direction of the Home Secretary, to complete his prison sentence. Any time spent in hospital will be deducted from the prison term. The court may grant a restriction order in the event that the psychiatric assessment of an offender indicates that he poses a significant risk of serious harm to others. A restriction order is added to a care and treatment order where detention in hospital is required. Restricted patients are managed under the supervision of the Home Secretary as they are currently under the MHA 1983. Where a prisoner develops mental health difficulties when in prison, the White Paper recommends that the Home Secretary should have the power to direct a prisoner to undergo a specialist assessment.[20] This power is not currently available to the Home Secretary under the MHA 1983. It is, therefore, hoped that greater opportunities for diverting mentally disordered offenders into the healthcare system will emerge from the introduction of this new power.

(d) Increased public protection

In addition to the procedural changes relating to compulsory powers, which are set out in Part One of the White Paper, the issue of public protection has become one of the Government's highest priorities. In July 1999 the Government published its consultation paper *Managing Dangerous People With Severe Personality Disorder – Proposals for Policy Development* to consider ways of introducing greater control over those who pose a significant risk to others.[21] Its publication followed the announcement by the Home Secretary, that powers would be established to detain people with personality disorders who represent a danger to the public (those who are classified as dangerous and severely personality disordered (DSPD)) on an indefinite basis.[22] Dangerous people with severe

20 Department of Health *Reforming the Mental Health Act* Cm 5016–I (December 2000) TSO, London, p 41.
21 House of Commons Select Committee on Home Affairs *Managing Dangerous People With Severe Personality Disorder* 1st Report HC 42 (2000) TSO, London; Home Office/Department of Health *Managing Dangerous People With Severe Personality Disorder – Proposals for Policy Development* (1999).
22 See House of Commons Select Committee on Home Affairs 3rd Special Report HC 505, *Government Reply to the First Report of the Home Affairs Committee, Session 1999 – 2000: Managing Dangerous People With Personality Disorder* (2000) TSO, London.

personality disorder are envisaged to be those who show significant personality disorder, present a significant risk of causing serious physical or psychological harm from which the victim would find it difficult or impossible to recover, and the risk presented appears to be functionally linked to the personality disorder.[23] Despite much criticism by mental health and legal organisations,[24] the proposals have continued to gain momentum. The White Paper has emphasised the importance of upholding and endorsing the aim of public protection.[25]

'[T]here will be specific recognition of the fact that for some people their plan of care and treatment will be primarily designed to manage and reduce high-risk behaviours which pose a significant risk to others'.[26]

New criteria for compulsory treatment under the new mental health legislation will form a crucial part of the new provisions. Powers will be given for the detention for assessment and treatment of all those who pose a significant risk of serious harm to others as a result of mental disorder or severe personality disorder. The criteria will separate out those who need treatment because it is in their own best interests and those who will receive treatment because of the risk they pose to others.

Those who pose a risk to others frequently find themselves in prison, under supervision of the probation service, or known to the mental health or social services. The Criminal Justice and Court Services Act 2000 will allow police and probation officers to assess and manage sexual or violent offenders and the new mental health legislation will enable the relevant authority to refer an individual for an initial assessment and from there apply for a 28-day period of compulsory care and treatment. Any compulsory care after the 28 days will have to be authorised by the Mental Health Tribunal. These particular individuals highlight the inability of the current system to deal with the challenges they bring. The MHA 1983 is not sufficiently flexible to provide for their healthcare needs and to ensure the risk to others is minimised. Currently, if such individuals are not considered 'treatable' then they cannot be detained. The restructuring of the assessment and detention process as proposed in the White Paper

23 Department of Health *Reforming the Mental Health Act* Cm 5016–I (December 2000) TSO, London, Part 2, p 13.
24 See House of Commons Select Committee on Home Affairs *Managing Dangerous People With Severe Personality Disorder* 1st Report HC 42 (2000) TSO, London. See also, Mahendra, B 'Ministering to madness' (1999) 149 New Law Journal 408-9.
25 See Bean, P *Mental Disorder and Community Safety* (2001) Palgrave, Basingstoke for a detailed examination of the increasing demand to protect public safety.
26 Department of Health *Reforming the Mental Health Act* Cm 5016–I (December 2000) TSO, London, para 1.4.

should assist with this problem as will the establishment of special units for those who are dangerous and severely personality disordered.[27] Furthermore, those who are already serving prison sentences may now find themselves directed for assessment by the Home Secretary.

Before this, those who represented a risk to third parties were difficult to manage. Many of them were considered untreatable and therefore not suitable for detention. The role of treatment in the current detention process can clearly be seen. Part of the motivation behind detaining a patient in a psychiatric hospital is to improve or prevent deterioration of their condition in some way, as detention should not be for detention's sake. However, the reform proposals suggest that care plans which are recommended for individuals after initial assessment must simply give therapeutic benefit or enable the management of difficult behavioural traits in certain individuals. The care plan 'must be designed to give therapeutic benefit to the patient or to manage behaviour associated with mental disorder that might lead to serious harm to other people'.[28] 'Treatability' is no longer necessary. For these people, their rights are to be superseded by the need to minimise risk. It is clear that in all high-risk cases, 'management' of the consequences of the disorder will be the priority and therapeutic efforts will be marginalised.

During the consultation process, two possible approaches to dealing with the particular needs of this group were considered. Option A suggested a strengthening of existing legislation so that 'high-risk' individuals would not be released from prison or hospital until they were no longer considered to represent a risk to the public. In addition, 'greater use of the discretionary life sentence, for example by improving the quality of the information available to the courts and extending its availability to a wider range of offences' was suggested.[29] Option B suggested that new powers (a DSPD order) in civil and criminal proceedings for indeterminate detention should be introduced for 'high-risk' individuals. The new service would be separate from both prison and health services. Separate specialist units may be desirable for several reasons. Placing DSPD individuals in units with other vulnerable people may lead to exploitation. It was noted in the Consultation document that those 'who are resistant to treatment can easily undermine the treatment of others ... and damage the mentally ill'.[30] Likewise, severe personality disorders often require

27 See below for further details.
28 Department of Health *Reforming the Mental Health Act* Cm 5016-I (December 2000) TSO, London, Part 2, p 2.
29 Home Office/Department of Health *Managing Dangerous People With Severe Personality Disorder – Proposals for Policy Development* (1999) Part 3, para 14.
30 Home Office/Department of Health *Managing Dangerous People With Severe Personality Disorder – Proposals for Policy Development* (1999) Part 3, para 7.1.2.

specific types of management, which are not available in general units. The order, which could be extended indefinitely, would be subject to appeal and periodic review. A final decision about which option to follow is yet to be made, although it seems that option B is most likely to fulfil the Government's requirements for public protection.

There are some clear legal and ethical implications arising from these proposals. The decision to detain an individual indefinitely because he suffers from a severe personality disorder is one that is made on the basis of risk assessment. However, risk assessment tools are notoriously inaccurate. If an individual's liberty is to be removed, more robust and reliable risk assessment methods need to be established. The European Convention on Human Rights, Art 5 enshrines the right to liberty and security of person. Article 5(1)(e) permits, in certain circumstances, the 'detention ... of persons of unsound mind'. It was held in *Winterwerp v Netherlands*,[31] that 'persons of unsound mind', 'obviously cannot be taken as permitting the detention of a person simply because his views or behaviour deviate from the norms prevailing in a particular society'. Detention under Art 5(1)(e) is justified on the basis that an individual is reasonably shown by *objective medical evidence* to be suffering from a mental disorder of a kind that warrants compulsory confinement. However, it remains to be seen whether current risk assessment procedures meet such reliability and objectivity requirements. To apply risk assessment techniques, those working within the field must be adequately trained in order to ensure consistent application. The threshold for indefinite detention, the definition of dangerous and severe personality disorder, must be clear and unambiguous. This is not currently the case and the White Paper makes little effort to define 'dangerous' and 'severe personality disorder'. It also needs to be decided how much risk to others must be evidenced. Would it be sufficient for an individual merely to pose *some* risk to others or must there be a *significant* risk? Indeed, would a significant risk be sufficient when the decision to indefinitely detain does not have to refer to past offences but merely that the individual *may* commit an offence in the future?[32] Part Two of the White Paper states that the '[n]ew legislation will be fully compliant with the Human Rights Act 1998'. However, the difficulties associated with the proposal to detain indefinitely the dangerous and severely personality disordered makes it difficult to see how this can be the case.

31 (1979) 2 EHRR 387.
32 House of Commons Select Committee on Home Affairs *Managing Dangerous People With Severe Personality Disorder* 1st Report HC 42 (2000) TSO, London, paras 70 and 83.

3 Future Moves

Where the White Paper will lead remains unclear. Expectations that a new bill would be included in the Queen's Speech in June 2001 were not realised. The next opportunity for inclusion of a new Mental Health Bill will be November 2002. Meanwhile, many problems exist with the proposals (most notably those that relate to the management of high-risk individuals) set out in the White Paper. Too many unknowns remain. Certainly, as far as those who have a dangerous personality disorder are concerned, there continues to be much confusion surrounding the concept of psychopathy and, consequently, many are subject to inconsistent sentencing strategies and treatment programmes. The new legal framework for when and how care and treatment should be provided may offer some improvements to the current position as set out in the MHA 1983. Change is long overdue. Yet, what must be avoided are short-term expedients, which are broadly aimed at removing political difficulties rather than dealing with the limitations of the current psychiatric system.

The simplification of the assessment and detention process as described in Part One of the White Paper is to be commended. Vulnerable patients have, for too long, been filtered through a complicated legislative process. Yet the proposed system also has flaws: not least the removal of 'treatability' in the decision-making process. It has been seen that the role of treatment dominates the decision to detain an individual under the current mental health legislation. There has to be a purpose for removing a patient's liberty. 'Treatability', despite the gradual broadening of its meaning, is pivotal. However, the proposed reforms to the mental health legislation may well marginalise this therapeutic objective in favour of minimising the possible risk to third parties. This is particularly evident in relation to those who are dangerous and severely personality disordered.

The reform proposals suggest a shift away from the 'new legalism' of the MHA 1983 and a return to the highly legalistic approach of the late nineteenth century.[33] It seems likely that the rights and status of the mentally ill, the mentally incapacitated and the personality disordered will not be improved in any dramatic way. The welfarist approach of the mid-twentieth century, which focused upon prompt treatment and therapeutic intervention by the medical profession, has been superseded by the more repressive system of legal intrusion and judicial safeguards. Risk assessment and management has become the focus for debate.

---

33 See Unsworth, C *The Politics of the Mental Health Legislation* (1987) Oxford University Press, Oxford.

Treatment and therapy are losing their significance. While this approach is favoured, the needs of those who are thought to represent a threat to others will be ignored and the administration of treatment without consent will be justified. Now that the European Convention on Human Rights and Fundamental Freedoms has been subsumed into the law of England and Wales with the Human Rights Act 1998, it must be questioned whether the reform proposals are completely compatible with Art 5 of the Convention.

The key to success does not hinge simply on a reformulation of the legal process. Psychiatric care has changed, priorities have shifted and public demands have become increasingly vociferous. The reform proposals have fudged around two essential issues. The first relates to the establishment of definitional boundaries. The definition of mental disorder continues to be broadly defined and evidence of specific diagnoses is no longer required. It is argued that this will allow the legislation to be more flexible in its application, yet broad definitions inevitably lead to greater numbers of people falling within its ambit. Certainly, this approach circumvents the problems posed by those with severe personality disorders but the numbers of such people within society should not be over-exaggerated. Moreover, while debate surrounds risk assessment tools and questions about the accuracy of these methods are raised, it remains difficult to justify the special control measures pertaining to the severely personality disordered that have been recommended in the White Paper.

The second factor, which might pose problems in the future, relates to resources. Certainly, the Government has made some clear statements regarding the funding of these services. The NHS Plan has committed £330 million over the next three years to the establishment of 24-hour staffed beds, assertive outreach teams and 24-hour services. However, considering the Government's reform plans, this money may well fall short of need. It must be recognised that in the health and social care arena, legal provision is only as good as its practical implementation. In addition, in the House of Lords Lord Clement-Jones noted that 'there is ... mounting evidence that the new money intended by the Government to improve mental health services is being spent on other NHS priorities'.[34] Lord Hunt of Kings Heath responded by saying that it was expected that 'NHS authorities and trusts ... [would] ... devote as much priority as they ... [could] ... to mental health'.[35] This offers little reassurance to a service, which has always been the Cinderella of the NHS.

It must be suspected that the political reality of these reform proposals will fall far short of actual need. Currently too many gaps exist both within

34 HL Deb vol 626, col 1083, 11 July 2001 (Lord Clement-Jones).
35 HL Deb vol 626, col 1084, 11 July 2001 (Lord Hunt of Kings Heath).

the proposals themselves and within current clinical and psychological knowledge. The Green Paper suggested that a research base on personality disorders needed to be established. This was affirmed in the White Paper. Such efforts must be applauded as too little is known about such disorders and how to deal with them effectively. Yet while these efforts are being made, any long-term reform plans should, perhaps, be re-considered. Unlike other areas of medicine, psychiatry will never be regarded as a popular and cutting edge field. Those suffering from mental health problems rarely receive social sympathy or support and are frequently regarded as misfits who cause trouble. Complete cure is seldom apparent and treatment techniques are rarely regarded as cutting edge or worthy of media interest. It is unlikely that these problems will be overcome and psychiatry will continue to be regarded as a peripheral service. However, it has been estimated that one adult in every seven suffers from depression, anxiety, or some other form of mental disorder.[36] Recent Department of Health figures have estimated that one adult in four will suffer from some form of mental illness at some stage in his life.[37] Clearly, mental ill health is not a small problem nor should it be regarded as someone else's problem. Therefore, any changes to the system of psychiatric provision should be thoroughly planned and well executed and should not be the result of media-fuelled hysteria.

---

36 Randall Kropp, P et al 'The perceptions of correctional officers towards mentally disordered offenders' *International Journal of Law and Psychiatry* 1989, Vol 12, p 187.
37 Department of Health Press Release 98/126, 2 April 1998. See also, Department of Health *Modernising Mental Health Services: Safe, Sound and Supportive* (1998) HMSO, London.

Chapter 9
Conclusion

This final chapter seeks to assemble some of the key issues raised in this book, draw some conclusions about the current state of mental health law in England and Wales, and consider its future prospects. Throughout this book it has been shown that the examination and assessment of mental health law must be carried out with reference to the context in which it works. Many people are regularly affected, both directly and indirectly, by the way in which mental health law operates. It must be recognised that this legal field is multidisciplinary in nature and, as such, those who provide and receive psychiatric care are affected by the inevitable tensions that arise between the application of legal rules and the execution of clinical practice. Yet, despite this conflict, it must not be assumed that mental health policy can never achieve an effective balance between facilitating access to therapeutic care, the enhancement of patient rights and harnessing public protection mechanisms. So far, achieving this balance has proved elusive, yet if the interaction between legal, political and social trends is more fully acknowledged within the context of mental health law, it may be possible to overcome some of the difficulties associated with past legislation and draft more appropriate laws in the future. The main aim of this book has been to explore the legal response to psychiatric care provision since the enactment of the Lunacy Act 1890 and to examine the way in which a changing social and political landscape has impacted upon policy development.

A struggle between proponents of the liberalist approach, which argues for strong legalistic intervention, and those who favour a welfarist approach, which prefers therapeutic intervention as directed by clinical discretion, has existed throughout the history of mental health legislation. During the eighteenth century, the mentally vulnerable found themselves spread around the country, in workhouses, in privately run madhouses, in their own homes and on the streets. As the lunacy trade became increasingly lucrative, private madhouses sprang up everywhere and fears that the sane would find themselves wrongfully incarcerated became widespread. The Lunacy Act 1890 sought to address this unstructured and exploitative regime of care provision and adopted a legal framework which firmly removed power from the medical profession and vested it in lawyers. The asylums of the late nineteenth century soon became great monoliths, where overcrowding was a common feature and stigma an ever-present problem for the inmates. The great efforts of the Earl of Shaftesbury and the Lunacy Commission to improve the conditions of 'lunatics' were soon forgotten as the early twentieth century saw the system as outmoded and inhumane. After the First World War, the political, social and legal mood shifted in favour of placing more power in the hands of the clinicians once again. This was in an attempt to 'humanise' the system and recognised the fact that psychiatry had developed as a profession in its own right. The development of new drugs and therapies, the acknowledgment that long-term inpatient hospitalisation was anti-therapeutic and the increasing presence of a human rights culture since the 1960s inevitably led to the questioning of the policy, which favoured institutional care provision. However, despite this gradual policy shift, legislation in the twentieth century has had difficulty reflecting these changes. Although the MHA 1983 in part acknowledges the greater importance of the community as a care environment, it still leaves much to be desired as detention still plays a key role.

As with many areas of public law where multidisciplinary involvement is visible, mental health legislation is always trying to keep up with current psychiatric practices. By its very nature, mental health policy is fluid, responding to changes in care practice, including new treatment techniques and reacting to evolving social attitudes. Legislation cannot hope to respond to such changes in this way and as such, may be outdated even before it reaches the statute books. As legislation cannot reflect the nuances of contemporary psychiatric practices, mechanisms have been adopted whereby current legislation is used creatively to develop pragmatic responses to challenges, which are brought about by new policy initiatives. During the 1980s and early 1990s, such activities took place on a regular basis. The result was ad hoc, unstructured psychiatric care provision, which left patients without appropriate safeguards. Inevitably this problem will always exist to some degree, yet what must be avoided in the future is law and 'policy-making on the hoof' which is beneficial to none and positively dangerous to all.[1] In the past few years, policy changes have been implemented as a direct Governmental response to

1   *The Guardian*, 5 January 1993.

specific incidents. The well-documented experience of Ben Silcock in 1993 led the then Secretary of State for Health, the Rt Hon Virginia Bottomley MP, to introduce the ten-point plan and supervision registers, neither of which were comprehensively planned or adroitly implemented, with the result that both initiatives have been heavily criticised and underused. Unfortunately, the Mental Health (Patients in the Community) Act 1995, which was heralded as the solution to failings in community care, has shared a similar fate. It is hardly surprising that people have become disillusioned with mental health care in general and the community care policy in particular. Patients, professionals and the public have seen their expectations unfulfilled. The provision of community services has been inadequately funded; inter-agency cooperation has been woefully deficient; and basic opportunities, such as the offer of appropriate housing and employment/occupational prospects, have been inconsistently applied around the country. This disillusionment has been paralleled in the criminal justice system, where mentally disordered offenders are usually expected to be diverted, when appropriate, into the healthcare system yet have not been. It is crucial that such individuals receive suitable care and support in order to avert the possibility that they be exploited and mistreated in the penal environment or pose a danger to others. However, the diversion scheme in England and Wales continues to suffer problems, not least from the fact that it has no statutory footing, lacks any agreed national standards of operation and is inconsistently applied. The notion of harnessing the healthcare system to provide for the needs of mentally disordered offenders continues to be supported by the current Labour Government. Yet, while the funding of such schemes continues to be dependent on central Government resources to pump-prime the system rather than on comprehensive local financing, the diversion scheme's longevity is open to question.

As a consequence of these wide-ranging difficulties with current mental health provision, continued calls for mental health law reform have inevitably been heard. The long awaited White Paper *Reforming the Mental Health Act*, which was published in December 2000, has fallen far short of expectations. With the White Paper being divided into two parts focusing on: (i) the creation of a new legal framework for when and how care and treatment can be provided; and (ii) outlining ways of strengthening laws and services to safeguard the public against those who pose the greatest risk, the emphasis has somewhat shifted away from the enhancement of a therapeutic environment in which care and treatment can be provided, and moved towards risk assessment and its management. This shift in emphasis has been the centre of much controversy and, indeed, it remains to be seen what will become of the proposals, as it is uncertain whether a new bill will be included in the next Queen's Speech in November 2002.

The proposals suggest that a total reformulation of mental health law will somehow solve the current problems that exist within the system, yet little indication is given about the actual implementation of this framework and the nature of the support services which are to be made available. It is clear that past disenchantment in mental health care provision has largely stemmed from inadequacies within the practical operation of the system. The White Paper does not truly confront these issues, so it may be assumed that similar problems could be faced by the new system. The White Paper certainly reinforces the Government's continued commitment to community care. The introduction of the Care and Treatment order, which can be applied in either a hospital or community environment, suggests that the increased flexibility of approach which has been called for by professionals and patients alike will be injected into the system. These proposals will go some way to answer the criticisms that the provisions of the MHA 1983 are obsolete and cannot adequately be applied to contemporary practices.[2]

Whether these proposals achieve these objectives remains to be seen. Yet what is not questioned is the need for further research on community care in order to ascertain whether the perceived benefits of this method of care match reality. Kathleen Jones outlines a vast list of possible areas for future research.[3] She includes the question of follow-up studies of patient cohorts, which would be aimed at establishing where patients end up after hospitalisation; longitudinal studies of patient careers to observe the experiences of the chronically mentally disordered in the community over long periods; typologies of care to establish which patient groups receive 'types' of care and to ascertain whether certain characteristics such as gender or race affect the care decision; planning studies to look at how local authorities plan their community care responsibilities; comparisons of residential settings to establish whether some settings lead to improved clinical outcomes; and housing studies to ascertain whether the mentally disordered experience significantly worse housing than other sectors of society and whether the law adequately responds to the needs of this vulnerable group. In addition to these areas of possible research, the Government clearly recognises the need for further research in the White Paper. For instance, clinical knowledge surrounding the thorny issue of dangerous and severe personality disorder needs to be deepened and ongoing work to improve risk assessment techniques is necessary if the Government's proposals in Part Two of the White Paper are going to stand up to scrutiny.

2   Blom-Cooper, L et al *The Falling Shadow: One Patient's Mental Health Care 1978–1993* (1995) Duckworth, London; 'Mental health law obsolete' (1995) *British Medical Journal* Vol 310, p 145.
3   Jones, K *Asylums and After* (1993) The Athlone Press, London, pp 247-48.

How effective community care can be in the future also depends largely on social attitudes. Despite the many criticisms that can be levelled at the recent White Paper, it must be acknowledged that the Government was, in part, responding to increased public fear and scepticism and the demand for greater public protection. This fear has emerged as a result of widely publicised community care failures where members of the public have been killed or seriously injured by a mentally disordered individual.[4] Therefore, greater efforts must be made to educate society about mental ill health and the realities of the risk posed by such individuals. Likewise, the effective implementation of any new proposals will depend on improvements in inter-agency cooperation, an area that has caused significant problems in the past. Such cooperation is dependent on improved education and training within the professions involved in providing care services. Greater opportunities for different professionals to come together to develop new approaches must be offered. Although increased education in all its forms is essential for community care to have a positive outcome, at the heart of any success will lie the provision of adequate resources. Although the NHS Plan has committed £330 million over the next three years to provide 24-hour staffed beds, assertive outreach teams and 24-hour services, it is thought likely that this sum will still fall short of need.[5] Inevitably the resource needs of the mentally vulnerable are never ending and demand will always outstrip supply, but every effort must be made to close the current financial gaps that exist within psychiatric provision at this time.

4   Wolff, G et al 'Community attitudes to mental illness' *British Journal of Psychiatry* 1996, Vol 168, pp 183-90.
5   HL Deb vol 626, col 1083, 11 July 2001 (Lord Clement-Jones).
6   Department of Health Press Release 98/126, 2 April 1998.

Index

After-care services
    community care policy, necessary for implementation of, 93
    compulsion, level of, 135
    constant duty of, 88
    discharge, triggered on, 88
    failure in discharge of duties, review of, 93
    funding, 90, 91
    individual duty of care, 87
    patients liable to be detained, extending to, 88
    rate of usage, 93
    requirement to provide, 86, 87
    responsibility for, 92, 96
    statutory provisions, 92
    supervision. *See* SUPERVISION

Asylum
    abuse, rising fear of, 11-14, 17
    application to detain person in, 18
    Board of Inspection, 15
    conditions in, 17
    county, 6
    detention procedure, revision of, 18, 19
    disuse of term, 22
    dumping ground, as, 16
    influences of, 7-11
    overcrowding, 10
    private, design of, 10
    public-
        inspection, 12
        system, call for, 12
        types of people in, 10

Asylum—*contd*
    purpose-built, 9
    rise of, 5
    sane people in, 12
    socially undesirable in, 16
    treatment regime, 10
    warehouse for the insane, as, 68

Bail
    conditions, 183
    right to, 182

Brain damage
    mental disorder due to, 46

Care and treatment order
    challenging, 210
    flexibility in use, 209
    Mental Health Tribunal, made by, 209
    mentally disabled offender, for, 210, 211
    proposal for, 208-211
    stages of process, 208, 209

Community care
    after-care services. *See* AFTER-CARE SERVICES
    campaigns concerning, 121
    Care Programme Approach, 91, 93, 94
    change, modern impetus for, 71-73
    community supervision. *See* SUPERVISION
    community treatment order. *See* COMMUNITY TREATMENT ORDER

Index

Community care—contd
 development of, 67-71
 disillusionment with, 145
 employment. See EMPLOYMENT
 failure in discharge of duties, review of, 93
 failure of, 203, 204
 families, by, 67, 68
 formalisation of approach, 121
 framework, emergence of, 67
 future of, 222, 223
 guardianship. See GUARDIANSHIP
 history of, 94
 hospital beds, reduction in, 85
 Hospital Plan, 66, 72, 95
 housing provision, disregard of, 146, 150-161. See also HOUSING
 inadequacies of, 96, 122, 143
 informal and ad hoc basis, 122
 informal, 66, 68
 institution, as alternative to, 65
 integration of patients, 146
 inter-agency co-operation, 147, 148
 leave of absence. See LEAVE OF ABSENCE
 long leash technique, 121
 mentally defective, for, 66, 69, 70
 mentally ill, for, 66
 modern notion of, 67
 needs of discharged patients, meeting, 171
 occupational or employment prospects, lack of, 147
 official order, 85
 pharmacology, reliance on, 85, 86
 plan, 92
 policy, implementation of, 145
 psychiatrists, creation of order by, 83
 purpose of, 65
 re-orientation of care provision to, 95
 revival of, 66
 SANE, work of, 121, 122
 services, definition, 92
 services, role of, 145
 statutory basis for, 70
 statutory recognition, 66
 structured approach, 65, 66
 supervision. See SUPERVISION
 therapeutic benefits, 124
Community treatment order
 application, 124, 125

Community treatment order—contd
 continuance of medication, ensuring, 125
 criticisms, 130-132
 debate on, 126
 discussion document, 123, 124
 effect of, 123, 124
 England and Wales, adoption in, 132-143
 international influences, 128-132
 legislation, 134-143
 medical treatment, permitting, 124
 medication, enforcement of, 144
 models, 128-130
 patients subject to, 124, 125
 ten-point plan, 132-134, 221
Continuing power of attorney
 effect of, 116
Court of Protection
 decisions by, 116, 117
 manager, appointment of, 118, 119
 new, 116-119
 powers of, 117
Criminal justice
 mentally disordered offenders. See MENTALLY DISORDERED OFFENDERS

Disability discrimination
 applications procedure, in, 165
 disability, definition of, 164
 fair and equal treatment, requirement of, 134
 forms of, 165
 harassment, 167
 limitations, 166
 long-term disability, meaning, 164
 main functions of job, impossibility of performing, 166
 protection for persons in employment market, 163
 scope for, 162
 unlawful, 163
 vicarious liability, 167
 working environment, adjustments to, 165, 166
Disabled persons
 provision of services for, 149
Drug therapy
 consent to, 57
Electro-convulsive therapy
 consent to, 57
Employment
 alternative opportunities, 170, 171

Employment—contd
disability discrimination. *See*
DISABILITY DISCRIMINATION
discharged patients, of, 162, 163,
172
opportunities for, 168, 169
positive impact of, 167, 168
rehabilitation, effect of, 168
schemes, 170, 171
social dealings, scope for, 162
unemployment, impact of, 169
work skills, effect of, 168
Enduring power of attorney
effect of, 115
replacement of, 116

Force-feeding
treatment, as, 104

Guardianship
application for, 76
coercive measures, illegal, 79
difficulties associated with, 78-80
failure of, 75
guardian, powers of, 70, 74-78
history of, 73, 74
introduction of, 66, 69
mentally disordered offender, order in relation to, 190, 191
nearest relative, veto by, 77
objections to, 77
paternalistic approach, 75, 76
patient compliance, 79

Habeas corpus
application for, 60
Health service
internal market, 148
management, 148
provision, system of, 148
Homelessness
ambit of, 156
community care, persons in, 157
definition, 155, 156
discharged patients, of, 159, 160
housing authorities, duty of, 156, 161
mental health problems, link with, 157, 158
Hormone
definition, 56
surgical implant, 56, 7
Hospital direction
conditions for, 195

Hospital direction—contd
criticism of, 196, 197
effect of, 195, 196
imposition of, 194
statutory provisions, 195
use of, 196
Hospital order
interim, 191-193
mentally disordered offender, on, 188, 189
restriction order added to, 193, 194
Housing
fair rent, 153, 154
homelessness. *See* HOMELESSNESS
mainstream, 151, 152
market forces, 155
owner-occupation, 153
persons in community care, provision for-
adequacy of, 159, 160
background, 150
disregard of, 146
needs, 153, 172
role of, 150
types of, 151-155
security of tenure, 154
sheltered, 151, 152
special needs, 151
types of provision, 151-155
Housing benefit
creation of, 154
Human rights
detention, lawfulness of, 52
European Convention, 27, 206
psychiatric hospital, unreasonable delay in discharge from, 88, 89
psychiatric patient, arrest and detention of, 137, 138

Ill-treatment
offence of, 61
Insanity
curable, claim of, 17
defence of, 186
doctors treating, 13, 14
early reactions to, 3-5
incurable, thought to be, 13
interpretation, widening of, 17
legislation, growing volume of, 15
madness, meaning, 13
medical control of, 14
physical or mental cause of, 15
relief, provision of, 6
review of system, 17

Insanity—contd
  special verdict, 186
Institutionalism
  culture of, 9
  patients suffering from, 11
Judicial review
  public authorities, proceedings against, 60
Leave of absence
  application of, 80-82
  authority to grant, 80, 81
  conditions, 83
  consent to treatment, continuation of, 82
  control, maintenance of, 81, 82
  extended leave, as, 80
  grant of, 80, 81
  long leash technique, 83
  objective of, 82, 83
  recall, 83-85
  renewal, 83, 84
  temporary, 81
Litigation
  immunities, 59, 60
Local authorities
  vulnerable, provision of services for, 149
Local Exchange Trading System (LETS)
  impact of, 170
Lunacy Commission
  discharge of inmate by, 18
  introduction of, 15

Madhouses
  environment of, 7
  evolution of, 9
  investigation of, 7
  legislation, 3
  Metropolitan Commissioners, 15
  private, setting up, 6, 7
  restraint in, 6
Madness
  meaning, 13
Medical profession
  common identity, 14
  insane, treatment of, 16
  strong position of, 16
  uniform standards, 14
Mental defective
  community care for, 66, 69, 70
  control of, 69

Mental defective—contd
  guardianship. See GUARDIANSHIP
  institutions, in, 69, 70
Mental disorder
  brain damage, due to, 46
  categories of, 41
  definition, 207, 216
  mental illness. See MENTAL ILLNESS
  mental impairment, 43, 44
  psychopathic, 44-46
  residual category of, 46
  severe mental impairment, 43, 44
  threshold criteria, 47, 48
Mental health
  approaches to, 219, 220
  care-
    attitudes, shift in, 22
    be-stigmatisation, 22, 30
  care and treatment order, introduction of, 208-211
  care in the community. See COMMUNITY CARE
  individual liberty, protection of, 20
  legal profession, role of, 20
  legal regulation, functions of, 34-36
  legalism, 2, 3
    revival of, 29-3
    rise of, 18
  legislative policy, shift in, 20
  pharmacological developments, 30
  resources, 216
  review of system, 17
  Royal Commission, 1924, 20, 21
  Royal Commission, 1944, 23, 24
  Scottish system, 17
  Seebohm Report, 72
  therapeutic division of labour, establishment of, 35
  treatment. See TREATMENT
Mental Health Act Commission
  independent review mechanism, as, 62
  introduction of, 62
Mental health law
  developments of, 1
  examination and assessment of, 219
  insanity, early reactions to, 3-5
  legislation-
    application of, 34
    current psychiatric practices, keeping up with, 220
    formal framework, as, 34
    growing volume of, 15
    reform, 204

Mental health law—contd
 legislation—contd
  reform—contd
   calls for, 221
   White Paper, 28, 29
   reformulation of, 222
   transformation, pressure for, 22
  legalist view of, 2, 3
  medicalist view of, 2, 3
  Mental Health Act 1959-
   disapproval of, 30
   effect of, 22-26
   ideology, 30
   legal regulation, restriction of, 30
   medical influence, high water mark of, 27
   new legalisms following, 32, 33
   optimism in psychiatry, reflecting, 29
   outmoded, becoming, 31
   public safety, threat to, 30
   shortcomings, highlighting, 31, 32
   voluntary admission to hospital, provisions, 36
  Mental Health Act 1983-
   diversion policy, 176
   ideology of, 62, 63
   legal regulation, functions of, 34-36
   social context, 29
   staff and patients, protective legal mechanisms for, 59-62
   therapeutic division of labour, establishment of, 35
   treatment provisions, 54-59.
    See also TREATMENT
 present challenges facing, 1
 White Paper 2000-
  assessment and detention process, 215
  changes in care, recognising, 206
  effect of, 215
  expectations, falling short of, 221
  legalism, return to, 215, 216
  mental disorder, definition, 207
  new standards, 206
  parts of, 204, 205
  public protection, increased, 211-214

Mental health law—contd
 White Paper 2000—contd
  reform plans, 205-207
  service reforms, description of, 205
Mental Health National Service Framework
 introduction of, 206
Mental Health Review Tribunal
 after-care supervision, application concerning, 142, 143
 applications for hearings, number of, 53
 conditions, deferring, 89, 90
 discharge of patients-
  conditional or absolute, 54
  suitability for, 53
 introduction of, 52
 judicial review of decisions, 54
 members, attitude and knowledge of, 53, 54
 powers of, 24, 25
 role of, 52-54
 style of, 25
Mental hospital
 closures, 85
 compulsory detention-
  assessment, for, 48
  duration of, 49, 51
  emergency assessment, for, 50, 51
  guiding principles, 47
  human rights provisions, 52
  initial application for, 49
  interim measure, 48
  necessary treatment, for, 48, 49
  number of admissions, 53
  power of, 39, 40
  protection of patient and others, for, 48
  renewal, 51
  threshold criteria, 47, 48
  treatability test, 47, 49, 50
 evolution of, 9
 formal admission-
  legal involvement in, 24
  medical decision, as, 24
 Hospital Plan, 66, 72, 95
 informal admission to, 24, 37, 38
 inpatient facilities, closure of, 71
 necessity of admission, 38
 remand to, 183-185

230 Index

Mental hospital—*contd*
  staff-
    false statements about patient's mental state, duty to avoid, 61
    ill-treatment by, 61
    immunities, 59, 60
    protective legal mechanisms for, 59-62
    wilful neglect by, 61
    wrong and misjudged decision by, 60
  use of term, 22
  voluntary admission to, 21
    acceptance of, 95
    basic principle, 36
    patient, rights of. *See* PATIENT
    statutory footing, 36

Mental illness
  attitude to, 217
  care and treatment, shift in, 22
  dealing with, inquiry as to, 1
  detention, threshold of, 42
  meaning, 42, 43
  medical interest in, 7
  metaphor, as, 28
  myth, as, 28
  number suffering from, 1
  physical illness, and, 20
  policy, upheaval in, 203
  problem of, 1
  provisional treatment, 21
  socially constructed concept of, 31
  statutory definition, lack of, 42
  temporary treatment, 21
  treatment, methods of, 8

Mental impairment
  behavioural criterion, 44
  meaning, 43
  removal from Act, campaign for, 44

Mental institutions
  abuse, rising fear of, 11-14
  alternative to, 65
  asylum. *See* ASYLUM
  charitable, 4, 6
  conditions in, 11, 12
  development of, 4
  mechanical restraints, use of, 6
  mental defectives in, 69, 70
  Victorian values, typifying, 66

Mentally disordered offenders
  appropriate adult scheme, 179-182
  bail, right to, 182, 183

Mentally disordered offenders—*contd*
  care and treatment order, 210, 211
  diversion policy-
    achieving, 176
    appropriate adult scheme, 179-182
    bail, right to, 182, 183
    criminal justice system, from, 173-176
    difficulties with, 199-201
    funding, inadequacy of, 200
    meaning, 173
    Mental Health Act 1983, role of, 176
    origins of, 173
    police, role of, 177-179
    practical problems, 200
    prosecution, proceeding with, 182
    sentencing, diversion before, 182-197
    sentencing stage, diversion at, 187-197
    stages of process, at, 176
    therapeutic opportunities, 175
  hospital, remand to for report or treatment, 183-185
  hospital, transfer to-
    power of, 197
    sentenced prisoner, of, 197, 198
    unsentenced prisoner, of, 198, 199
  insanity, special verdict of, 186
  medical reports, 187
  place of safety, detention to, 177
  pre-sentence reports, 187
  prison, in, 197
  punishment and retribution, effect of, 174
  therapeutic disposal of-
    guardianship order, 190, 191
    hospital direction, 194-197
    hospital order, 188, 189
    interim hospital order, 191-193
    psychiatric probation order, 189, 190
    restriction order, 193, 194
  treatment of, 173
  unfitness to stand trial, 185, 186

Moral therapy
  development of, 8
  objectives of, 8
  York Retreat, in, 8, 9

National Council for Mental Hygiene
  founding of, 19
National Health Service
  introduction of, 22

Patient
  after-care services, provision of, 86-94
  carers, claims against, 61
  classification, 35
  coercive powers over, 27
  community treatment order. *See* COMMUNITY TREATMENT ORDER
  control of, 2
  decisions concerning, 2
  detained, protection of, 36
  discharge-
    after-care services, triggering, 88
    clean break, 139
    conditions, 89, 90
    Mental Health Review Tribunal, role of. *See* MENTAL HEALTH REVIEW TRIBUNAL
    unreasonably delayed, 88, 89
  extended leave. *See* LEAVE OF ABSENCE
  formal detention, not subject to, 37
  lawful arrest and detention of, 137, 138
  leave of absence. *See* LEAVE OF ABSENCE
  legal status, 35
  normalising technique, 74
  professional power over, control of, 28, 34
  release of, 25
  rights-
    balancing, 63
    dispensation of supervision, application for, 60
    prevention from holding, 36
    promotion of, 28, 32
    recognition of, 27
    scope of, 35
  treatment. *See* TREATMENT
  voluntary-
    coercive powers, availability of, 39
    compulsory detention of, 39, 40
    consent to admission by, 38
    decision-making powers, removal of, 40
    legal rights, 37

Patient —*contd*
  voluntary—*contd*
    medical officer and nurses, relationship with, 40
    right to leave hospital, 39
    treatment, refusing, 37
Pharmacology
  drug depots, 85
  reliance on, 85, 86
Police
  mentally disordered offenders, diversion of, 177-179
  mentally impaired person, interviewing, 179-182
  public place, removal of persons from, 179
Prison
  health care in, 174, 175
  mentally disordered offender in, 197
  overcrowding and mis-management, 174
  restrictive practices, system embracing, 174
Prisoner
  hospital, transfer to-
    power of, 197
    sentenced prisoner, of, 197, 198
    unsentenced prisoner, of, 198, 199
Psychiatric probation order
  making of, 189, 190
  suitability of, 190
Psychiatry
  enlightenment, time of, 25
  gaoler, image of, 23
  intervention, control of, 32
  legal regulation, functions of, 34-36
  legitimacy of, 10
  modern age, beginning of, 19
  new legalism, emergence of, 32, 33
  oppression by, 31
  pessimism in, 63
  practice, development of, 30
  profession, emergence as, 19
  professional, control of power of, 34
  rise of, 13
  separate field of medicine, as, 14
  social standing, improvement in, 23
  therapeutic tool, as, 26
  World War I, effect of, 19, 20
Psychopathic disorder
  consultation paper, 45
  definition, 44, 45

Psychopathic disorder—contd
  detention of persons with, 45, 46
  treatability, 46
Psychosurgery
  consent to, 56
  definition, 56
Restriction order
  criticism of, 194
  duration, 193
  effect of, 193

Severe mental impairment
  behavioural criterion, 44
  meaning, 43
Severe personality disorder
  persons with-
    detention of, 212-214
    protection from, 211-214
Social security benefits
  persons with psychiatric problems, for, 163
Social services
  provision, system of, 148
  vulnerable, provision of services for, 149
Sterilisation
  non-consensual, 106, 107
Supervision
  after-care under-
    control, lack of, 146
    decision-making, consultation in, 141, 142
    duration of, 139
    effect of, 144
    enforcement, 136
    introduction of, 143
    legislation, 134-143
    medication, enforcement of, 144
    Mental Health Review Tribunal, application to, 142, 143
    patient subject to, 136
    powers, 136
    renewal, 139, 140
    responsible after-care bodies, 136, 137
    review of patient's position, 140, 141
    supervisor, role of, 135, 136
  community, 126, 127
  international influences, 128-132
  introduction of, 66, 69
  order, 127

Supervision—contd
  professionals, by, 70
  registers, 132-134, 221
  supervised discharge order, 135
  ten-point plan, 132-134, 221
Surgical implant
  definition, 56

Treatment
  community treatment order. *See* COMMUNITY TREATMENT ORDER
  consent on behalf of patient, treatment to which extending, 101
  decision-making, psychiatric support, 97
  decisions concerning, 54
  drug therapy, 57
  electro-convulsive therapy, 57
  freedom to choose, revocation of, 97, 98
  imposition, formula for, 55
  inferred authority for, 55
  mental capacity to consent-
    ability to rationalise and deliberate, 100, 101
    ability to understand and communicate, 100
    assessing, 112, 113
    best interest test, 113, 114, 119
    communication, facilitating, 113
    complete incompetence, 99
    continuing power of attorney, effect of, 115, 116
    definition, lack of, 110
    general authority to act reasonably, 114, 115
    incapacity, establishing, 99-102
    incompetence, determination of, 102
    informal patients, of, 108-110
    lack of, 98, 99
    legal, comprehensive definition of, 101
    mental disorder, treatment for, 103-108
    presumption of competence, 99, 100
    recommendations, 119
    reform of law, 110, 111
    test of, 112, 113
    threshold, 101, 115
  non-consensual-
    anorexia, for, 103

Treatment—contd
  non-consensual—*contd*
    best interest test, 106, 113, 114
    Caesarean sections, 104, 105
    conditions for, 139
    continuing power of attorney, effect of, 115, 116
    Court of Protection, decisions by, 116-119
    delivery of baby, for, 104
    force-feeding, 104
    general authority to act reasonably, 114, 115
    incapacitated individual, on, 109, 110
    making decisions, scrutiny of, 120
    manager, appointment of, 118, 119
    necessity, doctrine of, 108
    physical conditions, for, 102-108
    sexual deviancy, for, 103
    sterilisation, 106, 107
  patient's consent to-
    actual understanding of, 58, 59
    administration without, 98
    capacity. *See* mental capacity to consent, *above*
    capacity to understand, 58, 59
    drug therapy, 57
    electro-convulsive therapy, 57
    emergency, in, 58

Treatment—contd
  patient's consent to—*contd*
    formal safeguards, 55
    hormone, surgical implant of, 56, 57
    legalistic principle, 59
    not required, where, 55, 56
    reform, 55
    requirement of, 55
    validity of, 58
  physical conditions, for, 102-108
  psychosurgery, 56
  purpose of provisions, 55
  remand for, 183-185
  serious forms of, 56
  surgical implant, 56
  treatability test, 47, 49, 50, 58, 98
  welfarist approach, 98

Trial
  insanity, special verdict of, 186
  unfitness to stand, 185, 186

Unemployment
  impact of, 169

Vagrancy
  mentally disordered people, control of, 4

Wilful neglect
  offence of, 61

Workhouses
  development of, 4

Library & Information Resource Centre
Clinical Sciences Centre
University Hospital Aintree
Longmoor Lane
Liverpool L9 7AL